KASHMIR

AF011436

KASHMIR

TRAVELS *in* PARADISE *on* EARTH

ROMESH BHATTACHARJI

HarperCollins *Publishers* India

First published in India by HarperCollins *Publishers* 2024
4th Floor, Tower A, Building No. 10, DLF Cyber City,
DLF Phase II, Gurugram, Haryana – 122002
www.harpercollins.co.in

2 4 6 8 10 9 7 5 3 1

Copyright © Romesh Bhattacharji 2024

P-ISBN: 978-93-5699-694-6
E-ISBN: 978-93-5699-689-2

The views and opinions expressed in this book are the author's own and the facts are as reported by him, and the publishers are not in any way liable for the same.

Romesh Bhattacharji asserts the moral right
to be identified as the author of this work.

All rights reserved. No part of this publication may be reproduced, stored in a retrieval system or transmitted, in any form or by any means, electronic, mechanical, photocopying, recording or otherwise, without the prior permission of the publishers.

Typeset in 11.5/14.2 Adobe Garamond at
Manipal Technologies Limited, Manipal

Printed and bound at
Nutech Print Services - India

This book is printed on FSC® certified paper
which ensures responsible forest management.

For my granddaughters Keya, Sarah and Naira

Contents

Acknowledgements ix
Preface xi
List of Maps xiii
Introduction xvii

1. Banihal Gali to Kaukut Peak — 1
2. From Kaukut Peak to Putwalmarg Gali — 5
3. Patwalmarg Gali to Tuliyan Sar to Pahalgam — 17
4. Pahalgam, East Lidder and Sources of the Sind — 23
5. West Lidder — 35
6. From Tral, Chhumahai, Chhumanani and Other Lakes to Sumbal on the Sind river — 42
7. Baltal to Ganderbal on the Sind — 51
8. Vishensar, Krishansar and Gadsar — 57
9. Gangabal and Haramukh — 62
10. Kishenganga — 68

Contents

11.	Razdhainangan Pass to Wular	77
12.	Kupwara and Lolab	79
13.	More of Kupwara—Keran and Tithwal	89
14.	Of Bangus, Some Streams and Alps, Meadows and Passes between Kahmil Nala to Katha Kazinag Nala	97
15.	Baramulla and Uri to Gulmarg	102
16.	Ferozepur Nala to Peer Gali	110
17.	Peer Gali, Sat Sar and Kounsarnag to Didam Gali I	118
18.	Didam Gali I, Didam Gali II, Houen Heng to Banihal	127
19.	The Valley	131
20.	Srinagar	148
21.	Mughal Gardens of Kashmir	163
	Maps	179
	Glossary	213
	Bibliography	215
	Notes	217
	Index	219

Acknowledgements

The most important part of this book is its maps. I first made rough maps as untidy pencil sketches over two years. Then, my friend and mentor in everything to do with mountains, cartography and geography, Herr Hermann Soldner, of Bavaria, made sense of my untidy scrawls by redoing them patiently and determinedly. He is an investigative geographer and cartographer with a passion to study maps of mountains around the world—and to draw them. My heartfelt gratitude to him.

Most of the photographs in this book have been taken by my friends from Kashmir—Roshan Shehab a talented young photographer from Kupwara, Mohammed Amin Qureshi of Ganderbal and Mahmood Ahmed Shah of Srinagar. The last two work with the government. They are rare people who, though leading busy lives, are devoted to recording the splendour of their beloved homeland.

Mohammed Amin Qureshi and I have travelled in Kashmir for more than twenty years. He has been tireless in helping me with this book. He visited places that I had not been to. Revisited those that I had been to. He corrected my topographical errors by visiting places to check whether my memory was right or wrong. He got better pictures too. I thank him for taking so much trouble so selflessly to help me.

Acknowledgements

A part of the credit for these maps is due to the Survey of India, whose open series maps, though without heights, were helpful in resolving any doubts about the locations of some remote places.

My gratitude also to all my friends with whom I have had memorable visits to Kashmir over the past sixty years.

Without my daughter Jaya Bhattacharji Rose, co-founder, Ace Literary Consulting, this book would never have been completed. Jaya did the painful job of editing the manuscript and getting it published.

Thank you HarperCollins India team for helping me put this book together, especially Siddhesh Inamdar and Swati Chopra for believing in this book. Thank you Paloma Dutta who did the backbreaking work of squeezing sense out of an unwieldy manuscript. My thanks to the designer Amit Malhotra and proofreader Anju Christie.

Preface

Every nook and corner of Kashmir makes the heart jump and leaves the mind aching for more. There are no words to describe Kashmir convincingly.

I first experienced Kashmir in October 1963. Two of us, Adil Tyabji and I, young at heart and age, had tried to climb Mt Kolahoi, starting from Sarbal village and up the Durinar meadows. My last trek in Kashmir was in July 2010—the month of pointless violence—when I had tried to climb Mt Haramukh from Gangabal. Both my first and final attempts failed; the first, because our inexperience couldn't handle the steep descent from Lakhath gali and the last, because of age; I could not handle the steep ascent from Gangabal lake.

In between these years, I have been to Kashmir many times to trek, to travel and for work. Each visit is firmly planted in my heart and mind. This book is based on memories gleaned from faded diary entries, supplemented by extensive readings and numerous talks with Kashmiris. This is my tribute to the most spectacular and fascinating land that I have seen and to its long-suffering yet hospitable people. I have been to some of the areas I have written about in this book. The rest I have described after conversations with several helpful Kashmiris.

Preface

Before digital maps—which are still quite inaccurate—could be easily accessed on the net, there were no detailed maps available for lay enthusiasts. We had to rely on maps and routes published in books by English travellers in the nineteenth and early twentieth centuries.

This book describes Kashmir with the help of not to scale sketch maps. These maps have been drawn from experience and discussions with locals and garnered from books.

Each chapter describes a portion of Kashmir and has been named after the area's prominent physical features. The book and its maps are filled with names of places, especially ones worth visiting. All these names are likely to be confusing, and it may be impossible to understand the majesty and significance of these locations without consulting these maps. To describe each geographical feature of the never-ending fabled beauty of the Valley would be impossible in a book.

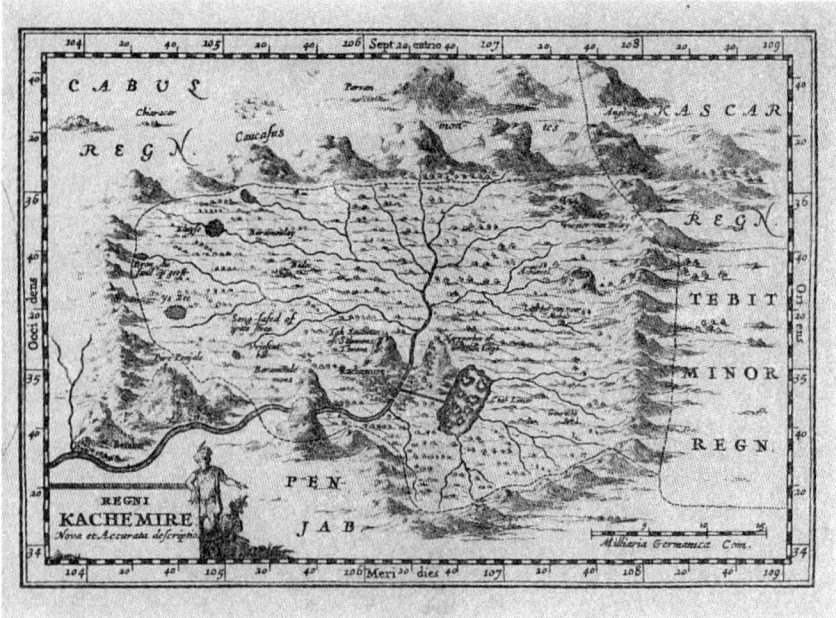

A seventeenth-century map of Kashmir based on Francois Bernier's description on Kashmir in Travels in the Mogul Empire—*a fairly accurate impression for that time.*

List of Maps

(These maps are not to scale)

Map 0: Some important rivers of Kashmir

Map 1: Banihal (2830 m), Verinag, Kaukut peaks (4100 m), Sangam, and Anantnag

Map 2: Kaukut peaks (4100 m) to Putwalmarg gali (4010 m) in east Kashmir

Map 3: Margan pass (3691 m), Chohar nag to Gaoran village in east Kashmir

Map 4: Putwalmar gali (4010 m) to Tuliyan sar in the north-east and Batkut on Lidder river in the west

Map 5: Tulliyan sar, Pahalgam, Mt Kolahoi, Mt Nishang, Amarnath Cave, Zoji la and Sonamarg, Sind

Map 6: Sheeshnag, Amarnath and Zoji la

Map 7: Pahalgam, West Lidder, Mt Kolahoi, Lakhath gali and Baltal

Map 8: Sangam, Tral, Mar sar, Tar sar, Chhumanai sar, Chhumahai sar and Deo Masjid peak

List of Maps

Map 9: Kolahoi nala, Sind river, Sonamarg, Zoji la, Bot Kulan Ganj, Gadsar, Vishensar and Mt Haramukh

Map 10: Kinari Darkush, Kaobal gali, Raman nala, Gadsar nala, Nilnai nala, Dawar, Kishenganga river

Map 11: Kishenganga, Taobat, Kanzalwan, Razdhainangan pass, Bandipora, Wular, Pohru river

Map 12: Sind river, Mohandmarg, Mt Haramukh, Gangabal lake, Madmatti nala and Sat sar

Map 13: Kahmil nala, Kupwara, Lolab valley, Kalaruch, Machil nala and Murdari gali

Map 14: Tithwal, Keran, Nasta Chun gali, Chowkibal, Rauta ki gali, Dudhnial and Kishenganga

Map 15: Hamal nar, Tangmulla, Limbar, Jhelum, Baramulla, Uri, Haji Pir and Gulmarg

Map 16: Gulmarg gondola, Zaisur gali, Hapat kol, Ferozepur nala, Kontar nag, Yusmarg, Tatakuti peaks and Pir Panjal (Peer) gali

Map 17: Romesh Thong peak, Peer gali, Yang nar, Rupri nar, Aliabad Serai, Shopian, Kounsarnag, Brahma Sakli peaks and Didam I gali

Map 18: Pir ki Gali (PKG), Shopian and Rambiara river

Map 19: Didam II gali, Shaliganga, Dudhganga, Banihal, Bandipora, Srinagar

Map 20: Anantnag district outline map

Map 21: Ganderbal district outline map

Map 22: Bandipora district outline map

Map 23: Kupwara district outline map

Map 24: Baramulla district outline map

Map 25: Budgam district outline map

Map 26: Shopian district outline map

List of Maps

Map 27: Kulgam district outline map

Map 28: Pulwama district outline map

Map 29: Srinagar district outline map

Map 30: Dal lake, Pathar Masjid, Hari Parbat, Shankarcharya and Burzahom and Gutlibagh

Map 31: Mughal gardens in Kashmir

Map 32: Chashma Shahi

Map 33: Nishat Bagh

Map 34: Shalamar Bagh

Map 35: Achhabal

Map 36: Verinag

Introduction

Understanding Kashmir

'IF THERE BE A PARADISE ON EARTH, IT IS THIS, IT IS THIS, IT IS THIS' IS THE best description of Kashmir's charm, though this couplet is wrongly attributed to Emperor Jahangir.[2] The only way of looking at Kashmir is with the heart. It overwhelms other senses and leads one to incoherence.

It would not be a stretch to state that there is no other place in the world that has a more immaculate and pleasing scenery at such a vast scale as Kashmir. And with time, the Valley is becoming easier to reach. Till a couple of decades ago, Kashmir had a few motorable roads. Today there are tarred roads along the numerous runnels, streams and tributaries of the Jhelum, reaching locations that are only a couple of days' march to the glaciers and springs that spawn them. Pretty hamlets, beautiful meadows, scintillating lakes, dramatic passes and exciting climbs are closer than ever before. Most of the roads in the interior regions are still not crowded. In an hour on these roads one can see all the expansive viewpoints which would only be possible with a five-day trek three decades ago. There are now four major roads to enter into Kashmir Valley, though the oldest one, through Banihal tunnel, still remains the only all-weather road.

The fertile Kashmir Valley (nearly 16,000 sq. km) is ringed by mountains. There are more than forty rivers and tributaries, and about 1230 lakes, tarns and other waterbodies. The following artistic interpretation of Kashmir shows why it is so agriculturally productive.

▲ *An imaginary, ariel, not-to-scale view of the Kashmir Valley and of the mountains girdling it. This image is not oriented to the north, which is to the right of this image. It shows how the Valley was a lake bed. The Pir Panjal is the curved rim from ESE to WSW. The snow ridge leaving the Pir Panjal at the bottom right connects it to the wide knot of the Himalaya at centre right. The Karakoram are the skyline mountains.*[3]

Kashmir's rivers and streams are what makes the Valley extremely fertile. Some of the rivers of Kashmir are explained in Map 0.

Map 0:

Unless one is an insurgent, one enters the Valley from Jammu either by road or rail at Qazigund, over Sinthan pass (3784 m) or over the Peer gali

(3485 m) to Shopian; one can also fly to Srinagar. I shall describe first the mountains that ring the Valley, by moving anti-clockwise from the Jawahar Tunnel, under Banihal Pass. The mountains that circle the Valley have been divided into sections in this book and marked by prominent passes, peaks, lakes or tributaries of the Jhelum.

1
Banihal Gali to Kaukut Peak

THE PIR PANJAL RAILWAY TUNNEL UNDER BANIHAL GALI (2832 M) STARTS at Banihal on the south of the Pir Panjal range and ends 11 km later at the north of the Pir Panjal near the village of Hiler Shahabad before Qazigund *(Map 1)*. The windows of the electric train are wide, enabling hearty views—stretching from the narrow confines of Banihal's mountains to the flattish poplar- and chinar-studded valley and the mountains encircling it. The beauty and seeming peace is striking. From the road the view used to be much more satisfying. It would weave through miles and miles of the fertile valley, crammed with orchards and villages and ringed by snow peaks. Now there's an expressway, NH 44.

Across the Jawahar Tunnel is Anantnag district. As one reaches the lay-by at the northern end of the Jawahar Road Tunnel, one is surprised by the many bare spurs plunging into the valley. This is not the verdant Kashmir one has heard so much about. A few kilometres beyond these bare hills, the fertile valley appears. It is vivid green in summer and often white in winter. It extends till the forested base of the surrounding snow-topped mountains.

The skyline ridges are around 3000 m above sea level and the peaks around 4000 m. Under clouds or snow, during autumn or winter, or at different periods of the day, the valley's colour keeps changing and is always captivating. A motor road over the Banihal pass was made in 1922, but it remained blocked during winter. The Jawahar Road Tunnel was opened in December 1956, after which Kashmir became accessible almost round the year. A broader road tunnel was opened in 2021, after ten years of construction.

For a few zigzag kilometres after coming out of the Jawahar Tunnel, the road weaves around treeless rolling hillsides overlooking the widening Omuwah nar to the east. Well before Qazigund and still in the hills, a narrow road branches off the NH 44 to the right, descends to the Omuwah nar and follows it till it meets the abundant and delectable waters of Verinag spring *(Maps 1 and 35)* in the Mughal Garden. Emperor Jahangir had a large octagonal tank of sculpted stones constructed around it in 1620. The garden, influenced by Persians, was made by his son Shah Jahan. The large spring at Verinag is a source of the Jhelum, or Veth as the locals calls it. This spring cascades out around the base of a fir-covered mountain on the lower fringes of a Pir Panjal spur. The waters from this spring meet those of Omuwah nar and Naugam nar to form the Jhelum.

Anantnag district sprawls all the way from south to east and then to north-east Kashmir. Verinag is at its southern end.

A short walk south of Verinag, through a jungle of pines and firs, on a northern spur jutting out of the Pir Panjal, there is a small point (around 2243 m away) from where one can see part-mountainous and part-valley landscapes up to Anantnag. On either side are the ragged ridges of the lowest part of the Pir Panjal. There is a satisfying day-long 15-km walk from Verinag over this peak to a broad ridge from which a stirring sunrise and sunset can be seen. All imaginable tones, tints and hues of a rainbow's colours are there. To the north is the second highest peak within Kashmir, Kolahoi (5425 m) *(Map 7)*. Beyond and far in the distant north-east are Nun (7135 m) and Kun (7077 m) in the Great Himalaya looking deceptively minor.

Go along this ridge traversing past a couple of small rock outcrops to reach a craggy peak (3280 m) in the Pir Panjal range. On a clear day—usually in autumn—a large expanse of the river-pierced, glowing green valley of Anantnag district as well as snow peaks to the north-east and west and north are visible.

There are three ways to return to Verinag from this peak. Retrace your steps for ten minutes to an alp extending on either side of the ridge. One route cautiously descends north-west over a patchy and wide alp, down the small Omuwah nar. To the north-east is a slightly steeper decline. This goes along the Naugam nar down to the large village of Shahabad Naugam. The third and more taxing way is to first reach the nearby, somewhat rocky Halan gali (3190 m) on the Pir Panjal, and then head north, down a wide gully and undulating fir-sprinkled meadows with bare patches that once had birch. The path ends at Halan village by the Sandran river. The Naugam nar is only a short walk through the fields and woods from the broader Sandran river, which, instead of flowing into the Naugam nar, turns west to link up with the nascent Jhelum beyond Verinag *(Map 1)*.

An enjoyable and easy circuit ends here. From Shahabad, catch a bus to Verinag or to the district headquarters at Anantnag or a taxi to Kokernag on the Bring river's left bank. Five decades ago, when there were none of the three bridges over the Sandran, a lively walk of about 15 km over Ren gali (2627 m) would take one to Kokernag from Naugam. Now only shepherds use this route—if uniforms permit.

The Sandran river, with poplar-bordered agricultural fields on both sides of the riverbed, begins to widen from Shahabad. There are short and relaxing walks on both sides of its bed. Upriver, from Naugam, is the village of Shekhpur. To the south of this village is a friendly peak called Kanari (3518 m)—an easy climb along a ridge that has forests on both sides. The accompanying map suggests several delightful trysts with hills and forests *(Map 1)*.

The views make one silent and wonder how any terrain could have so much splendour and grandeur in every square mile. But this is Kashmir, where such stirring sights are everywhere. It is not the grandeur of towering mountains and deep gorges of Zanskar and the Himalaya, but the beauty of the endless charming valleys and accessible peaks around them.

The wide plain near Anantnag splays out to the north, at the western edge of which can be seen glimpses of the Jhelum. Sandran river flows quietly now in its wide bed below. Towards the north-east edge of the valley, the snows of Kolahoi (5425 m) can be seen. To the north-west is Haramukh (5142 m). There is a road that goes to the south, up the fertile Sandran valley. Both its banks are covered with fields and orchards of villages that are so close that they look like unbroken green belts. In early September's mellow afternoon sunlight, before the golden paddy is harvested, it was a heady sight to walk above the clear blue-green waters of the Sandran river sandwiched between slopes of fir. Most mud-caked houses had bunches of red chillies hanging from their walls. All this under a dark blue sky dotted with lazy tufts of clouds floating by. Now a road has destroyed the silence. There is no question of walking along the river as smoke-spewing vehicles make it an odious experience.

Sandran's major sources—Shah kol, Chiwar nar and Chitar nar—are spread over about 20 km of the Pir Panjal, which includes a cirque of half a dozen peaks of around 4100 m each. These streams rise from the bases of Halan gali (3745 m) to Kaukut gali (3816 m) and Kaukut peak (4100 m) *(Map 1)*. The closest village near the sources of the Sandran is Chanpari. It is also the last village on the motor road. Below the road head of Chanpari, the Chiwar nar meets the Chitar nar to form Sandran. It was once completely submerged in thick fir forests from all sides. Not now, as deforestation preceded the construction of the road and continues surreptitiously. From here, there is an easy-to-moderately-difficult trudge up a tributary and through a thick forest to a hump known as Sundar Kanth (4137 m). It is on a ridge jutting north from the Pir Panjal. It sits astride the sources of the Sandran and the Ahlan. Its western slope is steep, patchily forested with a belt of lush meadow at the top. On the Ahlan side, the slopes are gentle.

Descending gently till Shekhpur, the Sandran nearly doubles its size after taking in all its tributaries. About 7 km later, a little beyond Verinag, is a road bridge leading to the Ahlan valley over a spur above the right bank of the Sandran. At this bridge, the Sandran comes out of its confines and spreads out wide as it enters the valley before meeting the Jhelum beyond Anantnag.

2
From Kaukut Peak to Putwalmarg Gali

East of Sandran, across a broad ridge, is the valley of the Ahlan—a tributary of the Bring, which is a tributary of the Jhelum. The wide ridge on a northern flank of the Pir Panjal, between the Sandran and Ahlan rivers, has charming, broad and long meadows at the very top. On either side of the ridge, dense bands of fir reach within a hundred metres, sometimes tapering off like an arrowhead when they reach the ridge. There are several passes to cross over to Ahlan valley from Sandran. One is the attractive viewpoint of Rangmandu gali (3357 m), which is above the long Rangmandu village now connected by a road. A walk along the gently undulating alp on the ridge is pleasant and relaxing. Rarely does one have the pleasure of walking many peaceful miles along a meadow-covered ridge with distant, unimpeded views in all four directions. Using the numerous shepherds' trails one can descend to any of the several villages in the Sandran and Ahlan valleys. Both valleys are fertile. Each village has shepherds' trails leading to springs, meadows and bare ridges of around 3000 m in height.

The sources of Sandran and Ahlan are below Nandmarg and Brari (4015 m) galis in the Pir Panjal to the south *(Map 1)*. One of the passes at the head of the Sandran is Nandmarg (3658 m). It is still being used by Gujjars and their flocks to reach the lower winter grazing grounds in Doda, Kishtwar and Jammu. They return the same way during summer and autumn months to the grazing grounds in Kashmir. In the past, visitors have noted indelible experiences on the way to these passes, with forests girdling alps, numerous lakes, tarns and ponds, and the hospitality of villagers on the way. Then insurgents came and soldiers after them. Today reaching these physically easy passes is impossible for civilians as they are crammed with check posts.

Chanpari (2450 m) is located in the neck of a narrowing valley from which forested paths branch out east and west to meadows, alps, snow fields, tarns, easy peaks and passes. One tarn that is a day's walk along a shepherd's trail from Chanpari is Gagan sar, a bowl-shaped lake on a steep wooded slope. Another shepherds' path traverses the western slopes of nearby Sundar Kanth (4137 m) and crosses Brari gali (4014 m) to Doda in Jammu. From Brari gali rises the Brari nar—the largest tributary of the Ahlan river. A shepherds' trail cuts across the Brari nar and goes to a bewitching alp around a drying lake called Hapat Talao (3234 m). Nearby is a fir- and birch-dotted alp called Poshbagh where there are several dokas, belonging to Gujjars. Gujjars are nomadic shepherds *(Map 2)*. Dokas are thick, flat-roofed mud huts built near alps and meadows.

The mountains that ring Kashmir Valley are not high and dominating. Their glaciers are few, at low altitude, and can be easily traversed. The most striking aspect of this ring of mountains—Pir Panjal to the south and the Himalaya to the north—is that they harbour a necklace of extravagantly beautiful lakes in every direction. There is no shortage of adventure or picturesque sights in Kashmir. There is only dearth of peace.

Many streams rise—like Brari nar, Poshbagh nar and Mawar nar—from the Pir Panjal in the south. They combine to form the Ahlan river, which is named after the village of Hera Ahlan. From Hera Ahlan too, there are many appealing walks. Hera Ahlan is one of the myriad Kashmiri villages at the head of valleys, from where formidable and marvellous trysts with extravagant beauty start.

From Kaukut Peak to Putwalmarg Gali

This is Kashmir's unique asset. Nearly every village in the valleys is a base for memorable walks to meadows and tarns, some of which, like Hapat Talao, are drying. Shepherd camps and dokas are in the most gorgeous locations.

At the head of Poshbagh nar is Kun gali (3975 m). To its north is Agashmandal peak (4154 m), which is reached after a strenuous scramble up a scree and some boulders. This effort is worth it for the jaw-dropping Himalayan view to the north. A long jagged range of white fills the northern horizon. In the foreground and about 80 km to the north-west is Mt Kolahoi (5425 m) *(Map 5)*—the second highest peak in Kashmir. To the north-east, beyond Sheeshnag lake, rise moderate peaks. Further north, is Nichang (5444 m)—the highest peak in Kashmir *(Map 6)*. A hundred or so kilometres beyond these peaks Nun (7,135 m) and Kun (7077 m) in Zanskar are seen.

At Agashmandal (4154 m), there's a fork in the Pir Panjal range *(Map 2)*. A 90 km long range heads north to meet the Himalaya, which it joins to the east of Amarnath Cave. The nearly 600 km long Pir Panjal starts from Domel, south of Muzaffarabad in Pakistan-Occupied Kashmir (POK). It heads south-east till Agashmandal, where it turns east-south-east for about 250 km to end at the easy dome of Deo Tibba (6000 m) and the difficult Indrasan (6200 m) in Kullu. Within Kashmir there are only a few small glaciers in the Pir Panjal. As Pir Panjal leaves Kashmir, the range gets higher and glaciers longer.

Across Pir Panjal in east Kashmir are about a dozen passes leading to Doda and Kishtwar. Most of them are used by shepherds and soldiers. Two have seasonal motor roads crossing them. A ridge turns north from Agashmandal. It is structurally different from Pir Panjal. It has more granite and several small but classical glaciers (with ice fields and ice falls)—perhaps an indication that this ridge is more Himalayan than Pir Panjal. It connects Pir Panjal in the south to the Great Himalayan Crest to the north.

In villages at the base of some of these passes were PWD and Forest Rest Houses from colonial times, appealingly embedded in clearings flanked by giant deodars and tinkling brooks. They were built for official use but often sheltered trekkers were never denied rooms. Near these passes are a number of 4500 m high peaks providing easy-to-exciting-and-challenging climbs and ski traverses. Such attempts at adventure are unthinkable now because of security problems.

After this macroscopic view I return to Hera Ahlan. Ahlan river runs through a fertile valley. Villages on both banks have rice, wheat and vegetable fields and orchards of pears, peaches, cherries and apples which were not there forty years ago *(Map 2)*.

A recently completed motor road to Hera Ahlan village could have made it an attractive tourist base. At present, it is mainly used by security forces; the gently sloped Wawdor peak (3999 m), with meadows and springs on its inclines and the lovely glade of Aryanbra, will have to wait for better days to thrill visitors.

The Ahlan river in its descent towards the north gathers the waters of the Razparyin nar and its tributaries and meets Naubug nar coming from the now motorable Margan gali (3691m) in the north-east at Vailu Bridge. This is one of Kashmir's more gorgeous valleys. After the confluence at Vailu, the combined waters are known as Bring river. Each of Ahlan's feeder streams has many tributaries running through fir forests to join them. Paths to the sources of each stream pass through lovely alps and thick forests, from which only glimpses of sunlight are had. Some of these can be explored in a week's stay at Daksum on the Soi nar and at Larnu on the Naubug nar *(Map 2)*. Soi nar's main source is below Sinthan gali (3784 m).

While walking in these grand woods and silent slopes years ago, no one could have imagined that the canopy of green would be reduced and the infernal combustion engine would sully the snow fields. Roads have gone up the Soi nar and the Naubug nar to Kishtwar, defiling nature with dynamite and by logging more trees than necessary. It is shocking to see roads scissoring up gouged, gashed and blown mountain slopes, where earlier birds filled the alps and forests and unblemished snowfields lay. Wildlife—especially bears—has all but gone. However, such roads

From Kaukut Peak to Putwalmarg Gali

are advantageous for the local population to market their ware, and for medical aid and higher education.

Daksum (2438 m)—16 km beyond Kokarnag, on right bank of the Soi nar and before its confluence with Razparyin nar—is in an ascending meadow surrounded by firs and fields. It was a quiet, small and charming village with a few houses and a rest house that was used mainly by trekkers till the early 1980s. Twice a year, in summer and autumn, migrating Gujjars and their herds would bring their cattle, goats and hustle-bustle on the way from or to Kishtwar over the motorable Sinthan gali, or Girsar gali to its east *(Map 2)*.

Daksum is now an urban village with several hotels. Everyday, from summer to autumn, many taxis, buses and trucks ply between Srinagar and Kishtwar over the Sinthan pass (3784 m), which is 37 km away from Daksum. From the pass, Srinagar is 131 km, Kishtwar 83 km and Jammu 315 km away. Previously, there were footpaths from Daksum through forests and alps to Kishtwar over the Sinthan gali (3784 m), Dringyan gali (4010 m), Shilsar gali (3961 m) and Margan gali (3691 m). There are many lakes and tarns on this crest connecting Pir Panjal in the south to the Himalaya in the north. The best time to visit Daksum is autumn when visitors are few, sunshine aplenty, with some flowers still adding colour, and the birches a glorious gold. Daksum is unfortunately a weathervane of political uncertainty. When insurgency is dormant, Daksum is busy, and when active, its hotels are shuttered.

These days, the Sinthan pass is a popular tourist spot. A road reaches the pass, first crossing slopes of needle thin firs, then white barked birches followed by meadows and rough detritus strewn on rolling mountain sides. It is no place to stop now in summer and autumn. Four decades ago, there would be only one hut to the west of the pass. Today, on either side of the dirty pass cars are parked on the road, and there are people, noise and litter. If one wants to soak in the heady mix of silence, clean snow fields, green alps and blue and grey skies, and forget the ugly, ravaged mountain sides, one has to trek along the ridge to the north. A three-day challenging hike under the scree slopes of

Wandar Dur (4334 m) will take you to Dringyan sar and gali (4165 m) and beyond to the east to two bottle-green lakes with tongues of ice licking them in Kishtwar.

A couple of hours walk south of Sinthan pass, across a broad ridge and over two bare mounds, is Girsar gali (3861 m) which is still being used by determined Gujjars despite army patrolling. Two hundred or so metres below this pass on the western side is the green Girsar lake set in a gray and mustard coloured rubble-strewn green meadow at its base.

After this fascinating area was cruelly desecrated—an area which once drove shepherds to poetic ecstasy—there is now a plan to build a tunnel under the Sinthan pass. It would have been better had the tunnel been built first, sparing the present environmental havoc caused by building the road over the pass.

Needless destruction lies around new roads as they snake into the remotest parts of the paradise called Kashmir. Grey landslips amidst green slopes, where earlier there were none, are frequent. During the idyllic days of no roads, even very steep forested mountain slopes had been held fast by the roots of giant firs and, higher up, by smaller birches. These slopes are now bare, and magnificent firs that lay dry on their sides, forlorn, have been collected by timber merchants. The timber contractors' lobby in Kashmir is powerful enough to do as they please. Similar devastation can be seen on the way to Margan pass (3691 m)—six passes away to the north from Sinthan.

Daksum is on Razparyin nar, which at Vailu meets Naubug nar flowing in from the north. For 25 km or so from Vailu (2050 m), up the valley of Naubug nar, till the last village of Gaoran (2465 m) on the Kashmir side are continuous and picture-perfect poplar-bordered terraced fields and neat orchards on either side of the road. To its left are slopes of giant firs, and higher up are snow ridges and peaks.

The old path to Margan gali after Goran used to go over endless alps speckled with firs, which gave way to birch trees near the top. It went past small, sparsely populated hamlets. The road has made getting to Margan, and beyond to Kishtwar, effortless. And the villages are larger now and prosperous. These new roads have connected people from Kashmir with those of Jammu. A few of the long slashes on the denuded hill sides sliced by roads are now sprouting grass, and perhaps soon there may be trees too. Progress is inevitable, but it could have been done with much less damage to the environment.

Margan (Death) Pass is heralded by boulders and rubble bordering succulent meadows, where thousands of goats and cattle graze in the brief summer. The pass is in an even defile that is about 2 km long. Midway are some solid tin and steel huts made for road-maintenance platoons, who leave after the first snow.

About 2 km beyond Margan, on the Kishtwar side, a stream coming in from the west-north-west is bridged. It is called Nilli nar. An energetic scramble up rock debris for two hours gives one countless heart-leaps. In the middle of a lambent green (only in August) meadow, a small round lake (3900 m) appears. It has ice floes, even in summer, and is surrounded by snow fields strewn on rounded hill sides with the eastern end being craggy and rocky. This is not all. There are three more lakes nearby, all of which are called Chohar nag (Persian for four) *(Map 3)*. From the largest of these lakes (4000 m) a stream plummets down to the south-west to meet the Naubug nar near some dokas about 2 km ahead of Goran village. Across Margan gali, to the east, is the valley of Warwan in Kishtwar. The pretty villages of Inshan and Sukhnai, in happier times, used to be on trekking and skiing routes from Lonivald pass to Zanskar. Margan slopes are now frequented by young Kashmiris for cross-country skiing and treks.

In an article in Greater Kashmir of 29 May 2007, an inadequately guided scholar from the University of Kashmir had suggested that these four lakes (Chohar nag) to the north of Margan pass be tapped for water.[4] It is an illogical article, but it might spark someone's imagination, and in the future this shocking proposal might become a developmental nightmare. On land that has water every few metres, such a scheme is unnecessary. Margan gali is the last pass till the far north Zoji la to be crossed by a motor road.

North of the Margan gali is Patwalmarg gali (4006 m) below which harbours the southern-most sources of the Arpat kol, another substantial tributary of the Jhelum which it meets near Anantnag, the district headquarters of this magnificent area.

It's interesting to note how the perception of beauty, which charmed one once, changes with tension. The tall, stately, dark green forests of fir sweeping up from both sides of Naubug nar were an impressive and pleasing sight while trekking from Vailu to Gaoran in the carefree 1960s. In 2003, when I drove through this area, aware of all the insurgency-related killings here, they appeared melancholic to me. The same happy forests now had an ominous air and reeked of evil. Perception of beauty is in the mind as much as in the eyes.

Before the nineties, Gaoran had a small and bewitching Forest Rest House, up the side valley of a tributary hidden by immense firs. During the Decade of Trouble, beginning in 1990, this idyllic and fertile stretch was taken over by insurgents and then the army. Families living nearby remember gun shots at night and finding bodies in the morning. For insurgents this place was a part of an important escape and supply route.

From Margan gali a ridge descends towards the west. One branch of this ridge goes down along the Narbug nar to Vailu and another to Kokernag further to the west on the Bring river. Over this ridge are several passes from which streams head north to Arpat kol, the river system that collects all the rivers of south-east Kashmir near Anantnag *(Maps 3 and 4)*.

The plains in the Valley that are contiguous to the mountains of east Kashmir need to be described now. At Vailu, Naugbug nar, Razparyin nar and Ahlan nala join to form the river Bring. A few kilometres later, at Kokernag, the gushing Bring is no longer in a rush. It stretches itself wide in the Valley and breaks into several murmuring channels. Kokernag is the subdivision headquarters of the entire area described till here.

It is known for its springs, agricultural research centre, a trout hatchery and a well-maintained Mughal-inspired heavily wooded botanical garden. The streams that flow through the garden have emerged from surrounding springs, which are supposed to have curative properties.

Kokernag has had a garden for many decades though only in the 1960s was an attractive and classical garden laid out. It gets its name from the streams coming out of the five springs that resemble a cock's (koker) claws. *Ain-i-Akbari mentions* that the springs of Kokernag satisfy both hunger and thirst and cure indigestion.

Kokernag is a sub-divisional headquarter town, whose importance has increased as civil and military roads to Kishtwar radiate from here. It is also famous for its trout hatchery. In the relaxed days of fifty years ago, when time wasn't counted in nano seconds and people could stand and stare for hours without being troubled by incessant mobile phones or diesel fumes, Kokernag was a small village with a post office. In 1967 we did a twelve-day circular trek from Kokernag. At Kokernag, the postmaster met us in the bazaar and gave me a letter from my mother. The address on the envelope simply read 'C/o Post Master, Kokernag'! In these days of instant connectivity, such simplicity and bureaucratic consideration cannot even be imagined.

Today experiences are shared at once with friends and families through smart phones. Kashmir is getting the kind of publicity its Public Relations Department had never been able to achieve.

Kokernag is 22 km away from the district headquarters of Anantnag, which covers all of east Kashmir from Banihal till Amarnath and Mt Kolahoi. Kashmir's most voluminous rivers—Jhelum, Sandran, Bring, Lidder, Arpat kol and Sind—have their sources in this largest district in the Kashmir Valley ***(Maps 2, 4, 18 and 20)***.

The Bring receives the tasty waters of Achabal spring, around which is a Mughal garden ***(Map 34)*** designed by Nur Jahan (1577–1645).

From Achabal, a leafy road heads for Anantnag, hugging the hill on its right and fields and apple orchards on its left. A few kilometres before Anantnag the road diverts to climb up an orchard-covered hill to Martand, where lie the stately ruins of a mammoth ancient Hindu temple. The magnificent sun temple of Martand is the loftiest in Kashmir. This immense roofless temple had been influenced by the Indo-Greek art of Gandhara. When it was completed during the eighth century, the temple roof might have been pyramidal like that of a smaller temple in Nuranag above Kangan, on the Sind river. According to the fifteenth-century *Tareekh-e-Hassan* (History of Kashmir), there was at Martand a city named Babul built by Raja Ranadatiya (AD 578 to 594). The construction of the first Martand temple was started by him. The present temple was completed by King Lalitaditya (AD 724 to 760) in the middle of the eighth. Below is a sketch by J. Duguid from his *Letters from India and Kashmir* (1870–1873) imagining what the Martand complex looked like when it was in use eleven centuries ago. The entrance is from the western gate that overlooks the valley.

Water seen in this sketch[5] was brought by a canal from River Lidder about 7 km away

The canal was, and still is, called the Martand Canal. It was built between the seventh to tenth centuries as part of the Martand temple project. It was renovated during Bud Shah Sultan Zain-ul-Abidin's reign between 1420–1470. The next renovation and expansion started in the mid 1980s and is still continuing. Today, the clear-water canal flows for some distance alongside the Pahalgam road, below the venerated Aishmuqam mosque.

The following photograph[6] was taken in 1868 by Jim Burke. It shows Martand's grand ruins standing in splendid isolation amidst a scorched earth because peasants impoverished by moneylenders under the Dogra rulers of the nineteenth century gave up agriculture. Today this area depicted in the photo has sturdy forests, fecund fields and lucrative orchards. The hill from which the photograph was taken by Jim Burke now has almond orchards and a cell phone tower.

Photograph by Jim Burke in 1868

The Bring, Sandran and Arpat kol merge with the Lidder, which flows into the Jhelum at Sangam a little to the north of Anantnag. Near Sangam is Bijbehara, with the remnants of a Mughal garden known once as Dara Shikoh Bagh. It has the second largest chinar tree in the Valley. This chinar has a girth of 19.70 m and is 13.30 m tall.

After the sources of the Jhelum, Bring and Sandran, which are in the south of east Kashmir, the next cluster of river systems are of the Lidder,

Arpat kol and Hapat nar. Lesser systems like Gagarpathar nar, Langinai nar and Sorus nar, and their many tributaries, join the Lidder. The Jhelum swallows all of them. Only the Sind in the north is independent of this combination of rivers, and it too is eventually swallowed by the Jhelum north of Srinagar.

3
Patwalmarg Gali to Tuliyan Sar to Pahalgam

A FEW KILOMETERS NORTH OF THE MARGAN PASS ARE PATWALMARG GALI (4007 m), Zambakach gali (4050 m) and three lakes (one dry). Two are below Nagaputan and one—Kon nag—is below Zajimarg gali (4040 m) *(Map 4)*. These passes are now exclusively used by insurgents, the army and by shepherds, if allowed. The Arpat kol has its other sources in these three passes and lakes which are on the ridge connecting Pir Panjal with the Himalaya. It also separates Kishtwar in the east from Kashmir in the west.

Arpat's most voluminous tributary is the Herbal nar which rises from Zajimarg gali (4040 m) and Kon nag. From Zambakach and Nagaputan galis flow several streams to form the Bajnal at the lovely village of Thimran, from where Putwalmarg gali can be seen *(Map 4)*. Bajnal and Herbal are the main sources of the Arpat kol and are of an average length of just 15 km or so. All descend, rapidly and noisily, through thick forests of firs and sedgy banks. Arpat starts at the point where Bajnal meets Herbal, near the several alluring villages of Rishpur, Bimar Nursar and Dardapur—all now connected by a road. Charar-e-Sharief, a mosque, had been built at Bimar Nursar in the early fifteenth century to honour

Kashmir's revered saint Sheikh Noor-ud-Din Noorani or Nund Rishi (1377–1440). The more-than-usually fertile valley of Arpat is bordered by forested side valleys, spurs and ridges.

Previously, there were many pleasant walking paths through forests and springs in the valleys made by these rivers and their tributaries. These walks have been shortened by good roads, which have even reached the last villages close to their sources—like in the valley of Arpat kol, and its large tributary like Herbal nar and small one like Halkan nar. There are passes on top of the ridges above these sources. Crossing one or two of these passes over a weekend from Srinagar is exciting and easy nowadays. Such trysts with beauty are all over Kashmir.

To the north-west of Rishpur is a short and stiff climb to Turigadalu gali (2812 m) followed by a pleasant descent to the Khaiyar Forest Rest House and a bus stop on Harpat kol *(Map 4)*. From the pass can be seen Mt Kolahoi (5425 m) to the north-west, and to the north-north-east are a few 4000 m high peaks and passes like Krepin gali (3885 m), which hem the long and rather unusual Langinai valley. Close at hand to the east and looking more domineering than its mere 3630 m height is Krasnak peak.

There are Gujjar paths over all these low and high passes. One from Chhatargul on lower Arpat kol goes along the motor road to Chugom and then climbs through forests and meadows to Badre gali (2888 m) to descend rather steeply to Matehund on the right bank of Naubug nar that comes down from Margan pass.

Kashmir is unusual in that it has an abundance of easy and visually rewarding walks close to road heads. Passes and peaks are aplenty. Finding a route has never been an issue in Kashmir. In the past, there were shepherds' trails and springs everywhere. As were the Gujjar dokas. These huts have thick mud-packed flat roofs supported by timber and usually have three rooms at least. They are spacious and warm, and till the 1960s, some owners didn't mind travellers camping on their roofs. Other shepherds used tents or build makeshift shelters with branches and stones. Even shortcuts were well-marked and one was never alone for long in those days. Now, I am told, only a suspicious soldier will greet you at such *settings*—if you get that far!

North of Patwalmarg gali (4006 m), the ridge connecting the Himalaya to Pir Panjal continues—it is strewn with peaks and passes that gradually increase in height and is dotted with about a dozen lakes on the Kashmir side of the ridge. From these, flow large and small streams to the west, roaring, gurgling and tinkling to meet the Lidder. The Anantnag–Pahalgam road bridges over them. Shepherds' tracks over the Himalayan Pir Panjal ridge go through thick forests of firs that thin out near the birch and glacial debris below the snow line.

So far, a feature of this Himalaya to Pir Panjal ridge, running north–south, had been that there were no classic glaciers with snow fields and ice falls. Sources of nearly all the streams had been snow fields, springs or lakes, but as this ridge approaches the Great Himalayan Crest, its average height from Sorus nag (3667 m) becomes about 500 m higher and harbours small glaciers *(Map 4)*.

Some of the subsidiary ridges, like that containing Langinai, which heads west for the Lidder river, are steep, gashed and serrated at higher levels, and forested and gently sloped lower down. From these subsidiary ridges, which are to the north of Langinai *(Map 4)*, are streams coming down from glaciers, snow fields and springs to Lidder valley. Their sources are surrounded by crumbling schist and moraine. As they flow down, there are juniper and birch trees followed by dense forests of magnificent tall firs till they reach the stony and fern-clad banks of the streams. At the head of these short valleys are charming pastures, and lower down are villages. Their inhabitants had made trails across these attendant ridges over galis or passes to take their flocks for trade or barter and negotiate marriages, preferring not to go down to the Lidder and then again up adjacent valleys. With motor roads opening up in these valleys, the passes are used only for shepherding and patrolling.

The first of Lidder's eastern tributaries to flow from the ridge connecting Pir Panjal to the Great Himalaya is the Harpat nar. If one is on a ridge-hopping trek from Rishpar on the Arpat kol to Langinai valley, the Turigadalau gali (2812 m) to the north needs to be crossed. Above the left bank of this nearly 15 km long Harpat nar are dense fir forests. Harpat nar rises from sources to the south of Krepin peak (4300 m) and Krepin gali (3885 m), which are on the 4000 m or so high ridge, south of the long cwm of Langinai river. Nearby is Gagarpathar gali (3795 m), which is the source of another of Lidder's left bank's copius tributaries—Gagarpathar nar.

As the Gagarpthar flows into the Lidder, after collecting tributaries from north, south and east, there is a large undulating plain on which is a hillock, about 130 m high, on which is one of Kashmir's most famous shrines—Aishmuqam. It's a mosque and a dargah built to commemorate Sheikh Zain-ud-din Wali, one of Kashmir's influential peers. He lived in the fifteenth century and was a favourite disciple of the most revered and famous sufi saint Sheikh Noor-ud-din. This shrine can be seen from the Anantnag–Pahalgam road.

Below this shrine starts the eleventh-century Martand canal, which once brought water to the Martand temple. The canal was built by King Lalitaditya and improved for agricultural use by Zain-ul-Abidin—lovingly called Bud Shah by Kashmiris—in the mid-fifteenth century. He reigned from 1420–1470 and was the eighth sultan of Kashmir. This part of Kashmir became such a land of plenty that in the mid-nineteenth century, Dogra rulers settled Sikhs around Anantnag to cultivate it. Subsequently, severe taxation ruined this land for a long time. The canal now flows out of a modernized barrage on the Gagarpathar nar.

Further ahead, on the motor road to Pahalgam from Anantnag, are the once idyllic and peaceful villages of Batkut and Lidru between which flows the Langinai to join the Lidder. The villages are about 3 km apart, but now the distance between them is closing in with increasing homes and hotels. An encouraging development is that there are now more trees (some are fruit trees) in the lower Langinai valley than fifty years ago.

On the right bank of the Lidder, opposite Batkut, comes a snow-fed torrent *(Map 4)*. It is called Owur nala and flows from snow fields to the west of Hodassar peak (4060 m). Here is a knot of small peaks around

Mt Kolahoi, which is part of the Great Himalayan Crest, according to Kenneth Mason's *Abode of Snow*.

The Langinai river rises from Langinai nag (3870 m), near Zajimarg gali, about 25 km away making it the longest tributary of the Lidder on its left bank. The Langinai has an east-south-east to west-north-west course. Both the leeward and windward side of the ridge above its left bank are well forested with firs. The steep, rocky serrated ridge above the right bank of the Langinai twists and weaves below high-altitude bowls containing at least six dramatic lakes—Chari nag, Zissar nag, Chirran nag, among them—all at around 4000 m altitude above sea level. *(Map 4)* There are challenging paths to these lakes from Karalnar village, the largest in Langinai valley.

All are pleasant and enchanting walks. The steep rugged ridge above these lakes, though only about 4000 m high, appears to loom large above them. Warwan valley of Kishtwar is on the eastern side of this ridge. There are two peaks of about 4700 m above Chari nag. On the northern side of these peaks is a glacier above Sorus nag, from which flows the Sorus nar. At its head is the first substantial ice field indicating that the Great Crest of the Himalaya is nigh.

It is a heady experience if one walks even 5 km up this river from Batkut. Shepherds' legends used to describe in poetic detail the sheep trails up to Langinai lake and beyond it to Kon nag (there are several Kon nags in east Kashmir) or Zajimarg gali (4041 m). From there they would descend either down to Kon nag, one of the sources of Arpat kol or cross over into the Zajimarg meadows in Kishtwar. These days, at least one trekking company in Srinagar is guiding trekkers to Langinai nag.

Between Lidru and Ganshibal villages, and about 4 km before Pahalgam, the first glacial stream is crossed. It is a combination of Sorus nar and Tuliyan nala, both glacial streams. Sorus nar flows out of Sorus nag (3690 m), which is fed by several runnels from small glaciers clinging to the cirque formed by three peaks of around 4700 m.

Across a ridge to the north of Sorus nar is the glacial origin of Tuliyan nala, which curves around a separating ridge to meet the Sorus about

3 km or so before the highway *(Map 5)*. Tuliyan glacier, though small, is a complete glacier having an ice field, an ice wall and fall, crevasses and a snout. The cirque enclosing this glacial lake is surrounded by half a dozen gently sloping peaks between 4000 m to nearly 5000 m in height. Further north of Tuliyan sar more glacial valleys appear.

4
Pahalgam, East Lidder and Sources of the Sind

THE ROAD TO PAHALGAM UP THE LIDDER RIVER FROM ANANTNAG ENTERS into a narrowing valley below the two Bumzo caves *(Map 1)* that have images of Shiv. The entrance to the Lidder valley is marked by two claw-shaped mountain spurs on either side. The Lidder valley starts narrowing imperceptibly from about 10 km before Pahalgam. The right and eastern side of the road have streams coming in from the ridge connecting Pir Panjal to the Himalaya.

A five-minute drive from Ganishbal leads one into Pahalgam (2110 m)—Kashmir's gateway to the Himalaya. Pahalgam is at the confluence of West Lidder and East Lidder, or Sheeshnag, rivers. The Sheeshnag, en route to Amarnath Caves, leads to religious solace and Aru to exciting climbs. Pahalgam is dotted with sparkling and lambent green meadows and alps and is encircled by the dark green of giant deodars. In summer the meadows are covered with so many flowers that stepping on them is painfully inevitable. This region has numerous dainty to imposing waterfalls.

The Aru and Sheeshnag lead to charming lakes, and heady climbs of moderate peaks, the highest of which are Mt Kolahoi (5425 m) and

Nichang (5444 m). Nichang is the highest peak in Kashmir, and Kolahoi is next. Kolahoi's western glacier is the source for the West Lidder. Nichang's western glacier is the source of the Sind. The V of Pahalgam, formed by the two Lidder *(Map 5)* rivers, has flower-rich meadows and many peaks, passes and lakes.

Pahalgam till the 1960s had blue pines. Some even lined the golf course. These have now gone. Where the golf course now stands, there were Gujjar camping grounds with their dokas and 'green lawns' as Francis Younghusband describes in his book *Kashmir* (1909). These were fringed by a deep, dark belt of firs, above which were white-barked birch trees.

Kashmir's valley and its mountains have been described as a diamond set in pearls. Pahalgam is one of this diamond's lustrous faces.

The upper part of Pahalgam town, to its immediate east, has the Sheeshnag river. To its north is the Mainpal nala. At its south is the Tuliyan. The lower part of Pahalgam, to its west, has the Lidder after it has been joined by the West Lidder.

Pahalgam till the early 1980s was a popular tourist resort with a bright financial future. Then came insurgency, followed by soldiers. Violence in the Valley started after the fraudulent election of 1988, when angry youth trained in Pakistan came back to fight for *azadi* (freedom).[7] Saving innocent lives was a massive headache in the 1990s. Following the abductions of seven foreigner trekkers in 1994, four of whom were later killed in the valley above Kokernag, many of Pahalgam's hotels and guest houses closed down. Only army boots could be heard during that era. Now peace returns and then vanishes for a while, but Pahalgam is prosperous and crowded once again. During peaceful times many short treks around Pahalgam are sold by the trekking companies in the Valley.

Around Pahalgam are little frequented trails going upstream that are memorable not only for their tranquility but also for the simplicity and hospitality of the people that one meets on the way—or used to meet. I have tried to revisit some of these areas in the past ten years by car. People remain the same, hospitable despite renewed anxieties, but there is no escaping the jarring fear of uniformed patrols and lurking insurgents.

Pahalgam, East Lidder and Sources of the Sind

I shall describe the right tributary of the Lidder—East Lidder or Sheeshnag—first and then return to go up the West Lidder.

On the right bank of East Lidder, and the couple of kilometres ahead of Pahalgam, is Nekbatun, nestled in the forested hillside. It was once an idyllic village with sheep and cattle grazing on fir-bordered alps with views of snows higher up. Now there is a road going through it and many hotels. More resorts are opening. There is more litter. The meadows are smaller with less green.

From this hamlet a gentle trail, dodging a couple of waterfalls, runs north up the Ath nar to the pass of Brarimarg (3540 m) and thence down Vimun nar (called Yemen by shepherds traditionally) and eventually to Hiurbagwan lake *(Map 5)* over a pass (4675 m) of the same name. From several promontories on the Brarimarg ridge heart-thudding and mind-blowingly extensive views can be seen of nearby Kolahoi (5425 m), which soars above in the north of the distant peaks above Zoji la in the north-north-east and of peaks to the east above Sheeshnag on the short range connecting Pir Panjal to the Himalaya. The faraway plains of Anantnag in the south can also be seen through a narrow window formed by plummeting mountain sides.

Hiurbagwan is now being called Harbhagwan. Hiurbagwan in Kashmiri means 'lake above the jungle', which is what it precisely is. But people from the Hindi belt do not feel comfortable with such names, and so they change local names to what's familiar to them in a fit of linguistic colonialism stretching from the north-east to north-west of India.

Both banks of the East Lidder receive numerous tributaries sparkling down from snow ridges above either side. Each tributary offers thrilling two-to-three-day walks through varying terrains, from green forests to grey icy debris and heady views.

The very next village on the road, along the right bank of East Lidder, is Phraslun bisected by Sezwatyar nar. It is formed by about half a dozen streams that have their sources in a kind of a triangular-shaped steep ridge over which there is probably no exit. An interesting and tough cul de sac—a minor sanctuary—is only a two-day return walk from the creature comforts of Pahalgam. This inaccessibility has not deterred shepherds from going up to succulent pastures closer to the snow tongues that come down the perpetually snow-covered ragged and rocky ridge. Gujjars have their dokas and Bakerwals, their temporary shelters and tents. Near the neck of the Sezwatyar nar is a green forested crucible where most of its tributaries meet. A short climb up any of these enclosing spurs gives out views of steep forested spurs, streams, meadows and alps and peaks across the East Lidder to Hagoon valley and far above it to the peaks and ridges of the Tuliyan and Langinai watersheds.

Several fingers of a voluminous rivulet called Hagoon meets the East Lidder on its left bank opposite Phraslun *(Map 5)*. The Hagoon valley has an unusually wide mouth (around 300 m) as the rivulet murmurs to its meeting with East Lidder. The views are stunning from the moment one enters this valley from Pahalagam by turning a spur near a Gujjar hamlet. A short walk through a fir forest above it leads to a ridge at the south of Hagoon nar from where breathtaking views of the entire valley can be had. It is a large, gently ascending (2400 m and higher) lush and lambent green meadow enclosed by a 4000 m ridge to the south and east, and a low ridge of forests and alps to the north. It is a stupendously pleasing sight of firs and willow-sprinkled meadows and snow peaks. Similar panaromas are there in the adjacent valleys of Wokhabal and Tramkazan nars. The reason why Hagoon is popular and makes people swoon is that a Bollywood movie called *Betaab* (1983) was shot here. A road from Pahalgam stops at the Gujjar dokas before the now-famous but always picturesque verdant cwm-like valley with wave-like peaks cleft with passes. Recognizing its public appeal, a silly government encouraged the use of Betaab as the valley's new name. Three nearby valleys, each as pretty, lie ignored.

From Pahalgam, along the left bank of the East Lidder, is a gratifying five-day ramble that is only occasionally tough. It follows a shepherds' trail. It begins from opposite Nekbatun village. Soon, one is in the thick dark Pahalgam forest filled with sun-dappled glens. After the forest are large meadows leading to a couple of tarns, several waterfalls and a glacier at the northern base of a cirque formed by four peaks of around 4600 m high. There is a col (3800 m) to the south-west that leads down a steep schist to the lovely lake of Tuliyan sar.

The motorable road up the right bank of the East Lidder ends at the vast open ground of Chandanwari (2895 m), bordered by firs, which is called Thanin by shepherds. It is in a triangle between the confluence of Harwat and Sheeshnag *(Map 5)*. The combined waters are known as East Lidder from here. Before the confluence many streams flow into both tributaries to increase their combined roar. The Amarnath pilgrim route starts from Chandanwari. There's a fir-capped knoll at its southwestern edge above the Harwat. During the busy two-month long pilgrimage season, here is a corner of silence for those pilgrims who want to escape from the teeming hordes in the tent-filled, crowded meadow below. The grass in a once-large pasture has given way to semi-permanent structures that accommodate myriad pilgrims every year.

The popular route to Amarnath starts from the road head of Chandanwari. It goes up steeply halfway to Pissu Top, and at about 3200 m levels off to gently climb to Zajibal, from where it takes one to above Sheeshnag (3600 m). One can veer off to the right to visit Sheeshnag lake. For the pilgrim in a hurry, a path heads north to climb to Mahagunas pass (4420 m) along Bratabal nar and thence down Kel nar to Panjtarni, Sangam and finally to the huge 40 m high cave of Amarnath before the head of Amarnath nala.

The Sheeshnag lake gets much of its water from the Sheeshnag glacier and the iced ridges south and east of it. Avalanche runnels from the ridge, and a few 4000 m peaks ornament Sheeshnag *(Maps 5 and 6)*. To its south-west, beyond a knot of rock knobs, the highest of which is 4242 m, is another pretty lake, Sona sar. It is fed by a 100 m high impressive semi-frozen waterfall fed by a small glacier. The channels from both these lakes pass through patches of birch and meet in a stony open ground near which there are some government pilgrim huts.

To the north of Sheeshnag lake is the Himalayan Pir Panjal ridge where the topography is decidedly Himalayan. The glaciers are longer, ice fields thicker and peaks higher. From Sheeshnag's north bank can be seen a 5000 m high peak that is south of Nichang, which at 5444 m is the highest peak in Kashmir.

Close by and directly east of Sheeshnag is Gulol gali (4391 m), across which is the Kishtwar valley of Warwan. The route to Gulol gali cannot be missed. It is simpler to access and prettier in May–June, when fairly firm snow still lies on the way from the semi-frozen Sheeshnag and the few bare patches have flowers. Gulol gali is an enjoyable but tough 5 km long icy trudge from Sheeshnag's eastern shore. The way is up the Bratabal nar, which comes in from the north for a while and then turns right to enter the unmistakable snow-filled gully leading to this pass.

From the spacious pass can be seen magnificently steep snow-capped mountains to the east and west. Especially to the east. By walking a few kilometres beyond the pass, down the deep Warwan gorge, one is overawed by the rugged western windswept faces of five sharp rock peaks looking taller than their 5000 m. The one in the centre is most impressive. It's a steep, perfect triangle of rock adorned with a smattering of shining ice. By climbing a spur to the west of Gulol gali one can see the entire Sheeshnag valley and peaks that surround both banks and in the distance beyond Chandanwari, the lower forested ridges that surround Mt Kolahoi. To the north and south, the view is blocked by two small peaks guarding Gulol, but by climbing them more can be seen.

Nothing—no written accounts, not even videos and pictures—prepares one for the immense cave of Amarnath. It's an inexplicable incongruity. It is wide and huge. It's a massive arched cave in which resides the waxing and waning ice lingam, which is what attracts devotees here. The proportions of the cave are mammoth, Himalayan—for that is where we certainly are now. There are other large caves in this territory drained by the Sind, but nothing as grand as this.

The Amarnath trek, for the initiated, is an intensely emotional experience, but even for the non-believer it is an exhilarating experience—provided it is done when pilgrims are yet to arrive or have left the Valley. To attain salvation and peace one needs struggle, and an epic effort is

Pahalgam, East Lidder and Sources of the Sind

required even though it is made easy by the state government, which has put up small self-contained cities of tents at various stages. About 500,000 or so pilgrims annually follow a rigorous path from Chandanwari. Another 50,000 take the even more difficult, steeper though shorter one from Batal, beyond Sonamarg, in the west. In these pilgrim campsites with tents, large stoves, furniture and helicopters, the damage to the environment is permanent. For the yatra starts in late June when plants are struggling to shake off the long freeze and ends in early August, three or so weeks before winter buries the survivors again. The yatra takes two to five days to complete.

There is a more challenging and scenic path to Sangam, but it is rough.

North of Chandanwari a shepherd track weaves along the right and left banks of Harwat nala, the main feeder stream of the East Lidder. A day's march from Chandanwari is the large and wide Astaanmarg meadow miserly sprinkled with fir and birch *(Map 6)*. 'Astaan' means a place of meditation made sacred by a holy man. There are several Astaans in Kashmir. This splendid grazing ground is green for a few weeks in late summer when it is crowded with shepherds and their flocks. The views vary, from steep mountain sides near at hand to 4000 m high peaks to the east, above Mahagunas and Saskat passes. At the eastern edge of this meadow, the Sarankut stream flowing in from the north-west joins the Harwat. One source of the Sarankut is in snow fields at the base of a 4000 m high peak to the east of Kon nag, which appears impregnable from here. Yet, two young men from Kashmir had come down this way after climbing Buttress peak near Kolahoi in 2015—a splendid achievement.

From Astaanmarg a pleasant walk up the Sarankut nala becomes risky and difficult as it heads into cliffs below Poshpathar gali (3983 m). The track is rough, scree-filled and so steep that few shepherds use it. After Poshpathar the track climbs gently up a wide snow-splattered gully. These tongues of snow are many even in late August. Down this gully comes the Sarankut from its main source south of Chhut gali (4278 m). To the north of this pass are several sources of the Nau nar, which flows almost arrow straight to Sangam (3514 m) in the north. Above either side of this easy gully are a few 4500 m high peaks.

Another divine way from Astaanmarg to Sangam is over Saskat gali (4200 m) *(Map 6)*. It branches off to the north-east, steadily climbing over scree and snow, and passes an awesome 100 m high, semi-frozen waterfall to the left. At the foot of this pass, partly hidden by a knoll, is a pretty ice floe dotted circular lake with the sinister name of Hatiara talao. 'Hatiara' means killer. According to the cricketer and explorer Godfrey Vigne (1801–1863), pilgrims used to go down over the Mahagunas pass to Panjtarni along the Kel nar and then reach Sangam. After visiting Amarnath Cave they would go up the Kel nar from Sangam till a confluence of streams coming from these two passes. Some would then branch out left to Hatiara talao and some towards Saskat gali and down to Chandanwari, which he also calls by its original name—Thanin. This route has not been used much since the end of the nineteenth century as it is dangerous.

Sangam (3514 m) is where all these paths to Amarnath converge. It's a wide, pebble-strewn meadow with a helipad for the rich who want to fly to salvation. The view is as magnificent and imposing as it has been on the various routes till here. To the south can be seen the gully leading to Chhut gali (4278 m) above the Nau nar. From Sangam, the way to Amarnath Cave lies to the north. There are, as expected, captivating views in each direction.

If one looks back, from the first turn in the gorge to Amarnath down the way till Sangam, it's an impressive sight in pilgrimage season. Above the right bank of the Amarnath nala stretches an unbroken stream of heads with colourful headgear jerkily moving up a sterile grey ragged landscape dotted with snow fields and dominated by craggy peaks. The Amarnath nala's roar occasionally reaches the endless nala of humanity puffing their way to the Cave. High rock faces dominate either side.

Amarnath's huge yawning cave is flanked by seemingly impassable cliffs. Half a kilometre to its east is a steep ice riven gully that looks improbable but is accessible only in August. It leads up to the Himalayan

Pahalgam, East Lidder and Sources of the Sind

Seki Pantsal Pass (4575 m). It has been in use, occasionally, for hundreds of years by shepherds, but it was first climbed and described by E.F. Neve, the early twentieth century Kashmir explorer. He, along with his brother Major Arthur Neve, was at that time a doctor in Srinagar Christian Mission Hospital, which is now the Government Chest Diseases Hospital, Durgjan, Srinagar.[8] Arthur Neve, had published the first detailed trekking guide of Kashmir and Ladakh at the beginning of the twentieth century. It was updated and republished in 1921 by his brother E.F. Neve.

It is easier to cross this pass from the north. The way starts a short distance from the east of Gumri camp across the Gumri river on NH 1, soon after Zoji la is crossed. Zoji la (3530 m) is a noticeable watershed. All the waters south of this pass go into the Jhelum, and those north of it eventually flow into the Indus. A shepherd trail goes directly south along the gully of Gumur nar, which has snow bridges even in August. It skirts around the base of the steep and ice-ribbed western face of Machoi West (5200 m) and then turns into the eastern moraine of Gumur glacier, which E.F. Neve called Amarnath *(Map 6)*. The best way is above the moraine till the point where the Seki Pantsal pass can be clearly seen. It's an easy climb across the glacier to the top of the Seki Pantsal pass (4575 m). Once this pass is reached, distant peaks and nearby rock faces hypnotize. Tarry here and linger there, get your breath back, have a leisurely lunch and descend cautiously. The 700 m steep descent is tricky especially when there is little snow. The Amarnath Cave is to the right of the base of this pass.

This way was used by traders avoiding the tax collecting station at Baltal but seldom by shepherds. Shepherds preferred to take a longer route to and from Sangam, through the vast tiered meadows of Minimarg. Here the Sukh nala coming from south-east meets the Gumri from the west. The way is up the Sukh nala's sometimes narrow gorge for about 8 km. At the first large confluence and before a large crumbling scree leave the Sukh to head west-south-west up the Kibla nala till the mouth of the C-shaped Kibla glacier is reached. The Kibla pass (4580 m) can be seen from the head of the glacier *(Map 7)*. The route is along the right moraine of the glacier, which is crossed about midway of the curve at the widest part of the glacier's large snow field to reach the pass. The easy descent on the other side of the pass ends at the base, which is the source of the Amarnath nala. The path passes below the legendary cave to Sangam.

To east-south-east from Sangam the view is of mountain slopes and snow fields converging onto a fledgling Sind river. Look above and beyond this mess of rock and ice and one can see the west face of Nichang (5444 m) about 12 km away *(Map 6)*. It is worth an hour of pause to show respect—especially at sunset when the peak shimmers and glows as if it is gold. By moving higher up a slope, one can see much more of this peak. It is on the border of Kashmir with Kishtwar. A kilometre to its north is the source of the Sind river. Nichang is called Yishan by E.F. Neve in his article in the second volume of the *Himalayan Journal* (1930). He says that the local name for this knot of peaks was Koh-i-Nur or Mountain of Light—perhaps because it is the first in this part of East Kashmir to catch the early rays of sunrise.

Amarnath is within the Great Crest of the Himalaya. The same crest that harbours Everest far to the south-east. From Amarnath, heading west, it ends 200 km away at the ninth highest peak in the world—Nanga Parbat (8126 m), which towers above the Great Bend of the Indus. The Himalaya starts from Nanga Parbat. Heading south-east, the highest range in the world has another 2100 km to go before it peters out at Namche Barwa (7782 m) at the head of the Great Bend of the Tsangpo.

From Sangam, the Sind river, the pride of Sonamarg, becomes a tossing turning voluminous river, getting wider as it rushes down, picking up all kinds of tributaries—from gentle to turbulent ones. The Amarnath nar meets the Sind at Sangam.

The meadows of Sangam (3514 m) are at the southern base of a couple of black-grey rock and schist peaks called Kajpathar (4820 m and 4905 m). This is a dramatic rock ridge decorated with slices of ice. They are drained to the west by the Kajpathar nar that, just south of Zoji la, emerges out of a dark gully as a short and steep waterfall. This can be seen from the road to Zoji la from Baltal, and one is struck by its inaccessibility. Yet, E.F. Neve and Kenneth Mason made a route along this waterfall and thence up Kajpathar nar stream through long snow and ice fields and reached Kajpathar. They then came down the steep rock face of Kajpathar peaks and met the path to Amarnath from Sangam.

There is a much shorter—done-in-a-day—14 km route to Amarnath from the tall, needle-firs splattered Baltal beyond Sonamarg on the Sind river *(Map 6)*. From Baltal (2890 m) a motorable road goes 5 km beyond to Domel (2933 m) on the right bank of the Sind. It is a tough walk requiring mental strength and religious fervour to get through. I knew a gutsy Tamilian lady journalist who, alone, on her first trek in the Himalaya, started from Baltal, early one summer day, reached Amarnath Cave and returned well past midnight, about eighteen hours later.

Domel despite being a sangam—a hectic and voluminous confluence of Hiurbagwan nar flowing in from the south and the Sind coming in from the east—is not a venerated spot. The Hiurbagwan gets its waters from a couple of peaks ranging over 4500 m, a lake of the same name and another one called Kon nag.

Domel is a fir-studded alp on a large green fan of alluvial-covered debris brought down from the steep mountain to its north-east. From Domel a precipitous footpath traverses flanks of forbidding cliffs well above the right bank of the Sind till Byari (cat) pathri. From here two paths fork out. A less steep path goes round a bend straight to Amarnath. Another one descends to Sangam (3514 m) where a night rest can be had. One has to skirt snow beds, avalanche runnels and snow bridges in the confines of a wild and grand rocky gorge, the grey monotony of which is relieved by intermittent patches of furze, grass and moss on both sides of the Sind.

The view from Domel is somewhat stirring. To the west is a shining peak of about 5000 m soaring above the scissor bends of the steep road to Zoji la (3530 m). To the east is seen the very top of Nichang (5444 m) and a subsidiary point to its north. In between are rock, snow and rivulets, and the Sind.

In late June maiden hair ferns dot the path along with more common ferns and many flowers. Jostling for space, but on the hill side across the Sind, are geraniums, gentians, primulas, thyme, the prickly spikes of the pale yellow *Morina wallichiana*, *Minuartia kashmirica* and many more. With the advent of September, the flowers in the higher reaches where shepherds still roam are gone, nights are cold and there's frost in the morning.

At this point I shall go back all the way to Pahalgam where the West Lidder meets the East Lidder. The East Lidder is famous for its religious significance. The West Lidder is favoured by shepherds and trekkers and takes one to supernatural grandeur.

5
West Lidder

The West Lidder is the name given to a union of many streams that drain lakes, snow fields and glaciers around Mt Kolahoi (5425 m), Kashmir's second highest peak. This river also collects waters from springs, ice fields and glaciers on the high ridges (4500 m) above its right bank *(Map 7)*. All its sources are located within this paradise.

The West Lidder starts from the elegant, vast and grand Kallan meadow (2920 m). Here the Kolahoi nala, curving in southwards, joins the Sosirwen nar flowing in from the south-east. This pleasing and spectacular confluence has huge fir trees standing like erect sentries that frame a looming, almost vertical, wall of rock below a snow ridge. It is as if Kallan's grazing grounds are a large amphitheatre, with a wall-to-wall carpet of green, striped with a few avalanche fingers that clutch the banks of both the rustling streams. Even in late summer. About 10 km to the north, up the narrowing cavern of the Kolahoi nala as it makes a 230 degree turn, one can see the friendly Basmai gali (4260 m). Above this is a 4660 m high peak, and behind it a pencil point 4860 m peak. Both hover above the Thajiwas glacier on the north. This ridge is pierced by the difficult Lakhath gali (4375 m). Sonamarg is only a few kilometres away from this pass and the snout of the Thajiwas glacier *(Map 7)*.

If there is a heaven, it must have at least one spot like Kallan. Above Kallan's meadows rise rugged mountain cliffs, which are too steep for trees. Gentler slopes have clumps of firs and birches. There's peace, perfect peace here. It's emphasized by the murmur of the two streams and tinkling of bells on horses of the Bakkarwals. There are permanent Gujjar dokas on both sides of the streams. In the brief summer there are also tents of Kashmiri shepherds and the Bakkarwals of Jammu. Further up, along both sides of the Kolahoi nala, are smaller pastures, which are filled with pastoral activities for a couple of months at best. A fond memory is of the green spongy turf curving over the banks of streams—unusual elsewhere but common in Kashmir.

About 2 km north from Kallan meadows on the Kolahoi nala is a cleft in a rock face above its right bank. Through this emerges the Riyul nar flowing into an ample side valley to meet Kolahoi nala. The Riyul drains Handil sar (3700 m) lake and a tarn at the eastern base of Gumbar gali (3877 m) *(Map 7)*. On the north side of a cliff above the bend of the Kolahoi nala is a yet another lake, the Sona sar, which is also the name of a small lake near Sheeshnag. In Kashmir, names are repeated even though the features so named are quite different. A stream called Basmai collects effluents from Sona sar and from the snow fields below the pass of that name and joins the Riyul. As is common with most lakes in Kashmir, the settings are striking and ravishing, each one unique. On the northern side of Basmai gali and Gumbar gali flows the Sind.

Two kilometres below Kallan is the much larger meadow of Lidderwat (2730 m). It, too, is in a magnificent location. Here, the fir forests are denser and wider as are the pastures. There is a confluence here of the Zajmarg flowing in from the west through a wide valley with gently ascending forested mountains with the West Lidder. The famous lakes of Tar sar and Chanda sar are two of its several sources *(Map 8)*. Some of its other sources are below Deo Masjid (4430 m) and Yamhar gali (4100 m), and also from peaks to the right and left of it. There are many alps along this river and its tributaries. The more favoured pastures are the ones at Dandabari (3320 m) and Sekhiwas (3430 m), as they can

West Lidder

accommodate many flocks at the same time. Shepherds believe that the higher the pasture the better the quality of the grass.

The Lidderwat campsite is across the West Lidder. Before crossing it by the log bridge, pause to admire, far above the right bank, the pinnacle peak of Deo Masjid (4439 m) through a V frame made of meadows and fir- and snow-covered slopes. Deo Masjid is an unusual Sanskrit and Urdu combination. Deo is Sanskrit for Devta and Masjid is Urdu. Both have been combined. Like Nanga Parbat's old name, Deo Mir (now Diamir), meaning mountain of the gods. In ancient times, there was much more warmth between the two communities than there is now.

About 4 km beyond are the shepherds' dokas at Sekiwas (3430 m) on Zajmarg nala. Before Sekiwas, a heady trail, along a tributary, branches off to Tar sar and Mar sar. After Sekiwas, another slightly more difficult path heads west towards Chanda sar, Hoka sar, Sona sar and more lakes. Peaks around 4000–4500 m high sprinkled between them ornament the splendour of the lakes. Nowhere in the Himalaya or Trans Himalaya have I seen such a spectacular tapestry accessible within a few days of a road head. If there is paradise on earth, it must be here.

There are two passes north of Sona sar and below the peak of Hokasar (4075 m). Paths go over these passes to Sumbal on the Srinagar–Leh National Highway No. 1, about 30 km before Sonamarg on the Sind river *(Map 9)*. All trekking companies in Kashmir, and some from the plains, bring tourists to this Elysian, this Garden of Eden, as it is the most accessible. These lakes, passes, peaks and splendid meadows can also be reached from Harwan forest (near Srinagar) to their west and from Khrew and Tral to the south. These will be described later. There are several other collections of lakes all over Kashmir. These are largely ignored.

Aru is the last of half-a-dozen villages above the left bank of West Lidder beyond Pahalgam, which is about ten kilometres away on a tarred road. Most shepherds and their flocks pass by Aru. So do trekkers and patrolling soldiers.

Aru's fir-speckled undulating, long and wide meadows are surrounded by receding forest-draped mountainsides. Aru is a paradisical spot to relax in. It is a base for an adventurous holiday too. Aru is in a lush triangle formed by the West Lidder river to the west, Armiun nar to the east and the Armiun ridge to the north. From summer till early autumn, Aru's flower-shrouded, fir-lined, lambent green meadows are besieged by all kinds of sheep, goats, cattle and humans—tourists, trekkers, soldiers and shepherds. Not far above Aru is a fabled Promised Land of alps, lakes, crags, rocks, springs, tongues of snow and ice, streams, glaciers and peaks.

The Armiun nar is formed by two streams—Girwar and Yemen—meeting about 3 km north-east of Aru. The northern stream is called Girwar nar *(Map 7)*. It descends steeply down from Katarnag gali (4763 m) on the southern shoulder of Kolahoi, and flows through two lakes enclosed in a narrow gorge of steep rock walls with loose scree at their base. Beyond the lakes, it hides for most of 2 km under snow bridges and then bursts out into a small pool. After this Armiun has a picturesque short way tumbling through alps and forests, more dense on its left bank than on its right, till it joins the Nafron nar above Aru. Yemen rushes down from a snow ridge to green fields in about 3 km. This flower sprinkled beautiful alp is called Honabacha (puppy). In comparison with the much bigger bowl-like meadow of Armiun it is small, and that is why the quaint name.

Nafron nar is twice as long as Girwar. It starts from the south of Hari Ghati gali (3856 m) and then swells a kilometre later after draining the Musa Sabin Qabr (meaning the grave of Moses) glacier *(Map 7)*. Musa (Moses) is a name that occurs several times in Kashmir's mountains. It is a reference to the Biblical prophet, who figures prominently as Musa or Alayhi Salam in the Quran.

More than fifty years ago, when I started trekking in Kashmir, there were few motorable roads and even a small trek would take a week. In November of 1967 a friend and I were trekking here. From Pahalgam we had to walk to Aru on a pleasant uphill track that passed through fir forests and then emerged onto the meadows of Aru. The log bridge over Armiun nar had icicles sticking to it formed by a spray from its tossing waters.

The chowkidar of the unkempt modest rest house was away but a neighbour let us in. Without us having to ask, they provided food for us. Such hospitality has remained intact through all the subsequent turbulent decades of violence. Aru is no longer a village struggling to live. Tourism has opened hotels and camps and shops and employment opportunities. No free meals now.

Aru became notorious in the summer of 1995 when six foreign, trekkers were abducted by insurgents from above here. Journalists put it in the spotlight. When normalcy eventually returned, with it came a smooth road, electricity, resorts and hordes of tourists.

There are many ways to reach the peaks, passes and lakes above Aru. To the east of Kolahoi are Kon nag (yet another one!), Har nag, Hiurbagwan nag, Dudh nag, four lakes of Sosirwen above Lidderwat and Dariyadar forests, the four lakes of Katar nag. Further to the west are the Tar sar, Mar sar and Chanda sar lakes, which can be reached from Lidderwat and also from Tral and Khrew in the south.

The ridges of Kolahoi and other attendant peaks are pierced by about a dozen passes. Each one has a shepherds' trail, but some are difficult, requiring the sure-footedness of a goat. The Kashmiri name of Kolahoi is the much more expressive—Gwasha Bor, meaning the Goddess of Light.

The Kolahoi group of three peaks, the highest of which is 5425 m, is a compact group on an offshoot ridge running west from the Great Himalayan Crest. On the east of this ridge is the pass Chut gali (4278 m) *(Map 6)*. It is to the south of the famous pilgrimage halt of Sangam (3510 m) in Sind valley. Its western end, the Zabarwan mountain, almost touches the crowded city of Srinagar.

One of the easiest and shortest enjoyable treks from Aru goes north over the Hiurbagwan gali (4290 m), past the lake of the same name and then down the river of the same name till it meets the Sind at Domel. Domel is connected by a motor road to Baltal, thence to Sonamarg, and along the Sind river to Srinagar.

A longer—about week long—trek starts from Aru. It goes up the West Lidder to the Lidderwat alp at the confluence of the Zajmarg with

Lidder. A charming but strenuous day-long walk from Aru curves along West Lidder and the many pretty alps along the base of the west flank of Mt Kolahoi and takes one to the lovely meadows of Lidderwat (2800 m) straddling both sides of the West Lidder. Cross the Lidder by a log bridge and go up the Zajmarg to circuit an exquisite emerald necklace of lakes of Tar sar (3795 m), Chanda sar, Sona sar and Koka sar, with Mar sar (3900 m) as a magnificent pearl pendant *(Maps 7 and 8)*.

The centre of interest, cynosure of all eyes, the Koh-i-Noor, of this part of Kashmir is Gwasha Bor, Mt Kolahoi (5425 m). Most people don't want to climb the second highest peak in Kashmir but see it from as close as is possible to view the entire massif. Its base can be reached from Sonamarg to the north and Aru to the south-east.

It is a classical pyramid-shaped peak more impressive on its north-eastern face which has alternating bands of rock and ice. Mt Kolahoi was first climbed by E. Neve and Kenneth Mason in August 1912 from Sonamarg.[9] They went up Durin nar through Sarbal forest. Then they climbed 1500 m skirting two sapphire lakes, one of which is called Nila nag, above a birch forest. From here they traversed to Lakhath gali (4375 m) on a ridge known locally as Kazim Phai bar (meaning, dangerous and hanging ridge). A steep descent of 1000 m brought them up against the ice fall of Kolahoi's western glacier, which they avoided by going up the West Lidder river to its source. Here they camped and climbed Kolahoi in two days. After this ascent there have been many, but their numbers have declined in the recent past. The most interesting climb was in the mid 1930s made through Aru by two women, one English and the other a Kashmiri from Laripora village, which is above Pahalgam's golf course.

The Lakhath gali route to Kolahoi's base is slippery, steep and risky. One is left wondering at the unusual ability of the shepherds who opened this route hundreds of years ago. This route is now more frequented by soldiers than by shepherds.

Kolahoi glacier has shrunk in area from 13.57 sq. km in 1963 to 9.88 sq. km in 2005 which is a loss of 2.88 sq. km in three decades.[10] In

1974, the glacier was about 5 km long and is known to have an extent of at least 35 km during the Pleistocene Age (2,580,000 to 11,700 years ago). A detailed analysis by Rafiq and Mishra reported that the glacier has shrunk from 35 to 09.88 sq. km.[11]

For many years now, only Kashmiri mountaineers have been climbing Kolahoi. They are pioneering new routes. More importantly they revived local and traditional names. One intrepid Kashmiri team led by Mohammed Amin attempted Mt Kolahoi from East Lidder in late August 1998, up the Ath nar that meets the right bank of East Lidder at Nekbatun. Going up Ath nar, they crossed Brarimarg gali (3560 m) and descended to what Gujjars call Yemen nar and Survey of India calls Vimun. Then they ascended the Yemen ridge to camp on Honabacha's stony meadow (where legend says Moses had transformed devils into stones). The next day, they traversed Harnag meadow which was brimming with flowers to some dokas.

They camped (at 4400 m) on the Musa (Moses) Sab-in-Qabr glacier and climbed to Katarnag gali (4763 m), to the north of which is Kolahoi (5425 m). Unexpected crevasses blocked their way but they climbed a 5116 m peak, that Neve called Buttress peak, to the south of Katarnag. They returned through Rabimarg, Kon nag to Astaanmarg (3300 m) after a dangerously steep descent, down the east shoulder of Rabimarg peak (4687 m). They described Kon nag, which had ice floes in it as 'green mosaic with chips of white marble'. A day later they were in Thanin, down the Harawat river.

Mt Kolahoi has two glaciers *(Map 7)*. The eastern one is smaller than the western one. Both are rather wide, about 300 m across, for a peak of this lowly height. At the south of the West Kolahoi glacier are two passes, Katarnag gali (4763 m) and Sosirwen (4629 m); below them are lakes by the names of the passes and seven more emerald tarns.

Kolahoi, despite the ease and speed with which it has been climbed, still kills. Two climbers from Kashmir were killed when they fell into a crevasse while dodging an avalanche in September 2018.

6
From Tral, Chhumahai, Chhumanani and Other Lakes to Sumbal on the Sind river

ABOUT 15 KM AHEAD OF SANGAM ON NH 44, FROM ANANTNAG TO Srinagar, is a culvert bridge between Tsaraligund and Larikpur villages. Under it, an innocuous sluggish tree-lined drain flows to meet the Jhelum. This is what remains of Tral's lively Arapal nar, which has had most of its water diverted for irrigation. A few kilometres before this confluence, Arapal is an energetic tossing and unrestrained river. I shall follow this river to its sources to the ridges in the north. It is a yet another enigmatic and outrageously appealing corner of Kashmir. Over the passes on this ridge are lakes to the west of Mt Kolahoi.

A few kilometres east of the Jammu–Anantnag–Srinagar highway, near Avantipora, are Tral and Khrew in Pulwama district *(Map 8)*. Tral is the sub-divisional headquarters.

In the eighties and nineties, from NH 44, chimney smoke could be seen billowing out in the east after the ancient temple town of Avantipora and before the famed saffron fields of Pampore. This was from Khrew's cement plants. There are eight of them. None of them spews smoke now. Pollution consciousness has ensured that. But, environmental degradation continues.

There are large ugly scars and pock marks on gashed hillsides all around Khrew and some around Tral. Limestone mining for the cement plants has caused this permanent damage. The springs and the Zanatrag stream that gave Khrew its drinking water are polluted and choked.

This could have been prevented but making money quickly mattered more. Yet, through these lacerated hillsides are trails leading to attractive meadows and snow fields in the north.

Tral (1690 m) is in a fertile plain drained by Arapal nar to the west and by Waltara nar to the east *(Map 8)*. On all sides, except in the south, it is bounded by forested mountains that rise from the outskirts of Tral. It has apple and almond orchards sprinkled on the many sixty or so metre high karewas. The water-rich plain of Tral has about eighty springs. It could have been a rich land had there been peace. The Arapal and the Waltara rivers wend their ways through narrowing valleys with mountains, hemming them in on both sides. No matter which tributary one follows or which forest one walks or drives through, there will always be memorable views.

Tral has a wildlife sanctuary that is about 150 sq. km of wooded area. It is between the Wasturwen (3000 m) and Kalultrag (2750 m) peaks *(Map 8)*. It is the habitat of the majestic antlered hangul deer and has helped in the rehabilitation of this Kashmir stag, which had once been hunted to extinction. Dachigam Sanctuary near Srinagar is the only other place where the hangul has been helped to survive. About 6 km to the east of Tral is Shikargah, a wooded village in a semi bowl formed by two spurs. This is the centre of the Hangul Conservation Project.

About 3 km before Tral is a karewa near Banmir village. In it is a deep cave known as Gufkral. Inside were found Neolithic-era domestic and hunting implements made of polished stone. Interestingly, the floor of the cave has been coated with lime from those ancient times.

In nearby fields and orchards, farmers work as in days gone by, but with one difference. Till a decade ago, Kashmiri farmers, while working in their fields, would carry attractively designed brass or iron samovars, in which tea would be kept warm by slow-burning coals. Sunlight would glint off them focusing the attention on a group taking a tea break. Lighter, more efficient but unattractive, thermos flasks have now replaced them, reflecting the imperceptible change in people's lives.

From Tral near the Arapal river, and nearby Khrew, are trails to passes and lakes to the west and south of Mt Kolahoi. Both these towns are in Pulwama district. Both have been affected by insurgency. Insurgents and uniforms leave no place for nature lovers.

Tral is the shortest but seldom used way to fabled lakes like Mar sar (3850 m), Chanda sar (3940 m) and Tarsar sar (3795 m) to the north and less-known but more exotic ones like Chhuhumanai sar (3780 m), Chhumahai sar (3900 m) and Pambach Khod lakes (3890 m) to the east. Such treks are merely a couple of captivating hours away from Srinagar. The Arapal and its tributaries, and the Waltara to a lesser extent, hold many enchanting valleys. In the meadows, nooks and crags by the side of lakes, in forests of fir and birch, and by dashing streams, roam Bakkarwals, Kashmiri shepherds and Gujjars.

The long and broad ridge where Arapal has most of its sources starts in the west from Zabarwan (2920 m) above Srinagar. It is known as Zabarwan range, a short medium-height sub-mountain range between Sind and Lidder valleys. One of its highest peaks is Mahadeo (3980 m); it looms above, to the east of Dal lake in Srinagar. It has Dachigam nala to its north. It ends about 30 km later in the east at Brahmoj (4100 m) and Angan gali (3795 m). This ridge, known as the Zabarwan, gradually increases in height towards the east. The passes on this ridge are Sangar gali (3500 m), Pir Pantsal Marg gali (3687 m), Pambach gali (4010 m) and Sinpathar gali (3900 m). At the last two passes, this ridge meets another one coming from the north, in which are Tar sar and other lakes. *(Map 8)*.

A pretty motorable road goes north-east from Tral along Waltara nar, skirting karewas and orchards, woods, fields and hills, till the village of Kahlil, below the pleasing confluence of Nagabal nar and Dudhmarg nar.

These two streams are separated by a 3000 m high fir-covered Mandwan peak. The ridge on either side of this peak has a dusting of snow even in early July. At the base of the ridge are gently sloping irrigated fans once made out of debris brought by these two streams and their tributaries.

One of Nagabal's tributary, Obliwas nar, comes down from the base of the craggy Banilmarg peak (3997 m). Immediately north of this peak is Banilmarg gali (3450 m). This pass is only 15 km or so from Tral, of which 10 km are motorable. Across it is the contrasting valley of Lam nar—lush green pastures at river level, with the alps, forests and scree slopes above leading to a snow-topped ridge. Lam nar meets the Arapal river at the big village of Arapal and has an exciting trek route along its banks. All these alps and meadows are sprinkled with idyllically situated shepherd camps. Centuries ago, it's these shepherds who had made paths all over the mountains around Kashmir Valley. Hunters and traders, and later explorers, followed them.

From the right shoulder of Banilmarg gali (3450 m) can be seen green wedges of alps and avalanche runnels on either side of the Wetharkut nar (later Lam nar) below *(Map 8)*. Towards the north are Hokasar (4075 m) and Deo Masjid (4440 m), below which are Tar sar and Chanda sar. The view to the south shows off more than 200 km of the Valley—wide, fantastic, rousing and mesmerizing. Most of the southern part of the Valley with Lidder and Jhelum, and beyond them the Pir Panjal range, are seen.

At the head of the sources of Arapal kol are several passes and peaks in the Zabarwan ridge. Two of them, from the east, are Pir Pantsal (3690 m) and Sangar (3520 m). Adjacent to these passes are easy and pretty peaks like Gagiari (3600 m). Across Sangar gali is an enjoyable descent of over 10 km of flower-sprinkled meadows with patches of firs to Harwan nala. Turn west and one is in the forest of Dachigam, close to Srinagar. There is a good road till the large village of Pranigam via Zuastan (2200 m). After this, a comfortable path goes through a forest, and a stiff climb later is Sangar pass. Bus services are irregular but taxis provide quick connectivity. Each village is populous and hospitable, seemingly prosperous with fields, orchards, shops and at least one mosque.

Turn east, after crossing Sangar pass, along a curving, sometimes rough, long track that fords the Nambalan nar (or Dachigam nala) and one will reach in three easy days the somewhat elliptical Mar sar (3849 m)—the source of the Dachigam nala. From Mar sar a stiff, slippery, rough trudge over a scree covered hill side about 500 m high takes an experienced trekker to Chanda sar (3940 m). From Chanda sar, a comfortable and pretty walk down a marshy and green alp surrounding a couple of S bends of the Zajmarg nar brings one to the shepherds' camps of Sekhwas in a day *(Map 8)*. Further to the east is another meadow called Dandabari. Here a stream coming from the south meets the Zajmarg. After a night's halt, one can go up this stream to Tar sar (3795 m) in the west. A right turn at Dandabari leads one to Lidderwat (2730 m). These numerous trails take one to enormous beauty—so generously displayed, so easily seen—and solitude.

About 15 km above Tral, two substantial streams meet Arapal within 2 km of each other. They flow in from the east. They are Lam nadi (confluence at the ziarat of Arapal town) and then the much shorter Brariangan nar (at the ziarat of Sotur).

Lam's source is a lake called Pambagai (3590 m), from which it flows south as Wetharkut nar. The Lam nar, a kilometre after emerging from Pambagai lake, makes a 90 degrees turn to the south directly below Pambagai gali (3760 m). It flows into a wide chasm filled with tongues of ice, snow fields, snow bridges and many meadows, each crowded with shepherds and their flocks in July and August. There are vast meadows, with clumps of firs, higher up above both banks of the Lam nar. For about two months from July, there are goats, sheep, horses, mules, tents, smoke and humans.

From Pambagai lake is a three-hour climb, over the Zabarwan ridge to the west, to another lake called Pambach khod (3887 m). 'Khod' means a whirlpool, which is formed during turbulent weather in August. Pambach khod is one of the sources of Brariangan nar, which flows south for half-a-day's march and then west to meet the Arapal at Sotur. Lam nar flows south for a two-day walk from Pambagai and then west at Waghabal to meet the Arapal river at Arapal town *(Map 8)*.

From Tral, Chhumahai, Chhumanani

Close to the north of Pambagai lake is a pass called Pambagai gali (3760 m). Below it is a lake called Hoka sar. Between these two features are two enormous and dramatic 300 to 400 m highs, and about as wide, perpendicular and frightening rock walls on the right side of the track.

From Hoka sar, two trails fork out to West Lidder river. The longer one goes north, over a nearby pass (3600 m), and meets the Lokut (small) Chhumahai nar a few hours downstream from its source in the lake Chhumahai sar (3897 m). Further down this stream is Nandakain (3100 m) grazing ground where the path and stream meet Bod (big) Chhumanai nar, which originates from Chhumanai lake (3784 m) *(Map 8)*. To Nandakain's north is Chhumanai gali (4000 m), over which is a way to Dandabari meadows. Dandabari is on the popular trek route to Tar sar and Chanda sar and more lakes from Lidderwat, which is a day's walk away to the east.

There is not even a small pocket in the mountains that gird Kashmir Valley that does not have shepherd's paths. Like the two lakes—Pambagai and Pambach. They are remote and troublesome to reach and yet are criss-crossed with centuries-old trails made by shepherds.

Wetharkut's (Lam nar's name near its source in Pambagai lake) left bank has four interesting and short routes to the Lidder. They go over two passes Veha gali (3920 m) and Lichudalai (4000 m) to reach Aru. There are at least three lakes below them to the east. These are Tson, Gandpathar and Munawar. The streams from these lakes surge into the Lidder through pleasant short valleys. Pahalgam is about a day's walk from any one of them *(Map 8)*. This variety in accessibility is what makes Kashmir so uniquely attractive. Many enticing paths lead to the same corner of paradise from different road heads.

To Munawar sar's south is a 3600 m high pass. Across it, after a gentle descent, is a spring from which emerges the Owur stream, which about 7 km later fertilizes the long and fairly wide green valley and fields of Owur across the Lidder from Batkut. Owur is on the Bijbehara to Pahalgam road on the west bank of the Lidder. Above Owur is the gently contoured Hodsar Bal peak (4060 m). This trek ends at the picturesque and once peaceful Batkut rest house across the Lidder river on its left bank.

Lam nar has an unusual course. Lower down its course, as it loses height, fir forests become thicker and widespread. At the long meadow of Waghabal (3130 m), the Lam nar makes another 90 degrees turn to the west. Its volume increases manifold as many streams from both its banks add their waters to it. The left bank has the 3200 m Banilmarg ridge at its south. The right bank, to its north, has the 3800 m Angan gali (3795 m) below which is the other source of the Brariangan nar.

A day's march to the west, the Lam nar escapes its narrow confines to start spreading wide from Lam village till it merges with the Arapal between the small towns of Arapal and Basantpura 3 km later.

The Brariangan nar as it meets the Arapal at Sotur also has as wide a bed as Lam's. Three kilometres before it joins Arapal, its bed starts widening from the pretty village of Narastan (2160 m), where there is a road bridge across the stream. An extremely short (about 10 km) but a pretty foaming stream, Sarai Bun, comes curving in from the Zabarwan ridge to the north. There are fields and orchards on both banks of Lam and Brariangan valleys, and picturesque terraces above them.

The motor road along Brariangan used to end at Narastan where the Sarai Bun stream meets it. Maybe it has gone on further by now. Narastan has ruins of a small eighth-century temple. There is a trail from this village above Sarai Bun to Pir Pantsal Marg gali (3690 m) in the north. It then descends into Nambalan or Dachigam stream, which flows into Srinagar's Dal lake.

A sanctuary is, I think, the best way to describe the peaks, passes, lakes and several small watersheds, at the centre of which is Mt Kolahoi (5425 m) *(Map 7)*. All are drained by just four rivers—Sind in the north, West and East Lidder in the east, Arapal in the south and Dachigam (Harwan) in the west.

Across the Zabarwan ridge, above the sources of the Arapal, flows the Nambalan nar stream. It flows out from Mar (death) sar (3850 m) lake. Then, it turns east, south and then west in a 260 degree arc towards

Dachigam forest *(Map 8)*. It feeds the Sarband reservoir after Harwan Forest Sanctuary where trout are bred. After filling the Sarband reservoir near the Shalamar Mughal Garden, a trickle flows into the north of the Dal lake. It's a minor watershed. The highest point in Dachigam forest is Mahadeo peak (4000 m) of the Zabarwan range. It can be seen from the Dal. From this peak, streams flow north, south, east and west. The main one is Mahadeo nar which meets the Nambalan nar in a glen in the Dachigam reserve.

Mar sar is a four-day rugged and sometimes gruelling trek up the Harwan nar. About a day's march before Mar sar is a hard shepherds' track that goes diagonally up from the left bank of the Nambalan nar to Tar sar (3795 m).

To the immediate north of the large Mar sar is a 4000 m high craggy ridge. There are three peaks of around 4300 m in height from which reach out three finger-like spurs. Within each of these nestle lakes. The largest one of these, in a gently undulating bowl, is Chanda sar (3940 m). Chanda sar is close to the north of Mar sar, but reaching it by a direct route is difficult as there is a ridge that has a steep rock and schist-filled crumbling slope for 300 m above the lake.

From Chanda sar flowing east is Zajmarg nar which picks up the effluents from Tar sar (3800 m) and about 20 km later merges with the West Lidder river at the unforgettable picturesque Lidderwat. The confluence at the meadows of Dandabari, where the Tar sar stream meets Zajmarg, is also a confluence of shepherd paths. One goes to Tar sar, another to Chanda sar, and yet another to lakes on the north side of Yambar gali (4100 m) *(Map 9)*. These lakes are on the Sind river side of the watershed.

The easier, and also very popular, way to Tar sar and Chanda sar is from Dandabari (3320 m) from West Lidder. The routes from Tral in the south are less known but more appealing because they are challenging.

To the west of Chanda sar are the two small lakes of Hoke sar and three of Sona sar. Each group is in a bowl separated by a ridge, connecting at the south the three peaks of Hangalmarg (4300 m approximately) to the twin peaks of Deo Masjid (around 4400 m). The combined streams from this clutch of tarns flow north through birch and fir forests to the meadows of Sonamus (3350 m), which have several dokas. Here streams flowing from the north of Deo Masjid peaks and from a 4100 m high pass combine to form Sumbal nar. The Sumbal flows north to merge with the Sind river between Sumbal and Sura Pharao villages on the latter's left bank. Above their fields used to be an old scenic rest house. Across the Sind is NH 1 connecting Srinagar to Sonamarg, Zoji la and Leh *(Map 9)*.

To visit all these lakes will take about a fortnight of relaxed walking. The best time to be there is in late summer, when the meadows are at their greenest and flowers brightest. The most common route is Aru–Lidderwat–Shekhwas–Tar sar–Mar sar–Chanda sar–Hoke sar–Sona sar–Sonamus to Sumbal on the Sind. Each of these lakes is an exquisite blue or green jewel, the lustre of which is increased by its sombre setting amidst grass patches, rock and scree. These colours are most vivid under clear skies and when the sun is way past its zenith.

The still water of Tar sar has ice floes till July. The lake is, only at best of times, sparkling blue, skirted with green grass sprinkled liberally with blue, white, purple, red and yellow flowers. On the east and west, Tar sar has plummeting slopes above this colourful strip.

There are no awesome towering peaks in Kashmir, and no long approach marches either. The endearing charm of Kashmir is that its glowing meadows, bordered by dark green forests, in and above which are lakes bordered by snow fields, are easily reached. Idyllic walks along murmuring brooks leading to sights of breathtaking beauty are literally round the corner. Reverence and awe are the most frequent emotions one feels in Kashmir. These descriptions of a few sights are teasers. They merely give hints of the vast opportunities for short and long trysts with this uncommon circle of friendly mountains cradling a valley lavishly gifted with glamour and beauty—a Shangri-la.

7
Baltal to Ganderbal on the Sind

THE NORTHEASTERN-MOST PART OF KASHMIR IS, NOW INDUBITABLY, IN the Great Crest of the Himalaya. The 5000 m peaks are not Himlayan in height but are stunning to see from the 2000 m high valleys they cradle. The northern-most area which is drained by the Kishenganga has Pakistan-Occupied Kashmir (POK) to the north, and thus trekking close to the Line of Control (LOC) is forbidden. These mountains can now be appreciated only by soldiers, although till the sixties there were hardly any restrictions.

The Sind flowing in from near Amarnath turns slightly to the north-east at Domel, where it meets the Hiurbagwan nar coming down from Hiurbagwan peak (4889 m), and then sharply turns to the north-north-west at Baltal where it meets Zojipal nar flowing in from Zoji la (3530 m). Fifteen kilometres down the river and on its left bank is Sonamarg.

On both banks of the Sind river are villages from which moderate to strenuous treks lead to lakes over the ridges. About half a day's walk westwards along Sind's left bank from Baltal is a large fan made by silt brought by the Durin nar, which has its source near Lakhath gali (4375 m). There have been concrete-free meadows on both sides of the stream for centuries now, but this is changing with resorts and affluent houses coming up rapidly. On the left side of the stream is the endearing Sarbal village, bordered by alps and pencil firs; from the busy and noisy Zoji la road above the right bank of the Sind, this pretty village can easily be missed. What one cannot miss is the massive polished grey-brown 30 m long boulder lying near the meeting of the waters of Durin and the Sind below the village. A footbridge is next to it. A motor road bridge is a few metres before it down the river Sind.

Up the Durin nar is a tough short trek to Lakhath gali (4375 m) made delightful by a diversion to a lake and a tarn. The way to the lakes forks out to the right, well below the pass. The bigger and higher sapphire-blue lake is Nila nag (4280 m), which only shepherds and soldiers get to see now. The southern side of the pass is exceedingly steep. The view of the contrasting peaks north and south of the pass is enchanting.

To the north, high above the right bank of the Sind, are a trident of imposing limestone snow-covered peaks (5020, 5025 and 5235 m in height), hiding the Bot Kulan gali (4480 m) leading to Ladakh *(Map 9)*. Two of these peaks can be seen from the road before Sonamarg as soon as it emerges from the Gagangir gorge at Satkari bridge over the Sind. These peaks are at the head of Nilnai nala (a tributary of the Nilagrar, which meets the Sind) and about 5100 m high. Seen from the pass, they loom above the spectator. The closest one, Sirbal, is a dark and fierce rock face that plunges steeply down from the peak. To the south and 1000 m high above the pass, and within arm's reach, is the grand ice serrated rock face of Kashmir's second highest peak, Mt Kolahoi (5425 m). Below it is the Lidder and its valley and to the north is the Sind valley, in the widest part of which nestles bustling ever-expanding homes, hotels and resorts of Sonamarg.

Sonamarg (golden meadow) is the name given to an appealing series of step-wise meadows. According to E.F. Neve, who had explored and climbed here in the early twentieth century, Sonamarg may have got its name from yellow flowers like ragwort and the tall mullein that were once abundant here. It could have also been so named for the golden leaves of birches in autumn or the golden glow of the meadows at sunset.

Till the mid seventies, Sonamarg's largest and only stable building was the four-roomed wooden forest rest house, in which Pandit Nehru stayed a few times and wrote about its incomparable peace and beauty. Sonamarg is now a beehive of commotion, frenzied construction and daily movement of thousands of infernal combustion engines from spring to autumn every year. There are more hotels in Sonamarg now than all the people that lived here half a century ago. Two long tunnels pierce the mountains below (Z morh at Gagangir) and above (Zoji la) Sonamarg. After their completion, there will be traffic throughout the year, but there will also be less green, and the pure white snow will have trails of horrifying diesel smudges.

Progress is necessary, but the pollution-free beauty and charm of the scenic Sind valley have to be preserved with urgency, extreme care, awareness, education and penalties.

In the late sixties and early seventies, the sound that stood out most was the mighty roar, even in autumn, of the Sind hurtling down the narrow echoing confines of the Gagangir gorge on the road to Sonamarg from Srinagar. We used to stop and relish its power and the thundering boom of a million kettle drums, and a few meters later below Satkari village emerge into sudden silence. These days, there is so much traffic that the Sind is barely heard and it is perilous to even stop for a photograph, for a traffic jam follows.

The meadows and mountains of Sonamarg (2686 m) appear suddenly if one drives in from the Srinagar side. One moment one is in a narrow and noisy gorge. A turn later, where the Thajiwas nar plunges into the Sind from the right, at the Satkari bridge, one is in a wide meadow with fir forests and not too distant snows rimming it. The devastatingly beautiful and astonishing unexpected view of the vast, spacious and spread-out triangle of the Thajiwas meadow (10 x 5 km), behind which looms a wall of glaciers and peaks, is an unforgettable sight. From the left, the Nichnai nar flows into the Sind. Several stunning lakes lie beyond the Nichnai pass (4070 m) above this river's source. The small Thajiwas and other glaciers are half a day's walk from the resorts and hotels in the lowest

Thajiwas meadow. The fragrance of flowers, grass and firs, even in a mist, is heady and so intoxicating that despite a chill one does not feel inclined to go indoors.

About 2000 m above the valley floor and straight ahead, looming over the road to Zoji la, and all the meadows and forests, are peaks with glaciers and rocks below them. The usually taciturn and unmoved E.F. Neve, who had climbed many mountains in Asia and Europe, wrote in 1930 '… it is one of the most impressive pieces of mountain scenery, not only in Kashmir, but in the world.'[12]

Sonamarg's meadows were most likely formed over millions of years when the once-massive Thajiwas glacier retreated. It is now less than a kilometre long. In summers of years gone by, these pastures used to be filled with short and tall, small and large flowers of many colours. Amid them were herds of peacefully grazing sheep and goats watched over by hefty sheep dogs. The only sound would be the occasional barking of the dogs or the tinkling of bells around ponies' necks.

Now one hears the braying of car horns and a racket from littering tourists. A good road has now gone 2 km beyond Sonamarg to its south and close to the fairly wide Thajiwas glacier valley. Thus, there are crowds and plastic muck crushing away what few species of flowers that may have survived. From about 2025, it will be mobbed even more and in winter too, when the 14.5 km long tunnel under Zoji la (3528 m) and the 6.5 km long tunnel under the difficult portion of Gagangir gorge before Sonamarg are completed.

Sonamarg is the base for many treks and climbs, and even short drives. The most stunning one is the drive to Zoji la if one is not carrying on to Leh. There is a shorter one to Domel on the road to Amarnath Cave and a short 2 km long drive through Sonamarg's terraces of meadows to the Thajiwas glacier.

Zoji la (3530 m) is the border between Kashmir and Ladakh. When a maharaja ruled Kashmir, there was a revenue post at Zoji la to collect tax on goods carrying caravans leaving and entering Kashmir.

Baltal to Ganderbal on the Sind

A steep road climbs above Baltal ('above and below') over excruciating gear-crunching hairpin bends. For one of the lowest Himalayan passes, Zoji la has an unusually high snow accumulation—up to 10–15 m. Zoji is a Kashmiri variation of the word Shivji. The steep road is impressive and dangerous. Despite several warning signs showing spots where vehicles have plunged over cliffs into the beautiful meadows of Baltal, they continue to fall.

Zoji la is a long defile where two decisive battles were fought. In 1557 a Yarkandi marauder Sultan Sajjad Khan Ghazi, also known as Daulat Beg, won a battle here and occupied Srinagar briefly. Then in the freezing mid November of 1948 General Cariappa brought seven tanks up to the pass to clear it of Pakistani invaders—a task he completed successfully.

The same Himalayan ridge on which Zoji la is twists north to Burzil pass (4100 m) and Nanga Parbat (8126 m), the world's ninth highest mountain and the north-west limit of the Himalaya. There are several passes on this part of the Great Himalayan Crest, all higher than Zoji la but the snowfall on the latter is the highest.

The next pass to the north *(Map 9)* is Bot Kulan Ganj (4480 m), where a successful diversion was made in late 1948 to harass those delivering Pakistani army supplies down Gumar stream to their soldiers pressing on Zoji la. This pass is down the north-west shoulder of Sirbal peak (5235 m) that towers to the north of Sonamarg.

There is a much-used trail to Bot Kulan Ganj pass from Nilagrar village on the right-hand bank of the Sind and a couple of kilometres from Sonamarg across the second Sind bridge. Go up the Nilagrar nar for half a day till it dodges a rocky ridge to its west. From here a path winds up to a tributary called Nilnai nar and on to one of its northern sources below the pass. Before Nilnai turns east to Bot Kulan Ganj, a 2 km long gently descending glacier can be seen on the steep south-west face of Sirbal peak. A determined person, familiar with ice climbing techniques can climb this peak and return to Sonamarg in three days. For such an attempt, guides are necessary. But they may not be as easily available now as they were till the seventies.

Beyond Nilagrar on the road to Zoji la is the valley of Kokaran nar *(Map 9)*. A short but tough one-day outing, crossing avalanche tongues even in August, can be made from Sonamarg to the southern rock massif of two 5000 m high peaks to the south of Sirpal. What makes this trek a must is a large cave in this rock massif and the view south towards Sonamarg. Any village elder from Nilagrar can guide you to this cave and tell of the myths and legends associated with it. The route is along the forested left bank of the Kokaran, a right-bank tributary of the Sind.

8
Vishensar, Krishansar and Gadsar

THERE ARE LONGER AND MORE CHALLENGING TREKS FROM SONAMARG TO lakes and passes in the north, above the right bank of the Sind. Before reaching Sonamarg, a bridge crosses the Sind. A little ahead of this bridge were a few huts of Satkari village. It is now a tunnel construction site. Now there are also shredded fir trees, long tin sheds and concrete structures. Not far above this is Sogput dhar (ridge), which has six passes, three of which are the Nichnai (4070 m), Babnar (4455 m) and Pandshur galis (4265 m) *(Map 9)*. After a few metres along the road, the Nichnai nar tumbles over a fan and under a bridge on the Zoji la road into the Sind. Up the right bank of the Nichnai is a well-marked path. It passes forests and meadows, skips over streams coming from the west, passes two confluences on the east bank and takes one to Nichnai bar (4070 m). There's a heartwarming 360 degree view of peaks, passes and valleys. A seven or eight-day trek over the Nichnai covers five to seven lakes like Vishensar, Krishansar, Gadsar, Satsar and Gangabal, etc., and ends at Nuranag in a side valley from Kangan. The first lake after Nichnai bar (pronounced *barey*) is the Vishensar, which gets overflow from its neighbour Krishansar.

More than fifty years ago these lakes had stunted juniper bushes, which, I believe, have largely disappeared. One reason could be that there are seasonal paramilitary check posts here, and they have removed them as fire wood as they burn well even if wet. Another reason is that this route has the largest number of trekkers in Kashmir and has become misleadingly known as the Great Lakes Trek. Misleading, because there are several larger treasuries of lakes all over Kashmir that can be included under this title.

From Vishensar a stream joins the Raman nala that flows north from its sources in some tarns and small ice fields on the northern side of Nichnai bar. From neighbouring Krishansar, an extremely steep track goes west up to Krishan bar (4060 m) *(Map 9)*. On the other side of this pass, i.e. the western side, is a somewhat risky descent, because of two small crevassed glaciers, to Gadsar. Some of these crevasses are covered with snow even in August.

If one is following an intrepid shepherd and his herd, one can wend an easier way over the Krishan bar pass avoiding the glaciers entirely. From these glaciers emerge streams that form the Gadsar to the west *(Map 10)*. Gadsar (fish lake), or Yemsar (lake of demons), is an oligotrophic lake, which has no algae and consequently has pure drinking water. Nearly all lakes in Kashmir are oligotrophic. Another way to Gadsar from Vishensar is over the Tsur bar (4200 m) in the west.

Krishansar flows into nearby Vishensar. All these lakes and tarns nestling under bare slopes have flowers in August, but the profusion and variety in Gadsar are much more, and colours are richer and deeper—even on its steep southwestern scree slope. From late July till August end the sides of these slopes bristle with masses of flowers and ferns—bracken, lustrous green maiden hair, gleaming blue delphinium, poppies and irises, hordes of white candles of Himalayan fox tail lilies, blazing red knotweed and buckwheat, clumps of vivid violet or pincushion flowers, blue gentians, yellow potentillas and flowering furze. Then there are medicinal plants like the violet *Aconitum violaceum*. Every colour of the rainbow encircles these lakes. And there are equally colourful birds.

Vishensar, Krishansar and Gadsar

The Gadsar nala leaves Gadsar to the north to join the Kishenganga at Barnai village on the left bank as Rakisin nala. By then it picks up waters from many runnels and rivulets and becomes a tempestuous stream. Gadsar and Raman *(Map 9)* nalas start within a kilometre of each other and their mouths at Kishenganga are more than 30 km apart *(Map 10)*. Raman nala has one source in Vishensar and another source in some palm-sized glaciers to the west of Nichnai bar. The Raman meets the Kishenganga at the village of Naruab. Only after the Raman mixes with the Kishenganga does the latter begin to look like a river.

More lakes are still to come. Over the Tsur bar (4200 m) one path turns north-east to Gadsar. And another leads above the right bank of the Tsur nar, which rises from some springs to the west of Tsur bar. This place is interesting hydrographically. The lakes to the east of this pass drain north into the Kishenganga. In the west this Tsur nar flows to join Mungshungan nar and eventually the Sind *(Map 12)*, which flows into the Jhelum. Both the Jhelum and the Kishenganga meet the Indus in Pakistan.

Mungshungan nar flows out of Gangabal and Nand kol lakes at the foot of Mt Haramukh (5150 m). The four-rock cluttered ice-clad summits of Mt Haramukh rise about 2000 m directly from the south and southwestern shores of these lakes. It is a grand sight, to put it mildly!

Adjectives have been inadequate and insufficient to describe Kashmir's never-ending appealing loveliness. Trying to search for the right adjectives to describe its majesty gives me a headache.

More lakes are lodged to the west of the ridge of Tsur bar. One fascinating set of lakes, arranged stepwise, have the combined name of Satsar (from 3600 m to slightly lower), which are a collection of seven (sat) lakes, but now, it is reported, that a couple are drying up. The drainage pattern of these lakes is interesting *(Map 10)*. Three of these lakes (one of them is also called Watal sar) flow north to Gadsar nala and then to Kishenganga as Satsar nar. The remaining lakes drain into a stream called Satsaran nar, which flowing south, takes in the Tsur nar at the forest-ringed, cliff-edged meadows of Chitardolu, which has some dokas. Three kilometres lower down Satsaran nar meets the Mungshungan nar, which collects the overflow from Gangabal and Nand kol. It flows past Nuranag and Wangat, below which is a small hydel dam, and then joins the Sind near Kangan as Kankanaz nala.

From Nichnai bar (4070 m) a twisting trident-shaped ridge, known locally as Sogput Dhar, of average height of 4000 m follows the norteast to south-west trajectory of the Sind till Kangan on the Srinagar–Sonamarg–Leh (NH 1) road. Many spurs jut out from this ridge towards the north and south. This ridge has forests and waterfalls on its southern side, passes on its shoulder and lakes on the north. It sparkles with peaks of about 4300–4700 m and is perforated by passes of around 4100 m *(Map 9)*.

On both banks of the east–west flowing Sind are attractively situated villages alongside its tributaries. The ones on the left bank (south) are far prettier and quieter. From both banks start rewarding treks. Several streams flow down to the Sind from the outskirts of the confines of the Kolahoi sanctuary. Some of these is Basmai nar, which meets the Sind near Kullan. Pashat nar meets the Sind near Reyil, and Kithol nar joins the Sind's left bank before Gund. Along each are fir forests and beguiling meadows, above which are the passes Basmai gali (4260 m), Gumbar (3880 m) and Yamhar (4100 m). Immediately across these passes are lesser-known lakes like Sona sar (3830 m), Doda sar (4055 m) and Handil sar (3710 m) and Yamhar gali (4100 m) *(Map 9)*. All are about a two-day march from the Sind. Just imagine the splendid location. Two hours out of Srinagar by road, and one is enveloped in perfect peace. Beyond these lakes are the well-advertised ones of Tar sar, Mar sar and Chanda sar, etc.

An old but renovated 15 km long aqueduct, from Sumbal to Kulan, collecting water from the right bank tributaries of the Sind, follows NH 1 above and sometimes below it. At Gund, the irrigation channel collects water from the Gund nar to its north. Gund used to be a small village in 1964, but today it is large enough to have a fire station, a bank, schools, shops, clinics and a large police station. It has expanded to the left bank of the Sind too. Along this road are many luxury resorts as well—eye sores but necessary for local employment and tourists.

An interesting short trek to Wangat-Nuranag starts from Gund Circuit, a heavily forested spur towering above the right bank of Gund nar, to reach an alp which has shepherds' camp sites. Above them are two passes, Mastrok bar (4025 m) and Dakteng bar (4120 m). To the south of Mastrok bar (pass) is a lake called Mangan dub or Mastrokhar sar (3910 m), to reach which one has to climb over a short ridge to the left of the path. If one camps here one can, on the following day, go to at least two or three of the half a dozen lakes in this area, only a couple of which are shown *(in Maps 9 and 10)*.

Dakteng bar is a little before Mastrok bar *(Map 9)*. Beyond it is the source of the Martshoi nala that curves to the west. There's an almost straight descent through alps and forests along this nala to shepherds' camps in the meadows of Baihak Sangam. Here it meets the Salnai sar, which starts far to the east from Salnai gali (4480 m).

From Baihak Sangam a path goes through forests skirting steep slopes. It criss-crosses Marchoi nala over comfortable log bridges, curving to the north-west to come out on the left bank of the Kankanaz nala between Wangat and Nuranag from where the trek to Gangabal starts. The Kankanaz meets the Sind near the town of Kangan. These are just a few of numerous short and exciting trysts with beauty that only Kashmir can offer.

A few kilometres ahead of Kangan are Chattergul and Manigam, after which the Sind river turns sharply south. The Leh–Sonamarg–Srinagar road that had been hugging the right bank of the Sind crosses it at Wayil bridge to Ganderbal. A few kilometres later a branch of the Sind flows through the marshes of dead Anchar lake and meets the Jhelum at Shadipora *(Map 18)*.

9
Gangabal and Haramukh

Between the lakes of Sat sar (mentioned in the previous chapter) and Gangabal is a ridge that has three passes. The most used of these is Zajibal[13] gali (4080 m) *(Map 10)*. This ridge has nine rocky knobs sticking out of it. If one is about 400 m up the north-east face of Haramukh around sunset and looks east to this ridge, one will be struck by the prominence of these rock features called Nau Kaan (nine ears). They resemble ears when lit up by the light of the dying sun.

The lake of Gangabal is at the northeastern foot of a steep rock face of the ice-ribboned, glacier-scarred and snow-topped Haramukh (5150 m). It is the third highest peak of Kashmir. It and its three attendant peaks look difficult from all sides, but they are not. One peak, Station (4877 m), is so easy and so broad that a large survey table was taken up and placed on it about 160 years ago *(Map 10)*. It is famous now as the point from where K2 (8,611 m) was first surveyed as the second highest peak in the world.

Away from the troubles of 1857 in the north Indian plains, a determined surveyor, G. Shelverton, camped for a week atop the 4877 m high and flattish Haramukh III (known as Station peak), to survey the peaks of the Karakoram and the Himalaya *(Map 10)*. He

Gangabal and Haramukh

had assembled a large fourteen-foot square survey table. On this he made angles pointing towards peaks he marked as K1, K2 and so on till K32 and calibrated their heights. K2 (8611 m) was, after triangulations from seven other survey stations, then declared as the second highest peak in the world in 1858.[14] The table was seen with a skeleton alongside it by Kenneth Mason in 1911—a former superintendent of the Survey of India and later professor of geography at Oxford. Both the skeleton and the table have gone now.

Nanga Parbat (8126 m), the ninth highest mountain in the world and the topographical beginning of the Himalaya, is just 90 km north-west from here and can be seen with a little luck. K2 (8611 m), the second highest peak in the world, is in the Karakoram, 210 km from here, and can barely be recognized. The view of the peaks is memorable. So is that of Srinagar. An overnight camp on Station Peak will give such an eye-popping view of the bright and twinkling lights of Srinagar that sleep will be impossible. A similar sight can be had from a halfway camp on the south ridge of Haramukh, which goes down to Tilwankain gali (4520 m) *(Map 10)*. Fifty years ago, Srinagar was quite dark at night and only a dim glow could be seen from this far. Since halogen streetlights and flood lights were added, the effect is magical from afar.

In Kashmir, bad weather usually does not continue for more than two days, even in summer. Only patience is required. Plan an outing for at least two days longer than suggested. If weather holds you up, watch the mists dropping down, rolling and lifting. Through gaps can be seen fleeting views of peaks or streams that will make you gasp. If nothing else, look at the flowers at your feet and talk to the shepherds. Shepherds are everywhere in Kashmir, no matter how remote a place may be.

Gangabal (2.7 km long and 3575 m high) is the largest high-altitude lake in Kashmir. A stream called Gang Ab flows from its eastern end to the lower and nearby Nand kol lake (3510 m), and from then on it is called Mungshungan nar. Its location is charming and stunning. Charming because of the flower-spangled green meadows, and stunning because of Haramukh (5150 m) looming above it. The meadows around the north, south and east of Gangabal are filled with wood smoke, tents, ponies, dogs, sheep and goats from June till early September.

The pyramid of Haramukh, when seen from Gangabal in the north-east, has steep rock guardians. On its northern side, the peak is smoother and has such a thick covering of snow that from above Loigul gali it looks like a generous helping of ice-cream in a cone. Above Gangabal's sedgy bank in the north-east there used to be a steeply sloping A frame log cabin made by the Himalayan Club in 1930. In 2010, even the platform had gone.

Haramukh (5150 m) means the face of Shiva. Haramukh has three other peaks. The next highest one is 4960 m. In spite of its modest height, it is a Himalayan peak. Unlike Kolahoi, Haramukh can be seen from practically all over the Valley and the ridges above it. A local legend claims that snakes are found in the Valley only in those places from which Haramukh is not seen!

Despite its fierceness, people have climbed it between sunrise and sunset from a camp at the west of Gangabal. R.L. Holdsworth, a former headmaster of Doon School in the fifties, included it in an article, 'Moderate Climbs for Middle-Aged Mountaineers', which he wrote for the *Himalayan Journal*, vol. 25. He climbed it in a day and had time to fish trout out of Gangabal lake before sunset.

Haramukh's base can be reached by several routes from the north, east and west. The most popular one starts from Gangabal in the east. The approach trail starts from opposite the ruins of an eleventh-century temple in Nuranag. After a stiff and continuous climb through a large forest, a huge swathe of which was deliberately burnt in 2010, a clear and wide path skirts the long alp of Trangkhul. In several clearings near the edge of this forest are rock shelters, dokas and shepherd tents during season. The long and steep gully of the Mungshungan nar, known locally as Wangat nar, and a classic saddle (3300 m approx) dominating the skyline above the nar can be seen from different points of the walk. Nearing Gangabal, the path skirts the Nand kol lake by a kilometre.

Gangabal and Haramukh

Another route to Gangabal is from the large and still-expanding village of Chattargul in the south *(Map 11)*. It is just off the Srinagar–Zoji la road and a kilometre before the turn to Wangat.

There is a famous ziarat here, and perhaps this accounts for its rapid expansion. Chattargul is on the Brahamsari nar, up which is a gentle path to its sources near Lawang gali (3970 m) and Brahm sar. Several small sources of this stream are in the ridge to the west on which is Tilwankain gali (4500 m). Beyond this pass are the lakes Chammar sar and Sarbal sar. Streams from these lakes are tributaries of the Erin river that flows through Bandipora.

The way to Gangabal goes through a dense forest and close to a couple of 30 m high waterfalls. After crossing easy Lawang gali (3970 m) and circuiting Kol sar (3740 m), which remains frozen longer than other lakes here, one reaches Trangkhul alp. Here it joins the route from Nuranag above Wangat.

There is one more route—circuitous, difficult and the least popular one—to Trangkhul and thence to Gangabal. This one is from a pretty alp above a forest. The way breaks away from the Srinagar–Zoji la road near the crowded village of Manigam and the J&K Police Training College. Drive up a narrow steep road till Andarwan village, beyond which it goes no further. Half-a-day's march above it, on a spur coming down from Kandalou gali (3400 m), is a picturesque meadow called Mohand Marg (about 3200 m) bordered below by firs.

Aurel Stein, the Hungarian-British Central Asian archaeologist, explorer and plunderer of Turfan gompas in the early twentieth century, used to camp here for months after every exploration. He would study, research and write in this wide-sloping alp. He was assisted in his translation and research by several Kashmiris, who would live with him here. This way he translated *Rajtarangini*, Kalhana's chronicles in Sanskrit written in the tenth century.

Kalhana had instructed the kings of Kashmir to tax the farmers so much that they would barely be able to live and thus will not be able to challenge the landowners and the king. The reason, he writes, is '…if they should keep more wealth, they would become in a single year very formidable … and strong enough to neglect the commands of the king.' This advice was strictly followed, sadly, by the rulers of Kashmir till the middle of the twentieth century![15]

There was a stone here inscribed by Stein himself, marking that he used to camp here. It remained there till 2007, when it was vandalized and even the pieces were then stolen. Aurel Stein must have selected this spot for its goosepimple-inducing view of the vast stretch of mountains and Valley. On a somewhat clear day one can see from the Pir Panjal above Gulmarg in the south-west, all the way till Margan pass to the East, the Valley below it, then Srinagar and the Zabarwan mountain above it, Mt Kolahoi, and the tip of Mt Haramukh nearby to east-north-east.

The Kashmir government is making an Aurel Stein Museum at Lar Marg, which is a little to the west of Mohand Marg.

Haramukh has about a dozen passes and lakes on all sides. The Great Crest of the Himalaya comes in from east-south-east and after including Haramukh moves north to Nanga Parbat. Its attendant spurs reach out in all directions. Within them flow streams, the larger of which originate from these lakes. Many of the lakes to the north-east, east, south-east and south of Haramukh are well known enough for trekking companies, even from outside Kashmir, to organize tours. But the lakes to the north, west and south-west are not as well frequented by hikers in present times as they are by shepherds who have their tents all over. Routes from the west can be explored from the district headquarters of Bandipora by going up the Erin nala from Wular ***(Maps 10 and 12)*** and or the larger Madumatti or Bod kol river.

To the west of Haramukh flow Chitrar nar and Kubbi nar which meet at a doka spotted alp in the once dense forest of Israntar to form the Erin nar, which flows past Bandipora into the Wular lake. Haramukh is usually attempted from this direction. These two tributaries of the Erin rise from the northern and western spurs of Mt Haramukh (5148 m). The northern source is to the west of Loigul gali (4045 m) and the western one is in Sarbal sar lake.

Gangabal and Haramukh

Across the ridge, above the right bank of Erin, are the several sources of the larger Bot Kul or Madmatti. To the north of Haramukh are several peaks of around 4500 m. In scree-lined bowls to the north and west of these peaks are several lakes like Madmatti sar (the largest) *(Map 11)*, Sainal sar and Chhiti Chhamri (white skin) sar *(Map 10)*. The Madmatti collects waters from all these lakes and from ice fields north of Loigul and Ganga galis or passes. It meets the Wular about 35 km away. On the ridges separating the Madmatti from Erin rivers are passes on bare ridges and lower down forests of birch and fir fostering diverse flora and fauna at their lower spurs.

Any foray here is full of surprises and terrain challenges—a heady and spectacular combination that makes Kashmir an unpredictable delight.

To the north of Madmatti sar is an exceedingly steep ridge that separates it from Kishenganga. Yet, there are several shepherds' trails that cling to this steep ridge and then cross over at least three passes that lead to Kishenganga valley. The easiest pass, in a manner of speaking, is the eastern-most one and is at the head of the narrowing Madmatti valley near the Madmatti sar as it curves west from the lake. This pass is Nilnai gali (4220 m). From the north of this pass flow two streams. The Pangwas nala meets Gadsar nala and then joins the Kishenganga. The other stream called Nilnai nar *(Maps 10 and 11)* meets the Kishenganga short of Dawar—the main town in rapidly developing Kishenganga valley.

The ridge above the right bank of Madmatti river is the furthest one of three ridges that emanate from Haramukh. The terrain gets drier as one crosses this last ridge to Kishenganga. The mountains are rather bare in comparison to those on the south. The lakes are few and quite small, the forests are not as dense, but views from some of the passes are imposing. Any walk here is full of surprises. One delightful treat is the view of the high mountains in POK, especially that of Nanga Parbat (8126 m). So near physically and yet so far politically. Rolling down these spurs on the Kishenganga side are clumps of white birch above patches of dark green firs plunging into the grey depths of its caverns, which are wide only in a few places.

10
Kishenganga

KASHMIR HAS TWO PROMINENT VALLEYS. THE LARGER ONE—THAT WHICH is drained by the Jhelum—is the charming paradise, the Arcadia, that droves of people visit. There is a smaller and narrower and rugged one beyond the mountains to the north of the Jhelum valley. This is the valley of the about 250 km long Kishenganga that cuts deep dark gorges. There are only slim pockets of cultivation on its banks.

The Sind valley is separated from the Kishenganga valley to its north by a sub Himalayan ridge that breaks off to the west from the Great Himalayan Crest at Bot Kulan Ganj pass (4480 m). It includes Haramukh peak. Raman nala flowing from the lake called Vishensar. Gadsar nala from Gadsar lake. All flow north to the Kishenganga from the Nichnai part of this ridge that is opposite Sonamarg *(Maps 9 and 10)*.

The politically and topographically important Kishenganga is born as Kinari gah on the Himalayan crest separating Kashmir from Ladakh *(Map 9)*. It flows out from the glacier hanging on the west of Kinari Darkush (5210 m) peak. A couple of kilometers later it swallows the Kaobal nala, which flows north out of Kaobal sar lake at the western foot of Kaobal gali (4130 m). Kaobal gali is about 7–8 km north of Kinari Darkush. Kinari gah cascades down as if it is in a hurry to leave the

Kishenganga

narrow dreary and dry confines of jagged icy cliffs with smooth, brown schist-covered slopes to soothingly meander in a wide bed and join the Gotum Shing stream coming from the north-east *(Map 11)*.

The mountains to the north of the Kishenganga are steep, furrowed and largely bare, except for pockets of fields and strings of birches and firs alongside tributaries joining the Kishenganga from the north. The spurs on the southern side are more gently sloped and have more and larger patches of green forests of fir and juniper and meadows. Till the confluence of Kishenganga with Burzil nala, before Dawar, nearly all agricultural fields and villages are on its right bank, which gets more sunlight. Dadareli Chak is the first village on Kinari gah and is on its right or north bank. From the next village of Abdulhun, Kinari gah is known as Kishenganga. It is a tributary of the Jhelum, which it meets much later below Muzaffarabad in Pakistan-Occupied Kashmir. The LOC is high above the right bank of the Kishenganga *(Map 11)*.

At the village of Naruab the Raman nala meets the Kishenganga. Naruab, like nearly all the villages on the Kishenganga, is on the right bank. From the north, the Naruab nala joins the Kishenganga here.

Nichnai bar (4070 m), the pass that has to be crossed to visit Vishensar and the cluster of lakes, has a couple of small glaciers holding its flanks *(Map 9)*. These glaciers and snowfields are the least of the four substantial sources of the Raman nala, which has a long downhill run. Only occasionally, before its confluence with Lokut Baib nar, is it rushed, when it has to pass through a couple of narrow ravines. But before its next confluence—with Baib nar—there are alps with flowers and forests and comfortable stretches. The Lokut (small) Baib nar and Bod (big) Baib nar rise from the west and east of Baib nar bar (4455 m), which is on the same ridge as Nichnai bar *(Map 9)*. About 5 km before Naruab, the Raman receives its last large tributary—the Makalwain nala—amidst sparse fir forests and vast swathes of green. The Makalwain is born in a small glacier below Pandshur bar (4265 m), which is a neighbour of Baib nar bar. Nearing Kishenganga, it spreads itself over a wide bed. A shepherds' trail—sometimes easy and often not—follows the Raman nala above its left bank.

Dadreli Chak is 56 km from Dawar on a fairly good, sometimes tarred, road. Between these two are fourteen villages along the Kishenganga. Most of the people here are Dards. All but two of these villages are on the right bank, which gets much more sunlight even in winter. The Kishenganga valley so far is between 100 to 250 m wide. It is fertile and the main crops grown are potatoes, maize, wheat and channa. Tributaries meet the Kishenganga from the south and north, but only up the streams bustling in from the north are there villages, about six of them. Of the about thirty villages in Dawar tehsil, about twenty are along or above the Kishenganga.

These villages, till about twenty years ago, were submerged in poverty and disease, and only Dawar—the tehsil headquarter—had some well-built homes. The hovels that were huddled together lacked maintenance and provided bare protection from inclement weather. After all of them were connected by roads, people became visibly prosperous. They started leaving the wretched crowded conditions and moving close to their fields in well-built wooden or log houses. Some of these even got homestay facilities as with the easing of restrictions, tourists from all over India began regularly trickling in. Home comforts like electricity, cooking gas, TV, mobile and internet are common. However, suspicious soldiers, sometimes overly anxious about security, can ask a bit too many unnecessary questions, like all over Kashmir.

Barnai is a large village with terraced cultivation on the right hand side of the Kishenganga. A stream called Barnai gah comes down from the south of Palat gali (3570 m) and meets the Kishenganga here *(Map 11)*. This village is on a fertile fan of sediment brought down by Barnai gah. The new motor road over Kaobal pass, from Dawar to Kargil, is above the village. There are patches of dense forests here on spurs above the river. The mountains are mostly bare, gashed, jagged and have crumbling cliffs. So steep, rugged and sunless are the sides of the Kishenganga gorge from Barnai, till its meeting with Burzil nala at Achhura before Dawar, that there are no villages.

Before Barnai is the village of Kashpat, on Kishenganga's right bank. A stream of the same name, flowing in from the north, meets it here. It has a somewhat wide bed, but the mountain slopes are steep above both banks. There is a path on the left bank of the stream leading up to two villages at its head. Tatri Krishdi is the last village below the LOC. From here is a thrilling view of the north face of Mt Haramukh. The people here would live in extreme poverty till; thanks to the LOC and Indo-Pak tensions, a motor road came here several years ago.

From Barnai, along the right bank of Barnai gah, a track climbs steeply to Palat gali (3570 m), below which flows west an ominously named rivulet called Shaitan Daku (Devil Bandit) nar! Its turbulent passage to Chorwan village is picturesque. The spur above its right bank is bare to the top except for a few firs guarding terraced fields at its base. This pretty stream must have done something devilish ages ago to have been given such a threatening name.

The narrow Kishenganga gorge ends at Achhura village, where the Burzil nala rising from below the Burzil pass (4100 m) meets Kishenganga on its right bank at the base of the striking pyramid-shaped forest-covered peak called Habakhatun (3989 m) **(Map 11)**.

Habba Khatoon (1554–1609), after whom this comely peak is named, was a beautiful Kashmiri poetess lovingly called 'Zoon' (meaning moon). Her husband, Yusuf Chak, was the king of Kashmir till he was defeated by Akbar, the great Mughal, in the late 1570s and imprisoned in faraway Bihar. A mourning Zoon escaped, became an ascetic and roamed Kashmir composing sad songs and poems which are still popular. This impressive peak that is a perfect triangle can be seen for many kilometres from the west of Dawar, the sub-divisional headquarters of Gurez valley.

A few kilometres above Achhura village, at the confluence of Burzil with Kishenganga, is Chorwan. The LOC, not far from here, rears its divisive fence crowded on both sides by soldiers. The village of

Chorwan sits tensely on both sides of Burzil nala, which comes down from POK's Burzil pass (4100 m). It has a school and a huge granary in which corn and other grains are stored for the five-month winter isolation. In its brief summer the sun is always mellow and in winter it has no warmth.

Dawar (2400 m) is not far from the confluence of Kishenganga (flowing in from the south-east) with Burzil nala (coming down from the north-east) at the base of Habakhatun (3989 m). It has the largest collection of buildings in Kishenganga valley and covers the widest spot in the rugged and beautiful Gurez valley. Gurez has been described by a cynic as a 'beauty under surveillance'. It had a population of about 40,000 that lived in some twenty villages. So bleak were employment prospects here that more than 10,000 of the young in Gurez valley shifted to Bandipora and Srinagar. It is about 150 km from Srinagar and about 80 km from its district headquarters in Bandipora. To get to Bandipora one has to cross the Razdhianangan pass (3560 m), which has a motorable road but is cut off by snow for five months. Most people who do not have the time to pronounce the unwieldy word call it Razdan.

Dawar, the headquarters of Gurez sub-division, once had only a pretty forest rest house with a large green lawn and a sturdy fence hugging the pebbly left bank of the Kishenganga. Now there is a well-constructed spacious tourist lodge built in a large meadow across the Kaobal road from the old quaint rest house. There are homestays in several villages. Dawar has many fertile fields that are sometimes damaged by avalanches. After Dawar, mountains hem in the river's alternating wide and narrow bed.

There is a recently completed motor road that goes from Dawar over Kaobal gali (roughly 70 km away) to Dras in Kargil. This road was made for security reasons, as POK is close at hand. The LOC cuts the mountains, ridges, valleys and tributaries above the right bank of the Kishenganga *(Map 11)*. Sometimes it is only 10 km from the north bank from Dawar till the village of Abdulhun below Kaobal gali to the east. To the west of Dawar, the LOC is even closer above the right bank of the Kishenganga. Above this bank of the fast-flowing Kishenganga are steep slopes covered with concertina wires and many check posts to prevent infiltration from POK.

Civilians can use this motor road all the way till Dras. At last the government has realized that permitting tourism means economic improvement for remote areas. And tourists (from abroad too) are flocking now to visit these spectacular areas for the pleasure of being amidst nature's splendid magnificence and infinite variety.

There are schools and hospitals, though in distant villages the only school or dispensary is run by the army. There is electricity in homes and a visible improvement in living standards. The Dards, the people who live in Upper Kishenganga from Sharda Peeth (POK) *(Map 13)* till Dras beyond Kaobal pass are not wretchedly poor any more. Some have made their homes comfortable enough for tourists to stay in. Many boys and girls go for higher education to Srinagar and Jammu and further away. All this seemed impossible even twenty years ago. At that time the road to Kaobal was still being built.

Dawar is a large sprawling town on the left bank of the Kishenganga. The town is cut into two by the Kisar nala which flows past Dawar's Juma Masjid to join the Kishenganga. Kisar nala has one source in the Kisar sar and another below Kisar gali (4100 m). Each is a tempting walk from the tourist hostel. The view from Kisar gali *(Map 11)* is skin-tingling as one is face to face with Nanga Parbat (8126 m), the ninth highest mountain in the world. Several other streams irrigate Dawar's fields, though the crops can be rather stunted if winter comes early.

Once suspicion and surveillance disappear from this strategic valley, Dawar shepherds will move with greater freedom on their traditional routes. And so can tourists. It can be a base to trek to meadows (Mianmarg, etc.), several lakes (Patalwan sar, Kol sar, Kisar sar, etc.) and passes (Patalwan gali, Mianmarg gali, Warli gali and Sukhnai gali, etc.) along the ridge to its south *(Map 11)*.

The Kishenganga has a dam before Kanzalwan—an ambitious and impressively immense 37 m high structure of grey concrete producing 330 MW. Nehru had called dams the real temples of modern India, and this one certainly is. The electricity is produced in an underground powerhouse before Bandipora after a part of the Kishenganga waters are diverted through a spillway tunnel deep under the mountain! This dam is a boon for this power-starved valley that is isolated for five months each year due to snow. Environmentalists also need not worry as no villages were relocated and no trees were cut. This part of the gorge has severely steep tree-less slopes eminently suitable for a run-of-the-river hydel dam.

Beyond the dam, a few kilometres later, there's a fork at Kanzalwan on the left bank. The road to the south and left climbs to Razdhainangan pass (3641 m) under which the spillway tunnel is. Another road carries on alongside the Kishenganga. It goes a little beyond the numerous terraced fields of the large village of Tharbal towards the narrowing Taobat valley *(Map 12)*. Halfway up the narrow Taobat valley the LOC and POK start. Taobat village is in POK.

The distance from Dadreli Chak below Kaobal pass to the LOC at Taobat is about 100 km. Within this the road descends about 700 m, which means a gentle decline. The part of Kishenganga in POK is beautiful too and well stocked with trout and luxury resorts. The Indian part of Kishenganga has only now *allowed tourists and homestays*. The Kishenganga is known as Neelam in Pakistan-Occupied Kashmir.

About 60 km beyond the LOC in Pakistan are the ruins of an important seventh-century pilgrimage centre for Kashmiri pandits called Shardapeeth *(Map 13)*. It is above the left bank of the Kishenganga where a small stream meets it. In pre-Independence days, before the motor road, Hindu pilgrims from the Valley would visit it for blessings. Shardapeeth had a temple and was also a centre for learning with a vast library once. The tenth-century ruins are similar to the medieval ones at Martand, Avantipore, Nuranag, Pattan, Pandrethan and (Datta Mandir) Buniyar.

Many decades ago, at the Kanzalwan *(Map 11)* bridge was a signboard. Painted on it was a tribute to several Gorkha soldiers who had died at Kanzalwan, Razdhianangan pass (3560 m) *(Map 12)* and Tragbal between April and May 1948 while repelling Pakistani forces from Gurez valley. This pass, like Zoji la, had seen heavy and courageous fighting.

Kishenganga

Raiders from Pakistan came up the Kishenganga river from Muzaffarabad, took Kanzalwan and tried to capture Razdhianangan pass but Bihar and Gorkha troops prevented that in a ferocious close combat. They surprised the Pakistanis by going up a terribly tough side mountain gully along the Viju nar, a tributary of Madmati, and brought artillery to the pass, shocking the invaders into retreating. To ensure that their success was not short-lived General Cariappa had a jeep road built immediately after. The present road is built on that alignment.

The Razdhianangan pass is a large uneven field on which snow gathers easily and stays for a long time. On some days, Haramukh can be seen from the pass. The well-maintained road is so thoroughly buried under 4–5 m of snow drifts that it cannot be located in the midst of winter. Tops of telegraph poles sticking out of snowfields help those desperate enough to walk across. Snow closes the road for five months every winter. But not for long, it is hoped. A tunnel is being made to avoid the pass and all the generous views it offers. At the moment, there are huge granaries in each village that store food for the difficult winter, and there is also a temperamental helicopter service.

To check intrusion by insurgents from Pakistan, India has made roads that snake over passes and along steep ridges to the west of Razdhianangan pass that include Gosai (3420 m), Miyingul (3680), Dudrei (3540 m) *(Map 12)* Giyun (3240 m) and Zamindar gali (3150 m) *(Map 13)*. This rough high-altitude road carries on west till the end of this ridge beyond Rauta ki gali (3320 m) *(Map 14)*. Some are a few kilometres, or even less, from the LOC. There are camps on this dehumanizing, inhospitable, bitterly cold, wind-swept ridge, where supplies are dependent on good weather and an occasional helicopter visit in winter.

The mountains, forests and valleys are slightly lower and more wooded than in the eastern part of this ridge that starts from Kaobal gali *(Map 11)*. There is fear and ominous foreboding that reigns here because of the uncertainties of hostility.

The miserable state of the villagers to the north of this ridge, till the LOC, was unbelievable in the twentieth century. Fifty years ago, people lived in unbelievable poverty, illiteracy and superstition, waiting for divine intervention to improve their life. They told of the many times someone or other in their family or neighbourhood perished in crossing unbridged streams, or were buried alive under avalanches and landslides, or were starved to death. Now their life has improved. There are roads, health centres, schools and post offices. The Indian Army is the catalyst for improvement in these areas.

The Razdhainangan pass is on a ridge that has a 3990 m high peak in the west and a 4020 m high Viju peak to the east. From its west the Bo nar and from the east the Viju flows to the south. On either side of the Razdhainangan pass are more passes *(Map 11)*.

The ones to the east have shepherds. The ones to the west have army camps! Go west along the ridge from Razdhainangan pass (3990 m) and one is astonished at the sites where army camps are perched. No eagles here. These camps are on high ridges and higher passes that were once used only by shepherds, and a surveyor or two. The army stationed at such spaces have a tough life, but even though they will move on after three months of tough patrols and feeling trapped, the experience leaves most of them bitter against the land and its people.

11
Razdhainangan Pass to Wular

From Razdhainangan pass, a smooth but seasonal road darts down between aged tall fir trees to the district headquarters at Bandipora. On the way is an emerald-green meadow called Tragbal spread over many terraces *(Map 12)*. Below the western side of the road is the once dense fir forest of Bonar plunging down the mountainside. As the road winds lower from the pleasing fir-spangled meadows, there are a couple of prospect points off the road. From these can be seen the dying Wular lake in the Valley's edge, the narrow confines of Madmati nala and Viju nar and their confluence, and above them Mt Haramukh's shining white triangle. This lavish view has another icing. Beyond the edge of the Valley to the south-east and east is a long range of glistening snow peaks, the Pir Panjal.

Descending to Bandipora, past a couple of villages, the road goes above the Bon nar. This is the stream that is born in snow fields and springs to the west of Razdhainangan pass. Into this stream, the waters of the Kishenganga are released after powering three massive underground generators at Karalapora. The combined waters meet Madmati or Bot Kul nala at Khaiyar in a 3 km wide valley just before Bandipora. There's a bridge below Khaiyar now. If ever one has the time, a walk to the head of this valley in an early autumn afternoon would be treasured for long. The sun is mellow, trees are changing colour to soft yellow, Walnuts are ripening, the vast paddy fields are ripe and there are pretty peasant homes outside which hang strings of drying chillies. Above the valley on both sides are steep forest-dotted mountain sides. People are working in the fields, orchards and homes, and yet there's silence!

A motorable road goes further up the right bank of the Madmati till its confluence with Viju nar. At this place is the terraced village of Athwatoo, which, apart from the narrow views of three valleys, has an interesting legend *(Map 12)*. According to tradition, Moses after his escape from Egypt's Pharaoh settled here and is buried at a hilltop called Baal Bebo. The legend of Moses in Kashmir surfaces in several places.

From the confluence of Viju and Madmati an irrigational canal starts. It ends near Wadura village where it flows into the Pohru river as narrow as a drain *(Map 13)*. The left bank of the Madmati is green and forested as it has several brooks coming down from snow ridges above.

Madmati or Bot Kul nala flows south through Bandipora town to enter the shrivelled Wular at its north. The Erin nala coming in from the east joins the Wular a little below at Nusu ghat *(Map 12)*. Further down the east shore of the once large lake, the Jhelum flows in *(Map 18)*. Perhaps, one hopes, the waters of the Kishenganga, which are being diverted from the Kunzalwan dam on the Kishenganga, will help dredge the Wular of a part of the parasitic growth that is clogging it up. In the years gone by, this was the lake on which there would be furious storms that capsized boats. Now, much of its 250 sq. km is a swamp or has willows on reclaimed land. Unbelievably, willow plantations were encouraged from the sixties, and they helped in killing the Wular acre by acre, year after year. Willows are used to make Kashmir's famous cricket bats.

12
Kupwara and Lolab

East of the Razdhainangan pass till Kaobal gali, the sub-Himalayan ridges are somewhat narrow, and even serrated like saws, at some places. To the west of this pass, the wide ridge of the short mountain range known as Shamsabari has been levelled at some places for motorable roads. On these ridges border road engineers have shown remarkable feats of gutsy road building without any concern for the environment.

Security is extremely costly. With politicians having failed, there is no other way to prevent insurgency. If only the uniforms one meets could be trained to reduce tension among our own people, not increase it. Even tourists are handled roughly at the best of times. It is easy to imagine what humiliation the residents go through often at the hands of the insurgents and soldiers.

Forests have been drastically reduced by Kashmir's powerful timber lobby. A road is the easiest excuse to cut more trees than necessary. And pine and fir wood sells well. Here each patch of forest, no matter how small or degraded, has a name—Brarbaz, Koragbal, Kachhama Melyal, etc. The local folk cared for them so tenderly and protectively that they named each tract and strip of forest. Earlier, each family was allowed to cut one tree to build or repair their home. Now, this little comfort has vanished, and they buy wood at an enormous cost for themselves and enormous profit to the timber merchants.

The ridge that bears Razdhainangan pass twists above the left bank of Kishenganga *(Map 13)* to the west. Its average height is 3000–4000 m with some peaks only slightly higher. On it are several passes. Many spurs wend north and south from it. Between these spurs flow nars and nallahs to meet the Kishenganga in the north or Kahmil in the south. Streams flowing south down these spurs fall into tributaries of the Jhelum. The west and north-west of Razdhainangan pass borders the Kupwara district, with some villages close to the LOC. People cultivate fields almost upto the LOC and soldiers are everywhere.

The north–south aligned Kongdor (3400 m) ridge, west of Razdhainangan pass, marks the boundary between Bandipora district and Kupwara *(Map 12)*. Kupwara is a polyglot town. It has well-established Sikh and Hindu families living peacefully with Muslims. In a couple of places, mosques and temples exist amicably side by side. Some shrines are revered and visited by all, like the Muqam Shah Wali Ziarat at Darugmul before Kupwara. Not too far away, in a scenic forest in Handwara sub-division, is the ancient temple of Bhadrakali. It was burnt down by militants in 1994 to the embarrassment of all. The army-renovated temple is just as popular as the ancient idol made out of a single piece of black stone.

Kupwara district is Kashmir's poorest and shabbiest, and it is also one of its four most attractive districts. It is the third largest apple producing and second highest dry fruit yielding district in Kashmir. The right bank of the wide bed of the Kahmil river used to be covered with garbage[16] and filth. The excuse for this municipal slovenliness was shortage of funds. There is a perpetual threat of money-guzzling insurgency hanging over it as it borders POK. Security thus comes first, not development. Had the latter been given priority maybe the former would have decreased.

Kupwara has many springs, beautiful inhabited valleys and passes. The contrast of squalour with the magnificence of this arresting, elegant

Kupwara and Lolab

and soothing land of mountains and valleys is both a delight and a pain to see.

The town of Kupwara is on a Y formed by three rivers—Lolab kol from the east-north-east joins the Kahmil from the west to form Pohru river that flows east. Before the Lolab joins the Kahmil, another river from the north meets the former. This is the Haehom kol, which has a short and interesting life. Its tributaries are Safawali nar, Kain nar and Haehom nar. They have their sources in Safawali gali (2937 m), Kripanwali gali (2920 m) and Atham gali (2960 m). These passes and several more to the west are on the ridge known as Shamsabari. Each comes down a fertile and crowded valley brimming with fields and orchards *(Map 13)*. None of these gurgling chattering streams has a run of more than 20 km. Each has roads along them. The road up Safawali nar goes past its source and over the Safawali gali (2937 m), and passes villages nestling within pretty fir-dotted meadows to almost reach the LOC, which here is on the south side of the Kishenganga.

In the most distant villages in the border areas, the army is the only source of relief from disease, unemployment, hunger, isolation and illiteracy. Sadly, as they are close to the LOC, they also live under perpetual and inevitable suspicion and shell-shocked stupor. After every incursion, they face an inquisition. This is routine operating procedure but it leaves them tense.

To the west of Haehom's watershed is Trehgam tehsil on the left bank of the Kahmil. It is at the end of a long fertile rectangle formed by two nalas coming down from Putakhan gali (2950 m) and another pass to its east. Vast swathes of idyllic fields, orchards and villages crowd both banks of the two streams from a few hundred metres below the ridge (3000 m). The largest villages are those of Ludarwan and Zarhama, famous for apples and apricots *(Maps 13 and 14)*.

To the east of Haehom kol is the Lolab river, which is a combination of many tributaries darting down from the 3000 m high and higher ridges in the north and a cirque of ridges 2000–2500 m high stretching from the east to south to west.

About 9 km east of Kupwara is the entrance to Lolab valley at Khumarial, where an old rest house has been made into a spacious new tourist bungalow. It was once known as the Indira Hut, as Indira Gandhi had spent her honeymoon here in 1942.[17] There is a big gate at the entrance promising 'jannat', i.e., paradise. Paradise is everywhere—in the galloping streams and spring-fed fields abundant with crops, trees laden with fruit and forest-covered mountains all around. Lolab valley is in a north-west to south-east direction. It has several small lakes, some of which are home to seasonal birds and also algae.

The Lolab's main tributary is Manchhar nadi. It collects several rivulets, streams, rills, runnels and brooks that sparkle out from magnificent forests of firs and pines on mountain slopes. These surround the bewitching four-finger-shaped green valleys at the east, south and west. They are dotted with springs, filled with paddy fields, lined by streams and ringed by almond, apple, apricot, cherry, peach, pear and walnut trees *(Map 13)*. This is the 5 km wide and 25 km long Lolab valley, one of the most charming, fecund and large valleys in all of Kashmir. The wide entrance of the valley has the large village of Sogam on the west and 7 km to the east is Krusan.

Lolab valley is the name given to a plain where about two dozen villages cluster around the sources of the Manchhar. It is around 120 km from Srinagar on a good road but visited by only a few tourists. Everyone who has been here swears that Lolab is the jewel in Kashmir's crown. Lolab is a fortunate fertile green valley. Even Kashmiris, used to abundant charm, swoon on seeing the valley of Lolab. Spring and autumn are the best seasons to be here.

In Lolab, there are also many ziarats and masjids. There is the grave of Kashyap rishi as well, next to a deep spring called Lavnag, near Lalpur to the east.

Sogam (1590 m) at the northern edge of the Lolab palm is the administrative headquarters of this Elysium. From it, roads go to the end of the attendant finger-shaped valleys. In four of them—Chandigam, Andarbug, Diwar and Maqam (Lalpora)—are rest houses and tourist lodges. The houses are sturdy, single and double storied. Each village has ponds or man-made tanks. With so much water, this valley is green till late autumn after which frost settles.

Maqam is at the entrance of a small finger-like valley jutting out of the main Lolab valley in the east. Its crescent-shaped terraced fields cascade down from the slopes around it to meet a stream and a road in the middle. Beyond the fields of Maqam, and above the encircling forested mountain slopes, is a shepherds' path over Nagmarg gali (2880 m) to Bandipora. From Andarbug too is a path across this ridge to Bandipora. Immediately below a curve of thick forests are the meadows of Nagmarg in the middle of which is the idyllic Rampur village *(Map 13)*. In these forests were once black and brown bears, an occasional leopard and deer. With roads penetrating these forests and anti-insurgency operations, these animals have disappeared. From Lolab, one could cross the Nagmarg gali and go down the thick fir and oak forest of Nagmarg and wend one's way through paddy fields and apple orchards and in half a day reach the motor road below the Alusa post office in Bandipora.

This is an enchanted valley that defies description. But you get out of your trance once olive greens appear and you see the apprehensive and helpless looks on the residents. Even under clear skies dark clouds are not far.

Each finger-shaped valley of the Lolab is separated by forested spurs of about 2000 m. The average height of the Lolab fields is about 1700 m. The one with the best tourist house in Lolab is Chandigam with a tarred road going right upto it. The next finger has *(Map 13)* yet another pretty village called Doruswain in which are several fish-stocked ponds. In 2016, after the insurgent Burhan Wani was killed, all three tourist houses in Lolab were burnt down despite constant army and police patrolling. Such is the cunning reach and insidious influence of insurgents.

At last winds of change are fluttering through the Lolab now. There is electricity, tarred roads, better A-frame houses, a variety of agricultural output, orchards of apples, apricots, walnuts, marketing facilities, telephone and mobile connections and even post offices. A better life seems possible if insurgency vanishes.

Roads are everywhere as part of development and security and have left ugly scars on forested slopes. Up steep hillsides, on ridges and through villages and valleys. Every stream with thrilling but precarious log bridges has concrete over it.

Fifty years ago, the forests of fir were thick, dark and deep, and one could walk in them without rude questions from soldiers and insurgents. Now the forests are patchy. While blasting forests and mountainsides to build roads, the builders let loose debris that destroyed grand deodars, buried deep many warrens and hutches of animals and nesting grounds for birds and clogged streams.

In July 2009, Earth Science India reported that deforestation led to severe soil erosion in the Kahmil river catchment area. 'In the moderate to severe erosion class, the total area in 1974–75 was 1908.8 hectares, which accounted for 3.7 per cent of the total geographical area. In the year 2000, the area under this class was 5980.1 hectares accounting for 11.7 per cent of the total area. This indicates an increase of about 8 percent.'[18]

At Khumarial, at the entrance of Lolab valley, Kalaruch nala from the north meets the Lolab. About 5 km to the north, along the right bank of the Kalaruch, is a place known by the same name. Kala is Persian for qila or fort, and 'ruch' is for Russia. Ancients must have had a sense of geography to have named it so! For there are long caves here and legend says that they reach Russia, *but there's no truth in it.*

Many years earlier when peace instead of war covered the land the entrance to the caves were partly hidden by bushes and even a tree. These caves were missed by surveyors in the late nineteenth century, though the people knew about them. It was only in the nineties when insurgency had increased that the army discovered that these caves were being used as a refuge by the rebels. So, they reduced their length by blasting the roofs down. The caves are a stiff half an hour climb from the road. They are surrounded by some young forests of pine, above which are grander firs. Below these caves are 8 m deep rockcut arches, called Satburn. They are

Kupwara and Lolab

old it is easy to see, but why they were made is unfathomable. Young men hang around offering to be guides.

A couple of kilometres above Kalaruch is a confluence of the northwestern Nawa nar with the Thaiyan nar at the Thaiyan village. Each of these carries waters of many smaller streams coming down from passes like Atham gali, Sonapindi gali, Nawan gali and Ura gali and more *(Map 13)*, which are close to the Line of Control. The courses of these streams are crowded with fields and orchards. The many villages around them are connected with roads that eventually lead to the Kupwara–Srinagar highway. Thaiyan has a rest house above the spring-dotted fields of the village. A wide, extensive and exciting view is had from here—from the confluence below, the entire Kalaruch valley till it connects with the Lolab, and beyond with Kupwara, to the snow-covered distant ridge above Gulmarg can be seen.

Another 4 km beyond Thaiyan is the confluence of Rangdori with Nawa nar below the village of Nagasari, which too has many springs. Springs are in many villages and are responsible for the healthy agriculture here. There is a good road till Nagasari. Beyond it a rougher road goes up along the Nawa nar and then switches steeply over many hairpin bends to a 3267 m high pass called Murdari gali *(Map 13)*. The Rangdori rises in snow fields below Ura gali (3137 m) and the peak of Rangtop (3485 m).

All these passes, and many more, split the watershed ridge that is entirely in Kupwara *(Maps 12 and 13)*. The streams to the south of this ridge flow into Kahmil nala, while those to the north meet the Kishenganga. This higher ground is in India while the LOC, which is much lower down, cuts access to Kishenganga.

The views to the north and south from some of the passes, like Murdari gali (3107 m), on this ridge are stunning. To the south one can see down the entire valley of Kalaruch and the several gullies from which its tributaries flow. In the middle can be seen a sliver of the Lolab kol and the dense forested ridge of Kandi forest above Chandigam. Further south are the plains of Handwara and beyond it is the Kazinag Dhar (ridge) above the Jhelum, with snow dusting its very top even in July and almost merging with the Gulmarg peaks and passes beyond it. Well, if this is not good enough, make a 180 degree turn to face north. Raise your eyes from the wider, less rugged and gentler slopes below your feet. Far in the distance, yet dominant, is the completely snow-covered immense hulk of Nanga Parbat's (8126 m) south face dwarfing all other peaks and ridges around it.

This is a view that only soldiers can see now. No civilians are that lucky. To make a tough life slightly easy, the army camps on Murdari gali and beyond are connected by a road that is blocked for three months by snow. Only an incurable optimist can hope for improved relations with Pakistan so that civilians can use them eventually.

The Thaiyan nar rises from the south of Ura gali (3137 m) and Jakhar peak (3496 m). Also, at the head of a tributary of Lolab called Shrant nar is Hunmar gali (3060 m). From these two passes and the peak flow streams to the north to form Machil nala in Machil tehsil—the once neglected valley *(Map 13)*.

The Machil stream is about 30 km long. Beyond Chuntwari village, it goes across the LOC to meet the Kishenganga. The heavily fortified notorious Machil tehsil was a convenient route for insurgents and is also known locally as the Valley of Fake Encounters. Wretched gloom, hopelessness and misery used to pervade every village in this once desolate valley. Today Machil villages are unrecognizable. Houses are sturdy with some offering comfortable home stays, there is electricity, development and prosperity.

In April 2010, three innocent labourers from Baramulla were killed as insurgents.[19] After Kashmir erupted in violence, killing about 100 more civilians, the army officers were sentenced to life imprisonment in 2014. But, in 2017, their sentences were suspended. There have been many more instances in and around Machil before this horrid killing. Tales of brutality in Kashmir, especially in the border regions, are all over this handsome and harried land. Only in a couple of places have I given examples to emphasize that violence and beauty are two faces of the Kashmiri coin.

Machaal (in Kashmiri) or Machil and Matchil (2450 m) (in Pahari) and its attendant villages, surrounded at a distance by partly fir-clad mountains, are no longer isolated. Once this sector was infamous for encounters. In the late sixties there were tall, dark fir forests hovering above the footpath and over a few depressing hovels amidst a majestic scenery.[20] The production from its fields was meagre. Most of the villages are on the right bank of the Machil river. There are eight villages in the Machil sector. Most houses are new and double storeyed and a few are even made of concrete as are the schools. The last school, 20 km away, near the LOC is Chuntwari Bala. Chuntwari means an apple orchard. From summer to autumn the rolling Machil valley is lambent green and bright with wild flowers. Yet another memorable corner in stunning and accessible Kashmir **(Maps 13 and 11)**.

Today all Machil villages (combined population about 25,000) have fertile fields and are prosperous. Pakistani posts can be seen from Chuntwari, the last village. Above Chuntwari is a mountain face called Hoi Bal, in which are caves. Many people hide in these caves whenever there is shelling from Pakistan. Occasionally people get killed.

Machil is a well-settled and wide-spread village about 70 km on a good paved road all the way from Kupwara. Villages are electrified, there is a bank, there are dish antennas over many houses in Machil. For a while, many houses had solar panels, but neglect ruined that good scheme. Batteries weren't charged nor were they replaced. All houses have gas cylinders. In wood houses these are kept in little cupboards outside the house next to the kitchen to protect them from fires if a cylinder explodes. However, despite facilities being present, the medical care is dismal. When winter snow lies deep people can only carry the ailing on stretchers to Sarikul. This has caused some people to buy land in Lolab valley where they shift for the six winter months.

There are cars and tractors here. The villages of Machil are renowned for their potatoes throughout the Valley. Their A-frame homes, like elsewhere in Kashmir, are large and sturdily built of wood, supported on stones and packed with clay about a meter and a half in height. These basements lodge their cattle and sheep in winter. In case of heavy snow, they can come and go easily. They have brightly painted tin or wooden roofs, which are a dazzling change from the caving dirty grey slatted roofs of decrepit hovels of fifty years ago. Some of these houses have begun offering clean and comfortable homestays. A valley that was on the insurgents' way is now confident enough to largely reject them.

Machil, which has its sources north of the Kupwara ridge, meets the Kishenganga, which has now entered into POK. The passes leading to Machil are Giyun (3240 m), Hummar (3060 m) and Zamindar gali *(Map 13)*. The motor road goes over Z gali (3150 m). From a bend below this pass can be seen Nanga Parbat (8126 m). The Machil nala has tributaries below these passes. The longest of them are Zand Dudinar and Pushwarnar *(Maps 11 and 13)*, which rise from the west of passes close to Razdhainangan pass. From the east come Seldori nar and Ringbala nar from Ura gali (3137 m) and Murdari gali (3107 m). There are villages on all these tributaries and, after they join the Machil, along it too. The last ones are Tsuntwari and Chuntwari. After that is the LOC and then the Kishenganga. Once, the villages in Machil, and beyond it, were a self-contained community not needing to go elsewhere for barter or for marriages.

13
More of Kupwara—Keran and Tithwal

AFTER KANZALWAN IN GUREZ, THE KISHENGANGA SWOOPS NORTH flowing through a narrow gorge, which has a couple of sprawling Kashmiri villages on the left bank. At the end of the gorge is the LOC and beyond is the pretty village of Taobat in POK on the Kishenganga. As mentioned previously, in Pakistan the river is called Neelam *(Maps 12, 13 and 14)*

From Taobat the LOC follows above the Kishenganga's left bank. It curves along spurs below and to the north of the ridge in India, and then dips down south from a little ahead of Dudhnial in POK. About 10 km later, the LOC comes down to the Kishenganga in Keran sector, the left bank villages of which are in India.

Keran (1580 m) sector was once underdeveloped like all border villages in Kashmir. And like all such villages it is now quite prosperous—all because of a motorable road and the easing of restrictions for Kashmiris and non-Kashmiris. It is much more than a blip on a map.

Earlier, some people had resettled in safer places to escape low yield from fields, poverty, infiltration threats, and occasional damaging floods. Their life was tough and unproductive. Over the past decade and a half, development and improvement in living conditions has come in with the army road. Agriculture has improved and several houses are new and well built.

Keran tehsil is in Kupwara district. The route to it is from Karapora and then over Parkyan (Farkhiyan gali, 2934m). Keran was on a trade route to Ladakh from Punjab before Partition. Also, before 1947 it was a longer but easier pilgrimage route to the famous tenth century Hindu pilgrimage site of Sharda Peeth that is now in POK. Sharda Peeth is about 30 km from Keran *(Map 13)*. It's on the left bank of the Kishenganga just as Keran is.

There are seven villages in hitherto remote Keran. The largest is Keran, which has about 430 houses spreading from the river bank and gradually ascending to spurs and knolls about 300 m above the river. From the ridge above the highest houses, a stunning view of the many shades of green in summer, and orange and light green in autumn, unfolds below. Beyond is the Kishenganga and further still is the Keran in POK.

Indian Keran has a population of around 4000. According to the 2011 census, remote Keran had a higher combined literacy rate, of 85.43 per cent, than the rest of Kashmir, which was 67.16 per cent. Schools and health centres were once helped by the army. There is a neglected state-run health centre now and well-managed co-educational schools. There's electricity too. Official neglect is gradually ending even though X-ray and other hospital equipment need maintenance. A double-storeyed wooden post office attractively nestles close to the Kishenganga river and the LOC. It has solar panels.

Maize and wheat are the main crops here. There are many walnut trees. Even some young chinar trees, planted by an optimistic and energetic Jammu and Kashmir Forest Department, are doing well here.

Recently, the army road over Parkyan has been opened to civilians and for non-Kashmiris getting Inner Line Permits is easier. Taking advantage of this relaxation, a Keran farmer has set up a tourist camp in a picturesque spot close to the left bank of the Kishenganga, and about 50 m from the LOC. It has tents, clean bedding and tasty food served in a neat tin shed kitchen. Tourists in taxis, cars and motorcycles from Kashmir and north India are slowly increasing in the seven months the road is free of snow. A couple of homes have been renovated as homestays. Keran is unrecognizable from the miserable hovel of many homes it was in the 1980s. It is prosperous too.

Keran is a sensitive sector as regular infiltrations from POK continue inspite of many being caught *(Map 14)*. The right bank in POK is by contrast has been well-developed for long. There are more than a dozen resorts, which advertise good views of Indian Kashmir!

Shalabhatu (fox on a mud wall) is the farthest of Keran sector villages to the east *(Map 14)*. It is an unusual village. The LOC divides it between India and Pakistan before it turns down to the Kishenganga. Many incursions from POK happen through here. Shalabhatu is across a stream of that name. It meets a lavishly named river, Kashmir Raha da Katha, which then meets the Kishenganga on its left bank opposite Pakistani Dudhnial.

The Keran in POK across Kishenganga (Neelam there) is a thriving town. It has more than a thousand houses, many luxury resorts and hotels, a busy highway and many markets and offices. The main attraction for Pakistani tourists is that of the LOC, and Indian Kashmir is sometimes less than 50 m away! Nearly a million tourists visit it annually. In India's Keran the number in 2022 couldn't have been more than a hundred. The good road in Pakistan ends at Taobat to the east where it becomes rough. Taobat is where the Kishenganga leaves India and enters Pakistan as Neelam. The road on the Pakistan side passes through settlements brimming with fine hotels and resorts.

Memories of an exodus much after Partition are still fresh amongst many families here as some people from Indian Keran live in the POK Keran across the Kishenganga. They moved out in the early 1990s. What made them make this shift so much after 1947? Insurgents from Pakistan had sneaked in here under cover of shelling from Pakistani guns above their Keran. They asked the residents to leave at once, as there was going to be a bloody war. They asked them to go to POK for a few weeks and then return. They never did. Within a couple of days about 500 residents of Keran left. Most did not. They preferred to stay and bear the brunt. Within ten days the tide turned. A Mahar regiment came down from Furkiyan gali and saved the villages of Keran. They were helped by those who remained. Some of these houses are dilapidated and some are not, and none has been encroached.[21]

The main reason for faster development of the Keran on the other side is that there is a low-level main road connecting it to Muzaffarabad, the capital of Pakistan-Occupied Kashmir, 93 km away. The second reason is that, unlike in Indian Keran, there is no Inner Line to hinder movement and investment. From 2021 most of the suspicions about Inner Line applicants in India vanished and permits are being easily obtained! A welcome change.

For a few kilometres towards the west, the LOC is along the river and then goes up cutting the spurs that are north of and below the high ground of the ridge in India, skirting Rauta ki gali (3200 m). A short distance later, it goes down again to the river till Tithwal in India from where it turns eastwards into POK.

Only a soldier or a shepherd can describe precisely where the LOC is. I can merely give an idea how difficult it is to understand its general location even. And for soldiers, it's a tough brutal life. They face howling winds, whiteouts and bitter cold. On patrols, conditions are worse.

The ridge in Kupwara, fortified with army camps even on passes, follows the course due west of the Kahmil nala till its sources in its south. The three prominent passes on this ridge above Kahmil nala are Kaiwali gali (2945 m), Farkyangali (2934 m) and Rauta ki gali (3320 m) *(Map 14)*. The road to Keran goes over Farkyangali, leaving the Kahmil valley at Kralpora. It winds past fields, orchards and homes and skirts forests. The last two of these passes are the main sources of the Kahmil nala on the south. Over these passes were trade routes, shepherds' tracks and pilgrim paths. In the north these passes have most of the sources of the Keran nar. Extremely steep and rough roads have been made on the windswept and treeless ridges for better and wider views of the LOC to check infiltration from Pakistan. Soldiers patrol here even in blizzards and at night.

Rauta ki gali (3200 m) is the furthest point west. To the west of this pass is the LOC, which is now in a north-to-south axis. To the south of it is Narazdan nar, the Kahmil river's largest tributary's—source. Studying the LOC I was confused by its whimsicality and capriciousness. What minds designed this asymmetry? Fortunately, all the strategic high grounds are with India. Below them, to the north, stretches the LOC across which is POK.

Like in the Machil sector, the LOC has separated family from family as elsewhere down the Kishenganga.

Similar is the case of villages beyond Putakhan gali (2950 m). In yet another superhuman effort, an army road goes over this pass. There are about half a dozen villages across this pass to the north and before the LOC. They live a tough life now made a little easier with the army's help but always under suspicion. There are several villages beyond Putakhan. The large village of Jumagund is the first one after the pass, and it merges with a couple of others *(Map 14)*. All are better off now than ever before. The second last village is Kainthawali. Both have forests and streams with their names. A few kilometres beyond and across the Shalabhato nar is the divided village of Shalabhato. Part of it is in India and the other in Pakistan. As expected, there are many alert army camps to respond immediately to threats from across the LOC.

Dudhnial, of the famous strike in September 2016 by Indian soldiers, is down the Jumagund stream as it meets the Kishenganga after the LOC. Before 1947, Dudhnial used to be an important halting point for trade caravans going from Delhi, Lahore, Muzaffarabad and Rawalpindi to Srinagar, Ladakh and Gilgit. The route to Srinagar was over the Putakhan gali. In the past, the quiet of this valley was only punctuated by the tinkling of bells on pack horses. It is gunfire now.

Till the late forties these passes, above the Kahmil, were on the Hindu pilgrim trail to Sharda Peeth's tenth-century ruins. Parkyan Farkyangali (2934 m) even had a Forest Rest House below it. It had three rooms and a wide 180 degree view to the south beginning from the soaring Haramukh to the east, the speck of Kolahoi in the middle and ending after encompassing Gulmarg's ridge at the peaks above Bangus valley. In between could be seen a large part of the Lolab valley, the Haehom valley, the plains of Kupwara and Handwara, with the Kahmil and Pohru flowing through them. Almost in the centre of this expansive view could be detected the glimmering blue of the Wular. Climb a hundred metres beyond Farkyangali and there was Nanga Parbat to stun you.

After Tithwal the Kishenganga turns west to go deep into POK. Soon thereafter the Kishengaga has a second dam built across it. The first one is at Kunzalwan in Gurez, India. The LOC goes south of Tithwal. Tithwal is one of the two places in Kashmir where people from both sides could cross over till three years ago. It is on the Katha Kazinag (Katha means stick, perhaps referring to its narrow width at places) nala after it has swallowed the much shorter Batemoj nar shortly after the sub-divisional headquarter of Tangdhar. Batemoj nar comes down from Nasta Chun pass (3130 m).

Katha Kazinag nar has an enthralling course because of politics. It is born in the snow fields above the lake of Kazi nag *(Map 14)* in India. This lake is to the west of the short Kazi nag Dhar range above the right bank of the Jhelum between Baramulla and Uri. For a while the nar flows in the Indian side of Leepa valley, enters POK and re-enters India before Tithwal. The lake of Kazi nag is no more.

After crossing the Nasta Chun gali, where there is an army check post now, the road goes along Batemoj (Rice Mother) nala past a string of villages beginning with the large Nachian. Many villages later is Tangdhar, the sub-divisional headquarters on the right bank of Batemoj nala. After that is the Tithwal bulge on the Kishenganga. This is on the LOC between India and Pakistan. Tithwal is 63 km from the pass and 15 km from Tangdhar—the sub division headquarter of Kupwara district. For a sub-division that can be cut off by rain or snow frequently, Tangdhar is a densely populated place. Some stretches of the road pass through narrow villages and their wide-green fecund fields for many kilometres. This strategic road is kept open despite the heavy snowfalls of winter. The steep climb on the east and descent down the west side of the pass has devoured, as usual, thousands of grand deodars.

At Tangdhar's south-east and about 30 km away by road is the village of Jabri (1300 m) *(Map 14)*. The LOC is quite near the well-maintained school at the far end of the village. It is marked by a simple wire fencing and is heavily mined! Jabri has improved so much that it is unrecognizable from the shabby village of three decades ago. Its population is about 400, almost equally distributed amongst females and males. The progress is solely because of the motorable road. It goes up to Magri gali (2850) and then comes down. After this pass are good views of the mountain ridge hemming in Bangus valley to its east. Jabri has a school, a health centre and, even though there is a check post at Magri gali, many taxis that come and go. Jabri's beans (rajma) are so good that they are welcome in north India. Across Jabri's LOC fence, near which is the school, is the Jabri in POK. Inner Line Permits can be easily got from the tehsildar of Karnah (Tangdhar).

Tithwal is about 40 km from Muzaffarabad, the capital of Pakistan-Occupied Kashmir. A few kilometres south of Muzaffarabad is Domel where the Kishenganga meets the Jhelum. This is the point where the Pir Panjal range begins. It ends 600 km later in Himachal Pradesh.

At Tithwal *(Map 14)* is one of the two Land Customs Stations in Kashmir. The other one is in Uri. Trade and passengers cross here in both directions. Tithwal is 195 km from Srinagar and can be travelled in six hours if the weather is good and more than twelve if it is bad. Despite its considerable population and strategic importance Tangdhar is still not connected by a government bus service. Only taxis provide this essential service and their fares increase according to the perversity of the weather.

Upriver from Tithwal on the Kishenganga an emotional sight was seen twice a month on the days that passenger crossings were allowed between India and Pakistan. Across the river is Chilhana in Pakistan. Before Partition, both villages had one name, Tithwal. From 2003 to 2019 two crossings a week for Kashmiris on both sides were legally allowed. On these days hopeful people would line the banks on either side and throw stones with messages wrapped around them or in bottles for their families on the other side. Some messages got home, most didn't. Yet they would throw, for hope springs eternal amongst desperate humans. Since 2019, there are no legal crossings.

Tithwal was once called Tirath Bal as it is near the spot where the Kazinag and Kishenganga meet. It was also one of the favoured routes to Sharda Peeth, the tenth-century Hindu, and also sometimes Buddhist, university. Near Tithwal and to its south, below a few houses, is a strong suspension bridge with fort-like gates on either side. This quaint, always freshly painted, well-maintained and attractive bridge, over the Kishenganga, was built in 1931. Halfway down this bridge is a white line painted across it. This is the LOC.

Tithwal is the largest village of Karnah tehsil, of which Tangdhar is the administrative headquarter. The population of entire Karnah is about 70,000. Two of the villages here have large Sikh populations. Tangdhar is spread lineally along the Batmoji stream.[22]

14
Of Bangus, Some Streams and Alps, Meadows and Passes between Kahmil Nala and Katha Kazinag Nala

THE KAHMIL VALLEY IS A RATHER SPACIOUS UNDULATING PLAIN AT A pleasant average height 1700 m above sea level. From Kahmil, good roads veer off north and south to the many fertile agricultural villages in the valley and in the mountains above. The valley is nearly 8 km wide. Starting from a little before Kupwara, it ends approximately 25 km later at Chowkibal. At Chowkibal, it enters a narrow thick fir-forested defile.

Roads go all over this valley and to the mountains around it. Perhaps the busiest road is the one to Tithwal. It pierces through the Chowkibal forest along the right bank of the Kahmil. The Kahmil has a narrow bed here, but wide enough for illegally felled trees to be dried and then floated down the river and collected before Kupwara. Kahmil is a tempestuous and fast-flowing nala picking up tributaries from north and south.

The Kahmil *(Map 14)* has two major sources. One is in the north and is known as Naradzan nar. The other is in the south and is called Drangyari nala. Both meet at the Transhipment Point (TP), which is about 15 km beyond Chowkibal. Many years ago, this was the end of the road to Tithwal. Goods were then carried by horses. Now the road turns left at this point to go along the Drangyari nala.

The Naradzan nar rises from below Rauta ki gali (3320 m). Drangyari nala starts from Bangus valley to the south. After a couple of kilometres along the Drangyari nala, the road leaves it to climb to Nasta Chun (Cut in the Nose) gali from the fork at Panzgam. This attractive descriptive name has been changed to a meaningless silly one, Sadhana Top (3130 m), after a Bollywood actress no less. Till the 1971 war with Pakistan this steep and attractive pass was still known as Nasta Chun gali. Its name was changed, most probably after the tarred road was built. This disgusting habit of changing names to suit the north Indian fetish for familiarity in a linguistically different land is found across all the Himalaya—from the north-west to north-east. It is insidious language colonization that litters the region with meaningless names from the plains. Once the name is changed in government records it will begin to be used widely, and after a decade or so the old one will be forgotten, as it happened in the case of Nasta Chun gali.

From Nasta Chun gali, an army road goes along the ridge all the way to Parkyan gali and further to other passes close to Razdiangan. This is a stunning engineering feat with heart-thumping views if one is fortunate to be allowed to go on it. At the moment, though, only army personnel can use it.

A road from the fork at Panzgam, below Nasta Chun gali, carries on ahead, climbing gradually above the left bank of the rushing Drangyari. There are graceful, glamorous and exceedingly pretty fir-lined, bowl-shaped meadows to the east of the Drangyari nala as it comes down from a snow ridge. The Drangyari nala flows south for a while through a declining deodar forest and then turns east, where it is known as Bangus nar. It drains three bowl-contoured bright green valleys surrounded by a receding fringe of firs.

The Bangus nar flows past these stunningly bewitching large meadows called Rahiwala Baihk (meadow), Lokut (small) Bangus and Bod (big) Bangus. Each has a pass at its head to the east *(Map 14)*, about 3000 m high. They are called Moldari (2890 m), Yadal (2545 m) and Bangus (2955 m) galis. Shepherd trails lead through mouth-watering forests (for forest contractors) to the Kupwara sub-division of Handwara. From Handwara, a road, I am told, has reached almost to the passes and then it's a short trek down to the flower-rich (only in late summer) meadows, in one of which the Jammu and Kashmir Tourism Development Corporation (JKTDC) was once building some log huts.

The Bangus meadows are one of the jewels of Kashmir. Each jewel is embedded differently and is uniquely elegant and magnificent. It is difficult to convey the beauty, grace and splendour of each. The Bangus meadows have rippling streams, and all around them are stately dark green deodar forests. And towards the west are views of an uneven bowl crossed by ridges and dotted with peaks of around 4000 m.

From these peaks rises the pretty Sokian nar, which flows east to join Bangus nar. A little to the east of the source of the Sokian is the ridge which has Gormatnar gali (3780 m) and close to its west Jatti gali (3799 m). Between these two passes is an unusual and eye-catching snow-filled cwm. It is marked by a 4100 m high peak and three lower ones forming a cirque from which emerges the Mawar river known here as Badroni nar, which collects water from small ice fields and countless springs lower down to become, first, the fast-flowing Haddan nar, and then, merging with other streams, becomes the gently flowing Mawar river which flows through the plains of Handwara. In the sixties one could walk for days and only occasionally meet Gujjars or Bakkarwals or their herds, and a couple of trekkers. Now it's an army patrol mainly, I am told. About 100 m above Jatti gali is a peak from where are seen the distant Karakoram and the end of the Himalaya. A stunning view of a not-so-faraway Nanga Parbat (8126 m) to the east dominates the horizon. Today, over these once long-peaceful ridges with fascinating views are army motor roads, connecting the Baramulla–Uri length of the Jhelum valley with Kahmil and Mawar rivers in Kupwara district. One hopes that in a couple of decades peace pervades in Kashmir and all these roads are accessible to at least our grandchildren's grandchildren.

Handwara is about 80 km away from Srinagar. It is a part of Kupwara district but suffers even more from insurgents as they somehow come through from POK's part of the Leepa valley. After the August 2019 abrogation of Article 370, the troop strength in Kashmir was increased three-fold, and it was claimed that insurgency was over. For nine months there was peace. It was shattered in early May 2020 when two strikes killed many Indian soldiers and policemen.[23] It has not been quiet ever since.

There is another path to Bangus. This one is from Handwara. Fifty and more years ago this trail too was popular with shepherds and occasionally visited by trekkers and climbers. Nothing technical in the climbs, but they were favoured because they were easy and offered scintillating views. Now no civilian dares go there. If peace returns, this tract will decongest Sonamarg, Gulmarg and Pahalgam—the only places that Kashmir is famous for now. Army roads reach all these heavenly spots and beyond. There must be some amongst the soldiers who take time off from their tough existence to admire the beauty that they are privileged to live temporarily with?

On a trek to Bangus through Yadal gali in the early sixties, we could not have even dreamed of a road here in a hundred years—so difficult the terrain seemed. But there is one now. Thanks primarily to insurgency!

South of Gormantar gali (3780 m) is a 4000 m high ridge called Pathri Jinjar. It heads south to meet the Kazinag Dhar ridge (4000 m) *(Map 14)*, which is high above the Jhelum. Near this junction is Kala Pahar (4398 m), and about a thousand metres below it to the west is a small spring and tarn called Kazinag. The Katha Kazinag nar descends west through the forested meadows of the fertile and seductive Leepa valley, only a small portion of which is within India, and meets the Batemoj nar before Tithwal.

To the west and below the Pathri Jinjar ridge is the largest village in India's Leepa valley—Channian. It is connected to Handwara by a seasonal road over this ridge. Channian, which in the troubles of the

1990s, was completely evacuated, now has its residents back. They have electricity, improved agriculture and its walnuts are famous.

There is a large army base here. A few kilometres beyond it is the LOC with the Katha Kazinar flowing across it. The larger and more inhabited part of Leepa valley is in POK. In September 2016, an Indian surgical strike into Pakistan's Leepa valley started from here. During the 1971 war with Pakistan, this lovely and elegant green bowl cut by the Lippa nala had seen fierce fighting.

The Kazinag Dhar is the border between Kupwara and Baramulla districts. The Leepa valley is separated from the Jhelum valley by Kafir Khan range. Two passes, Reshian gali and Brithwari gali, connect the two.

This is a yet another unforgettable and charming corner of Kashmir where land and families have been divided irrevocably. There is no hope during our time, but if peace returns, lost dialects along with filial bonds will be revived too.[24] The long separation has resulted in common dialects developing differently on either side of the LOC. Much earlier, in days that few can remember now, a Hindu pilgrim route used to go through this serene valley to Sharda Peeth on the Kishenganga.

As the Kazinag Dhar is crossed over the Sidh Kanu Shah gali (4100 m), the descent to the populous and fertile right bank of the Jhelum starts.

15
Baramulla and Uri to Gulmarg

THE KAZINAG DHAR *(MAP 14)* IS AN INTERESTING TOPOGRAPHICAL divide. Above Jhelum's right bank the link with the sub ranges of the Himalaya is finally severed. Now the dominant range is the Pir Panjal. It is on the left bank of the Jhelum. It has been steadily rising from the low height of 1000 m from Domel. The Pir Panjal enters India after crossing the Khalana nala beyond Uri *(Map 15)*. This nala is a left-bank tributary of the Jhelum.

The Pir Panjal rapidly climbs higher till it reaches Gulmarg's south, from where the almost permanent snowline starts. Continuing south beyond Gulmarg *(Map 15)*, its apex in Kashmir is reached at Tatakuti peak (4720 m) and Romesh Thong (Sunset Peak) (4745 m) *(Map 16)*.

In contrast to the northern parts of heavily forested meadows, the south face of Kazinag Dhar has fewer woods but many exceedingly fertile villages along the many streams coming down from this ridge. The fields start from a height of about 2500 m and extend down till the banks of the Jhelum at about 1500 m. The higher reaches have apple, pear, cherry and walnut orchards. This mountain side coming down from Kazinag Dhar has apparently the largest number of waterfalls per sq. km in Kashmir.

Each one is taller than Kashmir's best advertised 19 m high Aharbal fall on the Kounsarnag nar.

Uri is once again a bustling town as trade with POK has started. A spacious and vast Trade Facilitation Centre has been set up at Salamabad, about 5 km inside India's side of the LOC, for clearing trade goods in both directions. As Khalana nala, which rises in POK, meets the Jhelum on its left bank, there is bridge called Kaman, on the LOC. This is where bus passengers are checked and cleared.

Before Salamabad became known for Indo-Pakistan trade, it was known for growing *zaitoon*, better known as olives. It is the only place in Kashmir that grows olives.

Jhelum drains all of 15,948 sq. km of the Kashmir Valley and enters its last lap at Baramulla after flowing through the silted Wular. From Baramulla begins the 50 km long Baramulla–Uri–Salamabad *(Map 15)* road on the left bank of the Jhelum. The zone from Baramulla to Uri has considerable engineering and agricultural activity.

Here are two big run-of-the-river hydel projects on the Jhelum. Uri-I (Gingal) produces 480 MW in an underground cavern by diverting part of the Jhelum from the barrage at Gantamulla. Uri-II produces 240 MW. These are enthusiastic and ambitious hydel projects completed in the late nineties. What riles Kashmiris is that most of the electricity is for Chandigarh, Delhi, Himachal Pradesh, Haryana, Punjab, Rajasthan, Uttarakhand and Uttar Pradesh. Only a small slice of the electric loaf is left for Jammu and Kashmir. Had most of the electricity been for Kashmir, each village would have had electricity and there would have been no power shedding in the benighted Valley.

Only a small state-owned hydel power house works at Boniyar, where Hapatkhal nala, a southern tributary, meets Jhelum. The first hydel plant along the Jhelum was at Mohra above Boniyar. It was made in 1903, produced 1 MW of electricity and was abandoned in 1992. This project has now been revived to produce 9 MW of electricity. An interesting part of the earlier project was that water was brought from streams above

Jhelum's left bank in a long wooden flume. Parts of this flume still exist. From some places the wood of this flume has been stolen.

These dams did not submerge any villages. Though extremely beneficial otherwise, they have prevented fish that used to move up-river for spawning from doing so now.[25]

Good roads are on both sides of the Jhelum. The road along the left bank of the Jhelum is the busier one. Above the left bank are large swathes of dense patches of forests of pine and firs. Near Boniyar, by the side of the road, at the base of a dense deodar forest, is a now well-maintained twelfth-century Datta temple. It was noticed first by Baron Huegel, an Austrian traveller, in 1835. It had been hidden from view by a cluster of firs and covered by centuries of mudslides. It was completely excavated by 1865. It maintained its stolid stone-grey respectability for 175 years till some troops camped nearby, in a fit of religious enthusiasm, coloured the lower portion in a hideous red, installed a flimsy wooden door and painted it yellow. This well-meaning sacrilege is unaesthetic and unnecessary.

Above both sides of the river are fields and orchards but much more above the right bank of the Jhelum. The higher the village, the better the quality of apples, apricots, walnuts, cherries and plums.

Forests on the mountains above Jhelum have reduced considerably since the time when the cart road from Muzaffarabad to Baramulla via Uri was converted into a motorable one in the 1940s. This was the preferred route to the Valley in colonial days. Widening and relining over the years meant more trees were cut for heating tar.

Just as the valleys formed by spurs coming down from the Himalaya–Pir Panjal ridge above Pahalgam in East Kashmir are linked by low-lying shepherds' passes, so are the spurs on the left and right banks of the Jhelum here. There are passes linking spurs below the ridges above both sides of the river. Whenever normalcy returns, such trails could attract visitors who may still be able to see traditional Kashmiri villages, pleasant views and remnants of forests.

It is physically, but not politically, possible to experience an exciting and pleasant five-day trek (it was so fifty years ago) from Maidanan village, a short drive from Boniyar up the Hapatkhal nala *(Map 15)*. The passes crossed were Marg gali (2100 m), then Karamulla gali (3040 m) and finally over Urukshan gali (2980 m) to Saidpora village, which is above the confluence of Silpathar nala with Haji Pir nala.

Above Boniyar, forests have increased and so has wildlife. If one climbs the fir-clad hill behind the ancient Shiv temple in Boniyar, the Uri Hydel Project across the Jhelum is seen. Beyond the reservoirs of the Uri Hydel Project, above the right bank of the Jhelum, is the Limber stream disappearing in a detritus fan and meeting the Jhelum. Far above it is the snow-clad Kazinag Dhar around 4500 m average in height. Below are small patches of white-barked birches, thick forests of firs, spruce and deodars harbouring springs and criss-crossed by myriad streams.

This extensive view, from the snow ridge down to the Jhelum's right bank, can be seen from many an eyrie in the heights above Boniyar, which is on the southern side of the left bank of Jhelum. This is the demesne of the Kazinag National Park, which has been made by combining the Limber and Lachipora Wildlife Sanctuaries above both banks of the Jhelum. There are leopards, brown and black bears, deer, martens, flying squirrels and the rare markhor. The markhor is a huge goat with prominent horns shaped like large curving corkscrews. It had been hunted down to almost extinction. The western end of the Kazinag Dhar *(Maps 14 and 15)* dips into POK where the same markhor is welcome and is its national animal. With strict conservation laws on both sides, markhors are increasing.

The Hapatkhal nala that flows past Boniyar is also known locally as the Boniyar nala. It starts from the Pir Panjal ridge *(Map 15)* to the west of the Apharwat peaks above the Gulmarg ski lift and takes a circuitous route to meet the Jhelum below Boniyar, where it is locally called Boniyar nala. At one stage it skirts the LOC, perhaps even jumping across it. There is a good seasonal—for this is a region of heavy snow—motor road that goes to villages close to the LOC. It's difficult to believe, but on India's side of the LOC are a couple of villages that somehow manage to survive amidst the ever-present cross-border hostility and lack of transport.

The next big stream towards Uri in the west is the Haji Pir nala.

The Haji Pir pass (2637 m), from where the Haji Pir nala starts *(Map 15)*, was taken by the Indian Army on 30 August 1965 after a thirty-seven hour bloody battle. Along with this, they took control of the small town of Kahuta on the Betul nala. This spectacular victory removed an irritating bulge through which Pakistan sent insurgents. Sadly, an outstanding military action was neutralized five months later at Tashkent when it was handed back to Pakistan tamely. Had the area remained with India, the old route between Punch in Jammu and Uri would have reopened and the distance between Punch and Srinagar would have been only 150 km instead of the 263 km at present. An Indian Army general regretted this implausible return thus, 'Civilians don't read maps.' It is regrettable indeed.[26] Now Pakistani troops are well below north of Haji Pir and only around 15 km from the bridge over Haji Pir or Uri nala near Uri town. Today there is a road, I am told, beyond Saidpora to the last village till the LOC on the Haji Pir nala and army camps and helipads between Haji Pir and Hapathkhal nalas.

This very section used to be a favourite of people who wanted two-to-three-day-long treks about sixty years ago. There were springs, rivulets, forests, passes and ridges in between. There were astounding views of the Kazinag Dhar and beyond. On such walks there was no need to carry water as there were healthy springs all over. The view from a couple of points above these passes was what these treks were famed for. The depth of the view was stunning. Below, one could see the Jhelum at about 1500 m. Above it could be seen the entire course of the Limber nala *(Map 15)* and above it the passes on the Kazi Khan Dhar leading across to Handwara. Also seen were about a dozen streams foaming and twisting down from the ridge. Some of them joined each other. On either side of each of them were terraced fields and orchards cascading downhill like waterfalls. Like in the long and large village of Pahlipora and its ziarat.

Above it all, against the sky and far to the north rose the immense hulk of Nanga Parbat (8126 m). It's a view of about 6500 m in height, if the weather is kind! Well worth a short trek.

More than a century ago, some travellers who could afford the luxury would travel from Baramulla to Srinagar by houseboats. This smooth ride would take about twenty hours of non-stop travel, while the bone rattling journey on horses, dandi, or shock-absorber-less horse-driven carriages, would take two whole days. To Baramulla's east is the point where the Jhelum leaves the open valley and enters the mountains.

Villages, springs and forests abound on the mountain slopes above both banks of the Jhelum between Baramulla and Uri. There are more villages above the right bank, which gets a lot more precipitation and sunlight as it is south facing. In some of these villages were old folks who could tell stories of pilgrims and trade caravans passing through. The right bank of the Jhelum drains Kazinag Dhar and the left bank the Pir Panjal.

From Baramulla a good and scenic, but not yet popular, road goes to Gulmarg (2650 m). It has much less traffic than the year-round busy one from Tangmarg *(Map 15)*. Gulmarg's crescent-shaped bowl of softly shining green is so vast that a temple, a church, a ski run and a golf course fit in with room for many meadows more. Though for a golf course and club house to occupy so much green space, for a only few users, is a perversion in democratic times. In winter it is covered in snow, and in summer its gorgeous green is speckled with dainty flowers. At all times, it is stunning. There is a ring road around it with shops and hotels that range from seven stars to no stars. Beyond the crowds and noise, the meadows of Gulmarg are bordered by majestic ramrod straight giant deodars.

Gulmarg was first seen by H.H. Godwin-Austen, a surveyor with Survey of India, in 1860. There were dokas in the meadow and around it. Gulmarg soon became a splendid summer camp for the English. The ousted dokas moved up the rim of the crescent-shaped bowl. Today, their flat mud-caked roofs can be seen from the gondolas whirring away above.

Gulmarg now is crowded throughout the year with centrally heated hotels dotting it. Many trees—again many more than required—were cut down to make way for the hotels and the cable gondola *(Map 15)*.

After the English were charmed by Gulmarg's meadows and views, a cart road was made from Srinagar to Gulmarg via Tangmarg. The road in the Valley was bordered by Russian poplars that, with the passage of time, became majestic giants. Black and white photographs of these huge poplars hung in many studios of Srinagar. So attractive were they, they appeared in several old Bollywood films. Sadly, about a century and a half later these rare trees were cut down to make a four-lane highway. This slaughter made only the timber merchants happy.

Below Gulmarg is one of Kashmir's most revered ziarat, the three-hundred-year-old Baba Reshi, named after the Sufi saint Baba Payamuddin Reshi. It is in a clearing within a dark dense fir forest. The road from Baramulla meets the road from Srinagar–Tangmarg here. Gulmarg (2650 m) is surrounded by roads, army and civil, and saturated with noise. People who had trekked to the lakes and passes in Pir Panjal above Gulmarg four to five decades ago miss the perfect silence. There is a ski lift there, and terrible noise made by shrieking tourists, shouting hawkers, generators and infernal combustion engines—even at night.

Yet, these changes are welcome. There's comfortable accommodation for more than a thousand in Gulmarg. Earlier, a handful of people, apart from numerous shepherds, would trek to Apharwat. It would take a day. There was just one hotel at Gulmarg, Nedou's Hotel, and one could pitch a tent nearly anywhere one pleased. Now thousands go to Apharwat in fifteen minutes! Thanks to the kilometres-long cable car that connects Gulmarg (2650 m) to viewpoints at Kongdogri alp and Apharwat. From Apharwat, a heart-stirring view starts from the distant Kun (7077 m) partially hidden by Nun (7135 m) far away in the east. It then includes the lowly and closer Kolahoi (5425 m) and Haramukh (5148 m) before soaring to Nanga Parbat (8126 m), which one has to tilt one's head back to see. Across the ridge above Apharwat marg, where the ski lift ends, are some small lakes. The largest of them is called Alpathar (3780 m). Many years ago, it was a favoured spot for trekkers. Today, this is prohibited ground. The near-at-hand ever-sensitive LOC has ensured that.

To the west and north of Gulmarg, and quite close, are smaller meadows. The most unusual one is the large one atop a fir-clad hill called Budapathri (2824 m) *(Map 15)*. This curving mountain can be seen from some points in Gulmarg. It is at the end of a subsidiary ridge of the Pir Panjal, which goes north-east from Zaisur (3940 m) and Gurdali (3510 m) galis on the main ridge. At its northern base starts the Sultanpura kol, which in the Valley becomes Khursi nala.

There were, maybe still are, dokas on top of Budapathri and the many alps and meadows below it. Nearby is a large village called Scohalpathri (*pathri* also means meadow like *marg* does) in a lower and pretty meadow. Farthest is the little-visited meadow called Lokut (Little) Gulmarg (2800 m). All these grazing grounds are surrounded by fingers of dense forested spurs.

To the west and above Gulmarg is a curving ridge that has several peaks scarcely higher than the passes like Zarsur gali (3940 m) and Gurdari gali (3510 m). The highest are 4227 m and 4143 m. Both are known as Apharwat peaks. Both can be seen proud and glinting from Srinagar's Dal lake on every clear day. These passes are pocked with anti-insurgency camps and criss-crossed with roads built with incredible determination.

16
Ferozepur Nala to Peer Gali

THE MAGIC AND MYSTERY OF THE GALIS ON PIR PANJAL HAVE GONE AS they are criss-crossed by army roads. The Pir Panjal heads south from Apharwat. From there follows a 70 km or so section of the Pir Panjal range of an average height of around 3500 m, hosting a number of peaks and passes *(Map 16)*.

Gulmarg from Srinagar, by the most common and thus crowded road, is about two hours away. The valley is left a few kilometres before Tangmarg, which is on a spur above the Ferozepur nala. Along the Ferozepur nala was a route in Mughal times to Punch and thence to Punjab. It is yet another beautiful valley with yet another spectacular arrangement of alps, sky-hugging deodars, vast green flower-scattered meadows, peaks, passes and rushing streams.

The first village along Ferozepur nala is Drang. There is a road to it now. It is an expanding village as Drang's beauty is attracting many tourists, for whom hotels are coming up. Once upon a time, from a fir-covered peak south of Drang, one could see the meadows abutting Ferozepur nala as far as some of the peaks that shroud its sources and not see anyone but shepherds and their flocks. Now one sees large clearings in the forests, an indispensable mini hydel dam and many soldiers as POK is close at hand. The isolation enjoyed in the past is gone, even in winter. In winter, Drang is at the end of a long non-piste ski run, which starts from Apharwat.

The main sources of Ferozepur nala are south-west of Gulmarg in ice and snow fields, a lake called Kontar nag and an adjacent tarn below the passes of Nilkanth (3640 m), Dewar (3740 m) and Chor Panjal (3965 m) *(Map 16)*. From a ridge about 150 m above Kontar nag can be seen parts of the valley and Haramukh peak (5148 m). During the brief summer when only ribs of snow remain there is succulent grass that attracts shepherds and their flocks. Lower down at a large meadow called Lakshmidor the Ferozepur nala has its waters increased by a tributary from the south. Here is a place called Pandanpathri or Pandavlary where are big stones from a ruined eleventh-century temple. This is a fine location between the slopes of two gentle forested spurs below a 4158 m high peak and near an approximately 30 m high waterfall.

The Ferozepur nala flows north-east in a gully that has forests and meadows on both sides. There used to be scattered dokas here next to every alp and meadow reaching the edge of snow fields. These trails and many more used to be charming treks from Gulmarg in the days gone by, but now with the POK close by and army roads criss-crossing ridges and spurs and forests, no such trysts with beauty are possible. The only hope is that when eventually peace returns, civilians will be able to see this Shangri-la by using these roads.

A couple of hours' walk after Drang village is the Dhanwas forest, sheltering spacious meadows. Here in a gently undulating clearing, in a hill above the right bank of the Ferozepur nala, are the ruins of a tower. It was built during Mughal times as a revenue collecting post. Trade caravans to and from Kashmir had to pay taxes. This route wove along the Ferozepur nala to Nilkanth (3805 m) and Dewar gali (3742 m) and over them to Punch and Punjab. From Nilkanth can be seen the hills of Punch in India and the plains of Pakistan.

On the eastern side of Pir Panjal, that is Kashmir, is a bevy of lakes and tarns amidst the clutter and muddle of glacial debris. An exquisite setting that only nature can craft. There must be about a dozen on the Kashmir side of Pir Panjal stretching south till Peer gali (3490 m). As if that was not intoxicating enough, below these lakes are immense pebble-strewn meadows and pasturelands bordered by birches and, lower down, by majestic firs. The enthralling picture is completed with the snows of Pir Panjal hovering above them. But this stretch it is not unique. Still to come, further south of Peer gali (3490), is an even larger mind-boggling collection of lakes—but more about them later.

Ascending gently south from Pandanpathri is an ancient trail made by shepherds. After a few hours' walk through a long gradually ascending meadow above the tree line are the easy passes of Basam gali (3735 m) and Krala Nangal gali (3680 m). These passes are the sources of Behan nar and another stream, both of which are tributaries of the Ferozepur nala. From near both passes, looking south and east, long views of the Pir Panjal including Romesh Thong (Sunset Peak) (4745 m) can be had. The Sunset Peak is above Peer gali *(Map 16)*.

The peace of so many miles of meadows, forests, rivulets and lakes is shattered by an occasional diesel engine. Krala Nangal gali has an army motor road connecting Drang and Tangmarg to Tosha (Soft) Maidan in the south. It then skirts below the Kadalbal grazing ground to Budgam in the valley.

To the south of Basam and Krala Nangal galis is the vast rolling meadow of Tosha Maidan. Till 2017, the army had been using it as a firing range for its heavy guns! This can give you an idea of the size of the meadow and also of the environmental havoc caused by thirty years of heavy guns raining shells here. The guns have created craters and deep troughs that will take decades to be erased. Some of the tracks left by trucks have become roads for tourists. After thirty years of practice shelling by the army, including four for court battles, Tosha Maidan is once again with shepherds and myriad tourists.

Tourists drive to these meadows in a couple of hours from Srinagar. For some, their tour of beauty ends at dhabas and shops, around which

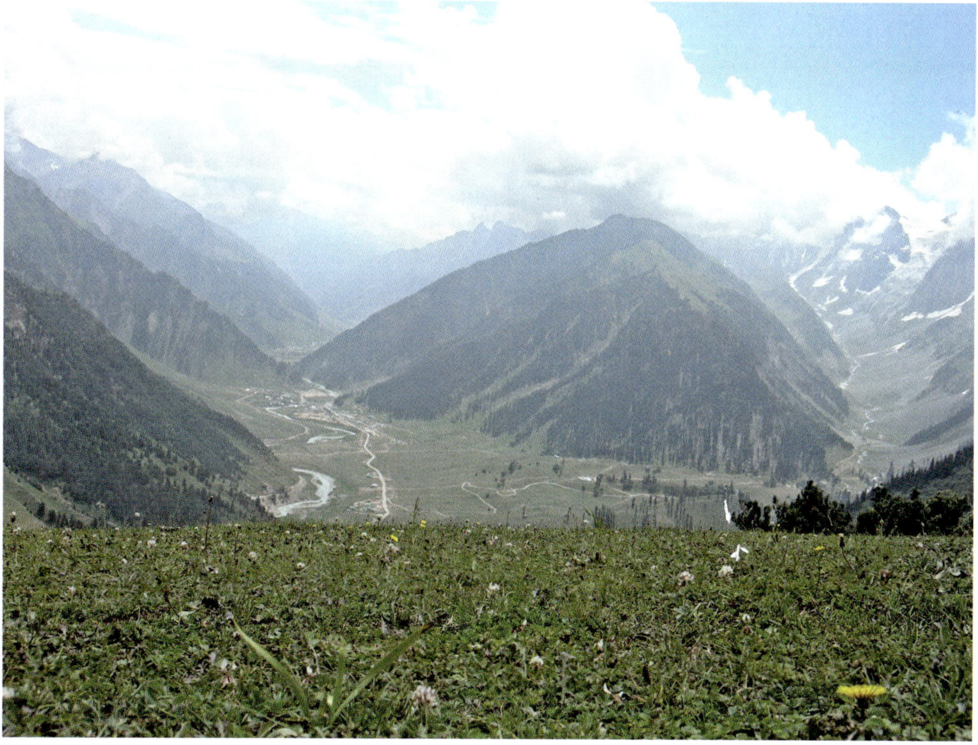
Photograph by Mohammed Amin Qureshi

Sonamarg and Thajiwas glacier from Ludharwas alp.

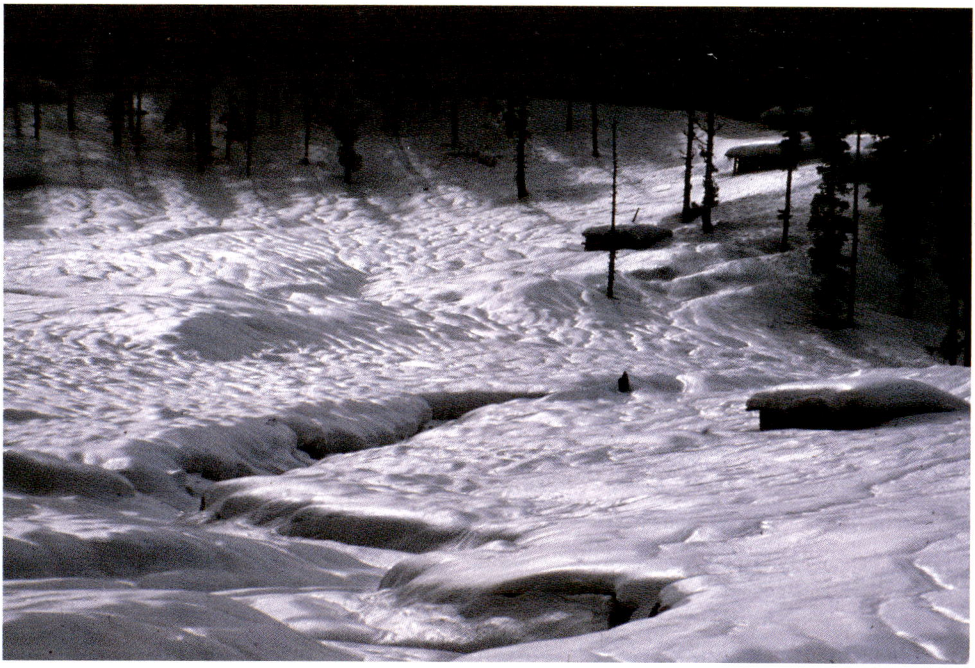
Photograph by Romesh Bhattacharji

Yusmarg dokas.

Tithwal: Looking for kith and kin in PoK (right) across the Kishenganga from Kashmir (left).

Nishat Bagh through Oonth Kadal, the old seventeenth-century bridge.

Zabarwan ridge above a freezing Dal lake.

Mughal Sarai at Aliabad below Peer gali on the Mughal Road. Mughal emperors used to camp here en route to Srinagar.

Burzahom's neolithic dolmen-grave of a clan leader built in ancient times. Harawar is the snow-clad peak to the right.

Shepherds moving camp from Tranghkul meadow. Haramukh looms behind.

120-year-old poplars once stood majestically on the Gulmarg–Srinagar road, now cut down in the name of progress. Haramukh at the background.

Kolahoi's striated north-eastern face with the main Kolahoi glacier to its right. The shrunken Hoksar glacier and an infant West Lidder can also be seen. Rare sight from Lakhath gali.

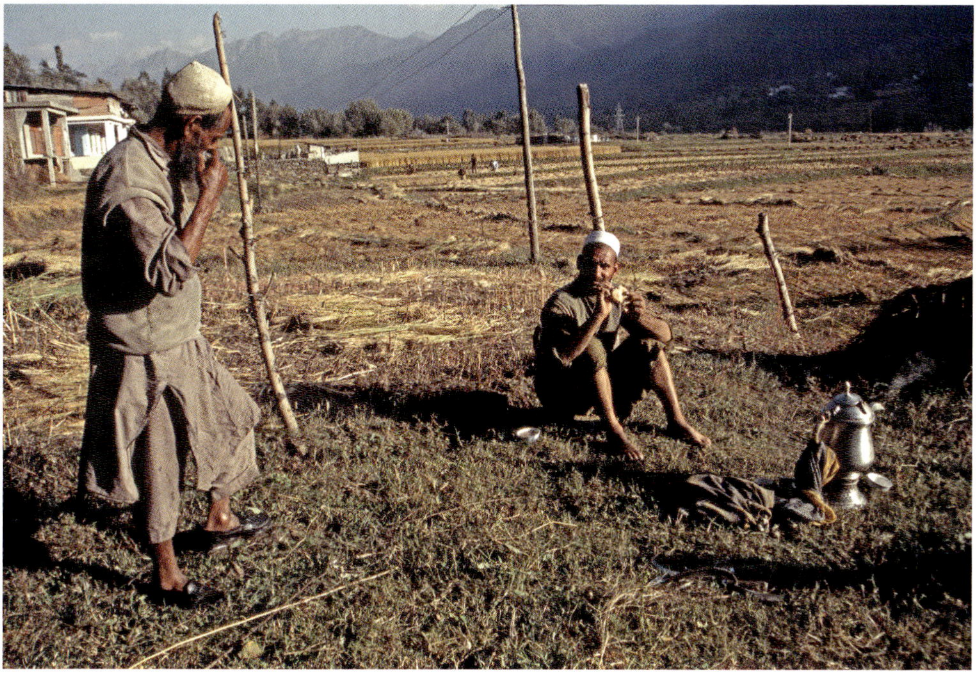

Photograph by Romesh Bhattacharji

Teatime in the recent past; the elegant samovar replaced by a thermos now.

Photograph by Romesh Bhattacharji

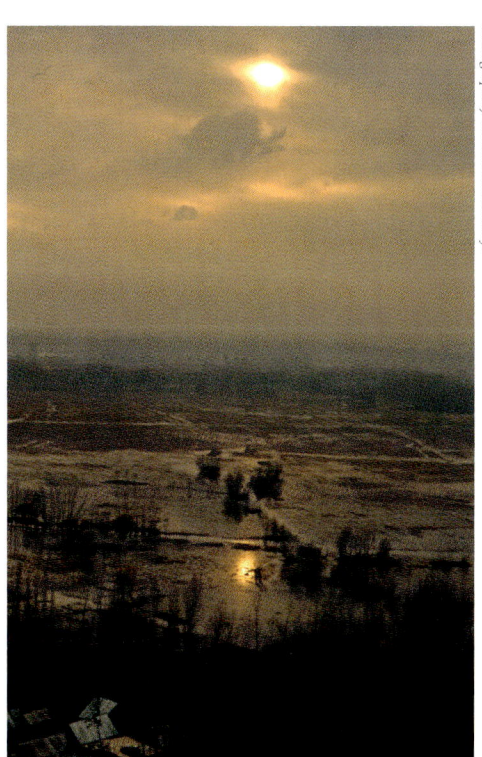

Wular, one of the largest fresh-water lakes in India, is degrading and silting.

Photograph by Mahmood Ahmed Shah

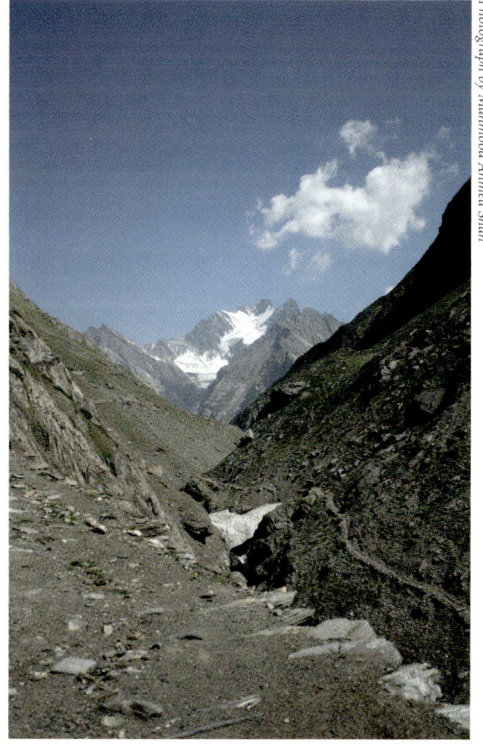

Nichang, the highest peak in Kashmir, is also the source of the Sind river.

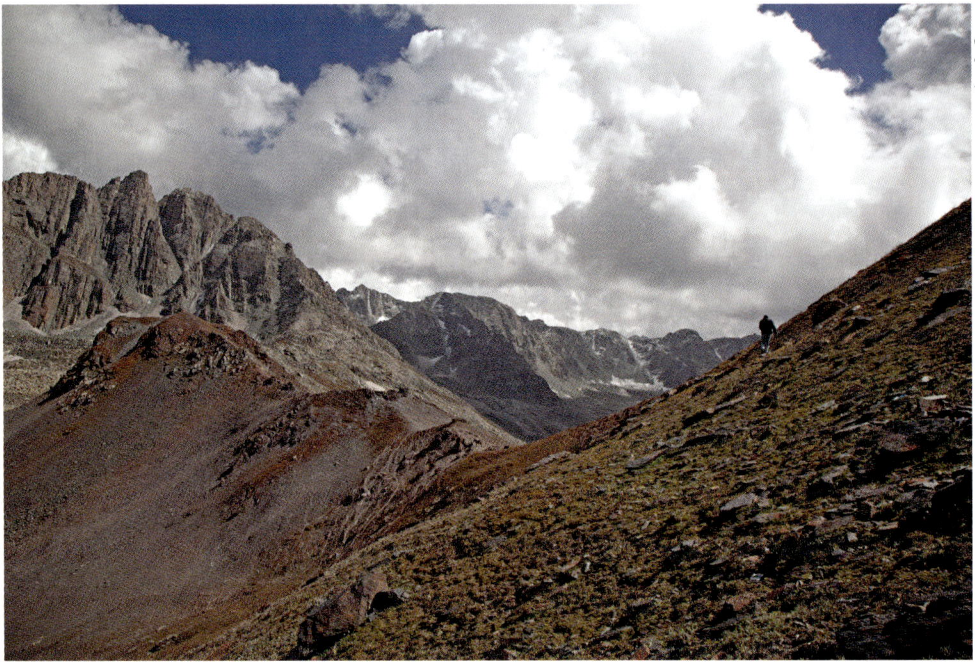

Photograph by Mahmood Ahmed Shah

Chor gali, to Jammu from Kashmir, called thus as it was used to avoid paying caravan tax demanded on main routes.

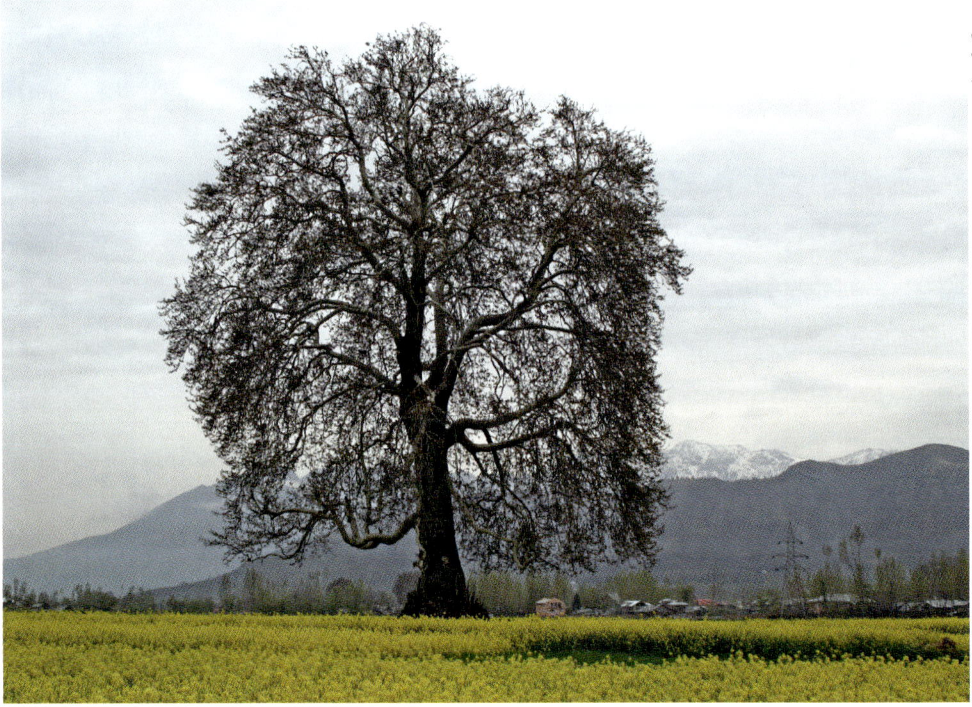

Photograph by Mohammed Amin Qureshi

The leafless grandeur at spring of a giant chinar soaring above mustard fields.

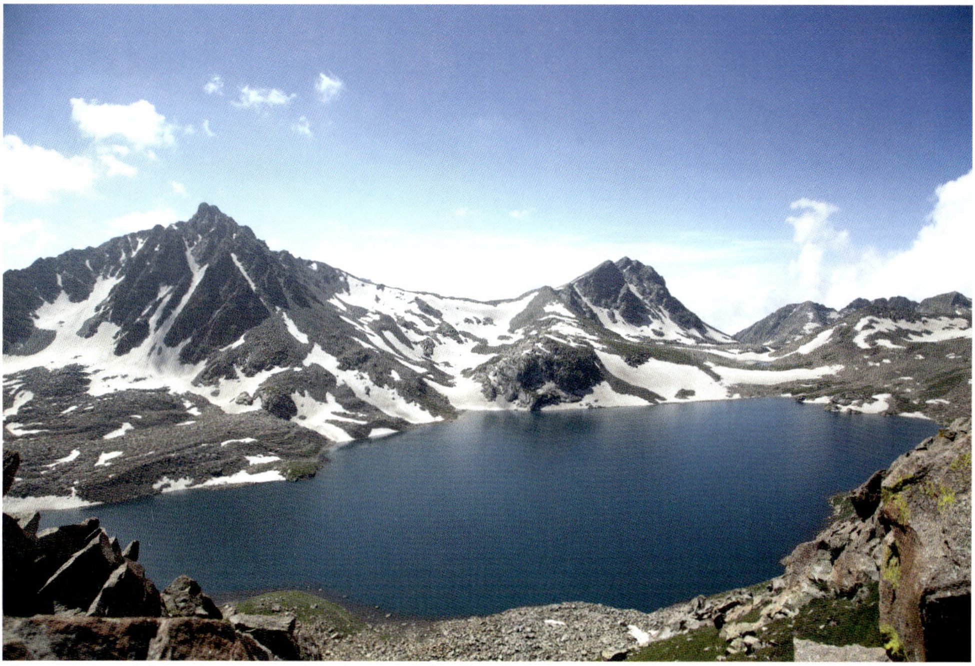

Photograph by Mahmood Ahmed Shah

Bhag sar, a vast lake in the Pir Panjal on the west side of Kashmir.

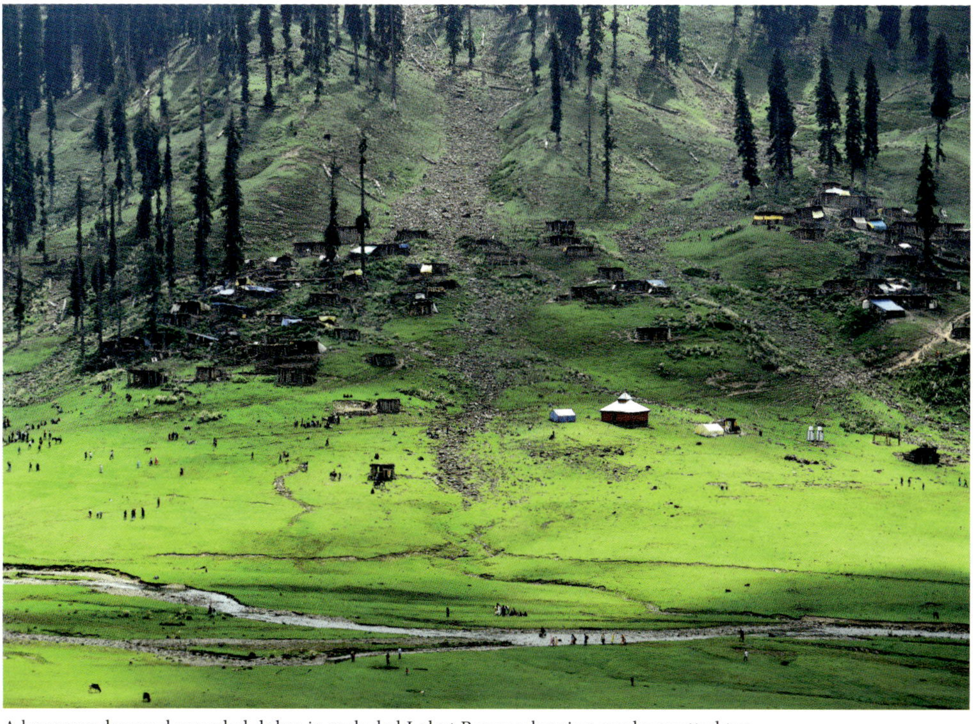

Photograph by Roshan Shehab

A busy meadow and crowded dokas in secluded Lokut Bangus; logging can be spotted too.

Didier's Tulips at the vast Indra Gandhi Tulip Garden in Srinagar.

Primula rosea and Saxifrage.

Foxglove.

Iris also known locally as 'flower of the cemetery'.

Primula rosea field in Bod Bangus.

Opium poppy grown secretly in Kashmir Valley.

Saxifrage field at Gangabal lake.

Moldavian dragonhead above Vishensar lake.

Photograph by Roshan Shehab

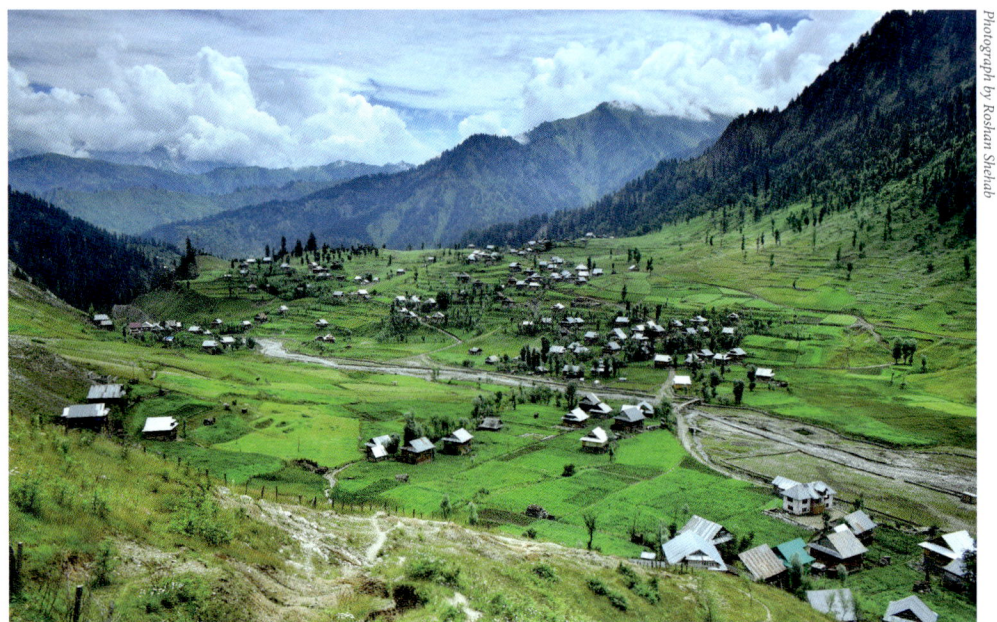

The now prospering border village of Ring Bala in Machil.

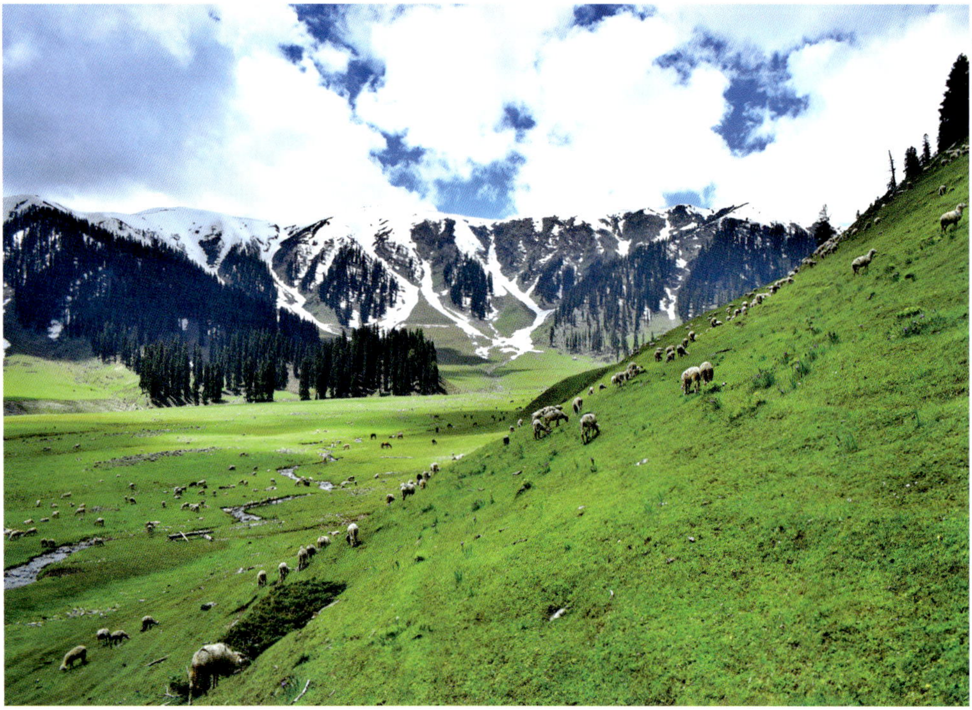
Photograph by Roshan Shehab

One of the many grazing meadows in Bod Bangus. On the skyline ridge are several passes leading to Mawar's valley.

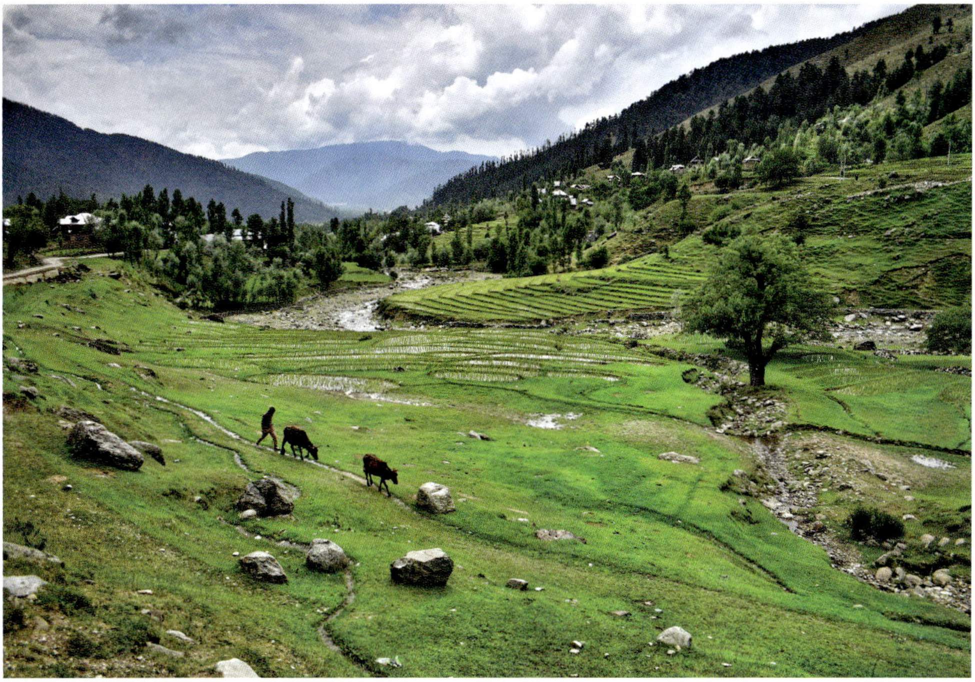

Photograph by Roshan Shehab

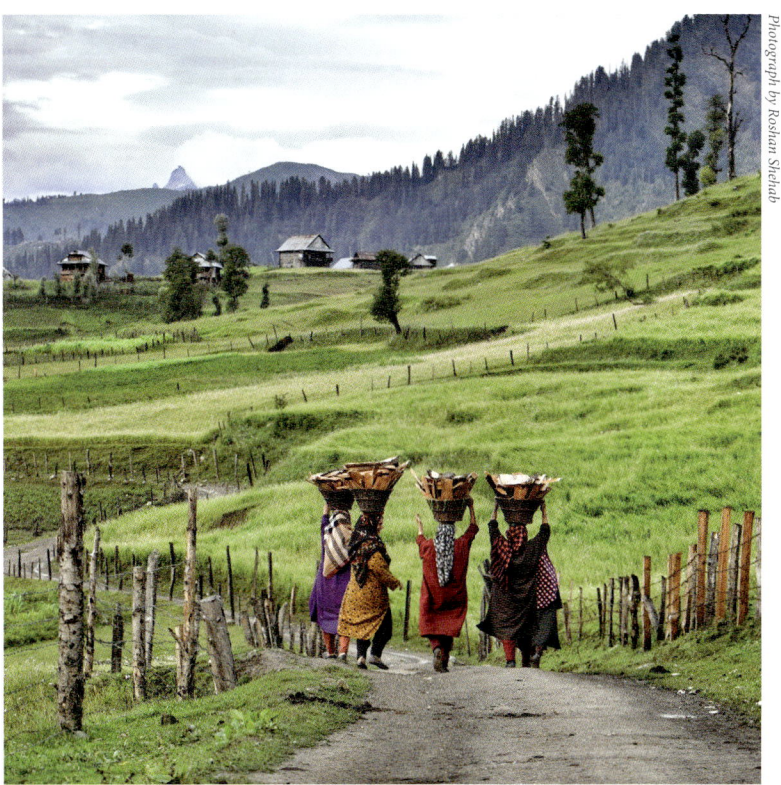

Never-ending shiny green for which Lolab is celebrated. Gratnar on Shrant nar on the road to Doban Lolab.

Photograph by Roshan Shehab

Smiles replace furrowed brows and roads dirt tracks in Machil, once a slough of despond. At the back is Toshain peak in PoK's Arang Khel.

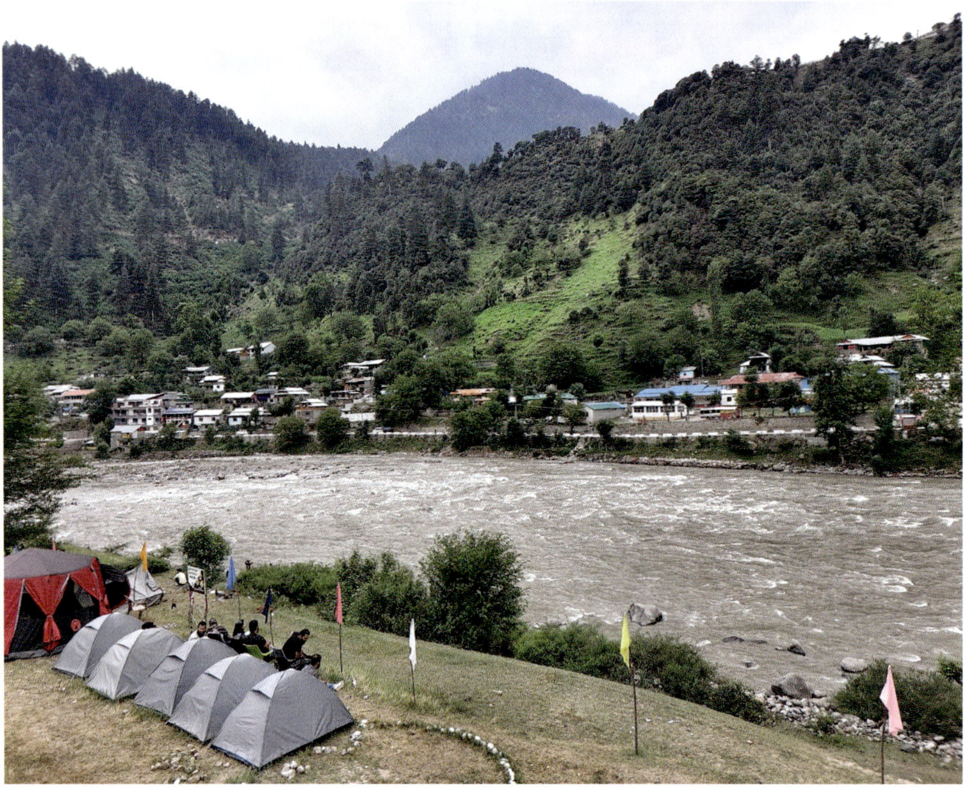

Photograph by Roshan Shehab

A tourist camp at India's Keran on the left bank of Kishenganga. A 110 m away on the right bank is PoK's Keran. Folk come from both sides to gaze at each other.

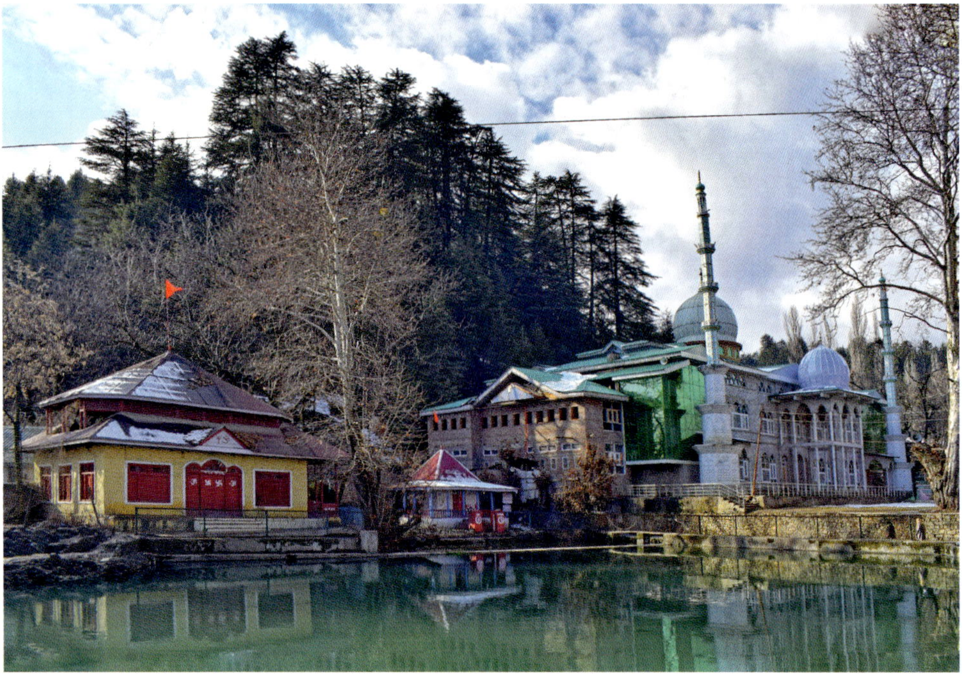

Photograph by Roshan Shehab

A frequent sight in Kupwara. Generations of undisturbed communal harmony in Trehgam.

Higher than the treeline, miles of unprepared ski slopes below Apharwat and above Gulmarg.

Photograph by Romesh Bhattacharji

Habakhatun peak in Gurez named after Kashmir's Nightingale, Habba Khatoon, of the sixteenth century.

Photograph by Romesh Bhattacharji

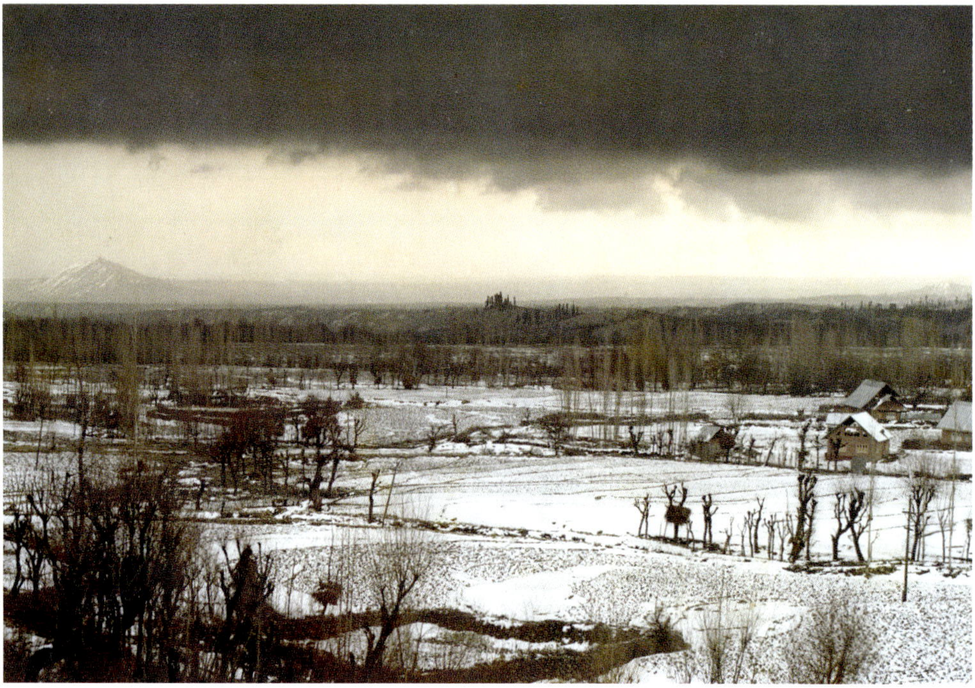

Photograph by Romesh Bhattacharji

An awe-inspiring sunset below Tangmarg after a light snow and before a heavier snowfall.

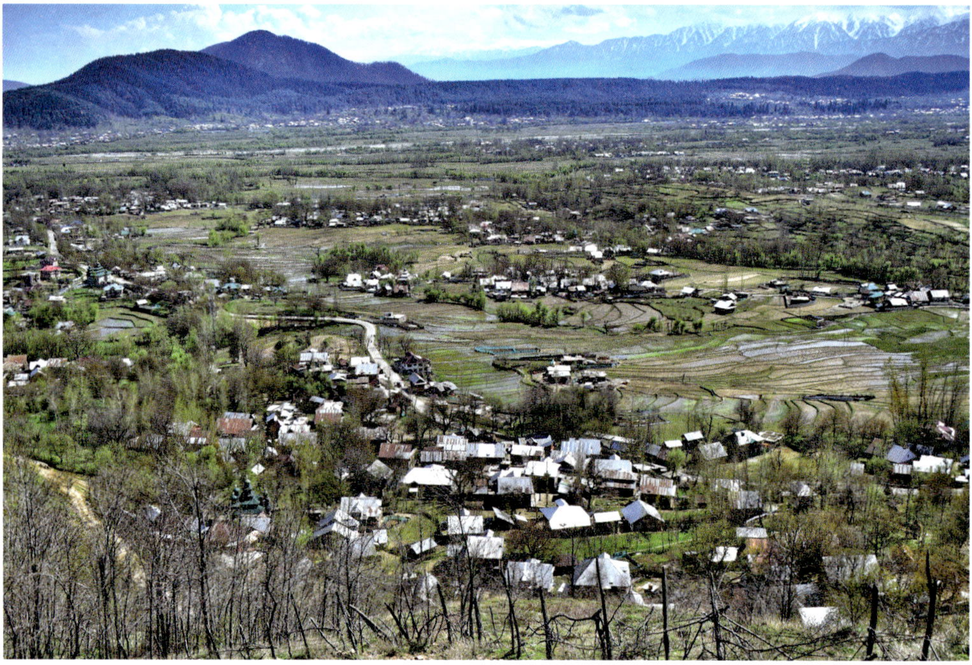

Photograph by Roshan Shehab

A sprawling Kupwara on both sides of Kahmil river with the Shamsabari range at the back; taken from Gulgam hilltop, 4 km north of the town.

A rare traditional kitchen that does not use gas, in Machil.

Homeward bound after work, an idyllic charming daily routine followed by hundreds on Srinagar's Dal lake.

Photograph by Romesh Bhattacharji

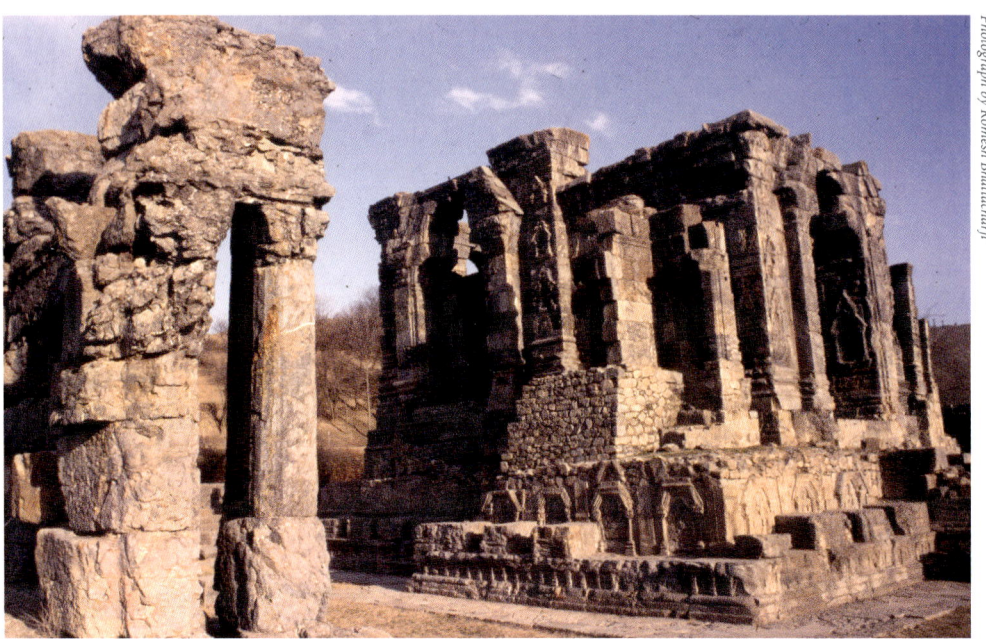

The enormous eighth-century roofless ruin of the Sun Temple at Martand.

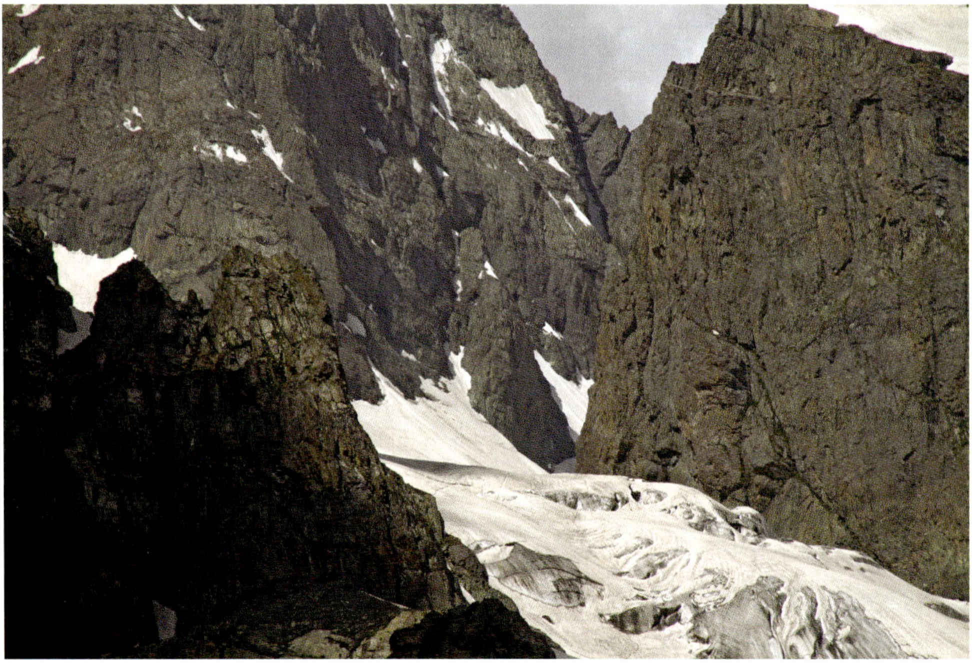

Photograph by Romesh Bhattacharji

Tumbling icefall from Haramukh's south face.

they litter. This is the sad lot of a part of Tosha Maidan and nearby Dudhpathri now.

The undulating meadows of Tosha Maidan are kept green in the short summer by many streams from Basam gali and Krala Nangal gali to the north and Daman sar and some tarns to the west. They join Godtar nala, which divides the meadow and separates it from the forested mountains of Sutaharan and Drang (another one) to the east. These two passes are a bridge between the Pir Panjal and a subsidiary range that starts from Drang village on the Ferozepur nala and ends on the left bank of the Rambiara river at Dubjan to the south of Shopian. If one visits these margs in August, there will be millions of flowers shining especially brightly in the clouds and cold mist.

Another linguistic change has been accomplished here. To the east of Tosha Maidan is a charming village called Sutaharan; it lies below a forested hill of the same name. The name Sutaharan has been changed by troops to Sitaharan—a word from Hindu mythology.

The sources of Godtar nala are to the west of Tosha Maidan in five lakes and tarns at the base of Chinamarg peak (4380 m) and Chinamarg gali (3870 m). Tosha in Kashmiri means soft as the wool of the rare shahtoosh goat. These lakes are surrounded by scree and trails of ice sliding down from several 4000 m peaks and two passes of the Pir Panjal rising to the west of them. This wind-chiselled ridge of passes and peaks can be seen frame by frame from points in the Tosha Maidan. For a better view one has to climb a fir-sprinkled hill to the east of Tosha Maidan and above the Godtar nala. It can soon be the Garden of Eden it once was, provided tourists cease littering and stop noise pollution.

There are about ten lakes between Chinamarg gali and Ashtaar gali (4190 m). They form an exquisite pendant to a necklace of moderate to tough peaks. Only now have folk from Kashmir, Punch and Reasi (in Jammu) started visiting these lakes. How times have changed! Fifty years ago, one would never find anyone from Kashmir or Jammu trekking here. These youth are writing about these less-trod paths on their blogs. This is an encouraging sign, for these routes will not be forgotten.

After peacefully rambling through this spacious treat of green packed with flowers, Godtar enters into a ravine close to the north of Kadalbal where there are some dokas in a forest clearing. It meets several streams and Bodhsar nar coming from Bodh sar. After this confluence it becomes Sukhnag nala. Sukhnag on entering the valley flows northwards to Magam on the Srinagar–Gulmarg highway *(Map 16)*.

Next comes the Dudhpathri meadow, which is cut by several streams that form the Shaliganga. This is yet another mesmerizing and exotic meadow. It is at the edge of Raiyar forest and has several Gujjar settlements. Dudhpathri has the Sukhnag nala to the north and Shaliganga to the south. Such never-ending delightful sights are what makes Kashmir unique. They steamroll the mind where it remains planted forever.

Dudhpathri (Meadow of Milk) straddles more than 20 sq. km of meadows cut by forests and streams and is less than a day's walk southeast of the larger Tosha Maidan. The legend is that Kashmir's most revered saint Sheikh Nooudin Noorani had meditated here, and when the time came to offer namaz, there was no water to clean his feet. He pierced his stick into the grass and milk came out. Seeing this, he told the spring that milk could only be drunk and not used for ablutions. Promptly, from the spring flowed water—the source of Dudhganga. That is the reason for a popular ziarat here. About an hour's walk to the south-west is an alp with an unusual phenomenon of large stones strewn around an undulating plain. The name is Palmaidan, and it has many shepherd camps.

Dudhpathri is at the eastern base of a long spur that heads east from the three Pir Panjal peaks of Tatakuti. This spur ends in Chhang peak (3699 m), which is also the name given to the large meadow and seasonal Gujjar village at its western base. Dudhpathri has a road connecting it to Budgam. That means there are shops and cafes and dhabas and parking lots and, of course, filth.

The Shaliganga nala starts from the small glaciers around the Tatakuti peaks to the west and the snow fields below Ashtaar gali (4190 m) as

Ashtaar nala *(Map 16)*. It flows through the part of the valley that is south of Budgam and later joins Dudhganga. The Dudhganga meets Shaliganga at Wahathor in the valley about 10 km before Srinagar. It enters the town through a brick fortified sluggish and filthy channel to eventually merge quietly with a drain, run off from Jhelum. A nauseating end to the once-bustling and bubbling clear water stream.

From Dudhpathri to Ashtaar gali and back is an enjoyable three-day trek. To the south of this troublesome and steep shepherds' pass leading to Punch is the lowest (4549 m) of the three Tatakuti peaks. Across its short cwm is another cwm of Tatakuti II (4591 m) and then of Tatakuti I (4725 m). Streams from them combine to form Shaliganga. The main source of the Shaliganga is a snow field between Tatakuti I and a rocky peak called Bod Angan (4251 m). From this rises Ashtaar nar that later becomes Shaliganga. In August, as most of the snow disappears, alps and moraine are exposed through which meander shepherds' paths.

Across another fir forested spur to the south is Yusmarg—yet another long, soothing undulating meadow cut by the sparkling Dudhganga. Its liveliest and cleanest part is in a thick fir forest when it hammers downhill in a spray of white (that is the allusion to milk). This is half an hour's brisk walk downhill from Yusmarg. Much of Srinagar's water supply comes from this river after it meets the Shaliganga at Lal Gam. There is lot more to be done for Yusmarg, and quickly, for otherwise litter will clog Srinagar's water supply.

Yusmarg is bordered by a forest-covered hill to its east and a large rolling meadow to its west. It is not far from the Valley further to its east and from one of Kashmir's holiest shrines—the ziarat at Charar-e-Sharief. Beyond the meadow are acres of boulders and pebble-strewn high ground leading to Pir Panjal. While all the meadows and alps to the south of Basam gali are close to Pir Panjal, Yusmarg is different. Its forest-ringed meadows are on hills about 20 km away from Pir Panjal, a wide swathe of which can thus be seen. Yusmarg is a popular meadow as it is just about an hour and a half drive from Srinagar, and it has JKTDC huts for tourists to stay in. It is accessible in winter, too, when snow has been ploughed away from the road.

Yus has been derived from Yousa, which is how Jesus Christ is known in Kashmir. According to legend, he crossed this meadow on his way to the Valley from Palestine. A couple of kilometres before Yusmarg is a pretty hamlet cut by the road that is called Yous. Yusmarg means 'Meadow of Jesus'. There is a legend in Kashmir that Jesus Christ was in the Valley and is buried in Srinagar. Of that later.

Across the vast uneven meadows of Yusmarg flow streams that form the Dudhganga. All these streams tinkle and roar past many alps and meadows. Dudhganga has its genesis about 20 km away at the northern base of Sunset Peak (4745 m).

Then close to the north and across a moraine is a standalone, unusual U-shaped rocky ridge, with the U pointing to the north-east. There are more meadows close to its mouth. This is called Musa Mashid—Moses's Mosque. On the west of it and north of the nearby Sunset Peak are half a dozen iridescent lakes and tarns that surface from their winter hibernation only during August. From these flow streams that form the Dudhganga.

From the eastern and northern shoulders of Sunset Peak are the Naba Pir gali (4259 m) and Kats gali (4229 m). The western faces of these summits in Punch are steep, rugged and rocky. *(Map 16)*

Over these passes is an improbable shepherds' trail to Yusmarg from Shopian—the district in which Sunset Peak is. The reason why shepherds choose such a difficult terrain is because of the healthy grazing grounds here, even though grazing may be available for a month or less.

The shepherds use a lower and easier way to return to Shopian via Yusmarg in autumn. They cross Khanchi kol and Gadar nar, and then, trudging over forested ridges and spurs, reach Hirpur and then Shopian—the apple town. From Shopian, the Sunset and Tatakuti peaks can be viewed in their awesome and immense majesty as they rise high above the noisy and crowded town famous for its apples. One turn after the town and they burst into the sky.

It is impossible to describe adequately the grandeur of these seemingly limitless swathes of green bordered by firs, birches, scree, tarns, snow fields and resplendent peaks. My head is on fire when I wrestle with adjectives that try to do justice to this gorgeous sight, but don't really.

Routes go through slashed forests and overused meadows to Dubjan and Hirpora. Anyone who had been here four or five decades ago would be shocked to see these forests. There are none left. Dubjan's elegant fir forest has gone, and only a vast green spur remains with a few tree stumps to remind one of their past majesty. The routes threaded now by shepherds were used by traders to avoid paying taxes to the Afghans, Mughals, Sikhs and then to the Dogras, who were installed and protected by the British.

Romesh Thong, Tatakuti and other peaks on the Pir Panjal range were first climbed by the Neve brothers in the early twentieth century from Yusmarg. They would climb them within four days of leaving Srinagar by a tonga (single-horse carriage). In these days of faster transport, even if ability and intention are there, restrictions will not allow such climbs. However, whenever possible, intrepid Kashmiri youth are the only ones climbing these peaks.

17
Peer Gali, Sat Sar and Kounsarnag to Didam Gali I

THE SOUTH RIDGE OF SUNSET PEAK (4745 M) DIPS SHARPLY TO A SADDLE at 3490 m, which is called Peer ki gali *(Map 16 and 17)*. The Pir Panjal range then carries on south, harbouring, as before, alps, meadows, lakes, passes, peaks, moraine, scree and streams. The old Mughal Road went over Peer gali. By this road the Mughal court escaped Delhi for the long summer. The road passed through Lahore and Rajouri.

There is a broad tarred road now. It leaves Srinagar and passing Shopian, Peer gali and Rajouri, reaching Jammu 330 km later. It is open for eight months.

Peer gali has a ziarat. More than 400 years ago, a Faqir called Seikh Ahmed Karim chose this spot to meditate a round the year. The Mughals venerated him. He was buried at Peer gali, and a shrine was built by a Mughal general. A kawah and sattu langar is run by his followers. Dinner is also provided to those who stay in the shrine. With the construction of this road the shrine receives donations of more than a million rupees each month that the road is open.

The new motorable Mughal road was opened in 2010. It is such a gift that apart from trade even marriages between the peoples of the Valley and of Punch and Rajouri have increased. A 20 km stretch over Peer gali has been so over-logged that the ground is unstable.

Nothing, however, excuses the wanton destruction of many more trees than necessary. Yet another forest that timber merchants have devastated. One common feature on all the newly built roads in Kashmir's surrounding mountains is the extravagant destruction of the giant deodars—be it over Margan pass or in the higher reaches of Kupwara or on the Mughal road.

From Srinagar the road crosses Rambiara river to Shopian—Kashmir's biggest apple market. Beyond it is the village of Hirpur and a wildlife sanctuary. The road follows the Rambiara river till Dubjan, where it is crossed and the climb to Peer gali starts. There's a well-positioned and attractive modern wooden gazebo by the side of the Mughal Road at Dubjan. One can see all the way up the valley to the forest shrouded confluence of Yanga nar with Rupri at Sokh Sarai dominated by a snow peak of Pir Panjal. Rambiara is the river after this confluence. Sokh Sarai is the name of an old Mughal Sarai, which is now roofless and crumbling. The moss-covered walls of one encloses a water-filled crater. The other one at Aliabad further ahead is much larger and partially roofless. No attempt has been made to restore these two ruined structures.

Yanga nar turns right and vanishes from view into a densely fir-wooded valley. The Rupri nar is visible for a slightly longer distance as it turns left to its sources in the Pir Panjal passes and lakes in the south. Two villages called Rupri are near here. One heartening sign is that young pines and firs have been apologetically planted around this Dubjan gazebo. A poor compensation for wiping out Dubjan forest.

Till three decades ago, the way to Peer gali was along the right bank of the Rambiara river from Hirpora (Hirpur)—much lower than today's tarred road. This was the old Mughal Road. The path skirted dense forests sprinkled with meadows and foamy brooks. On the left bank were thick forests till the high altitude and wind-swept south face removed all possibility of trees below the huge Mughal Sarai at Aliabad **(Maps 16 and 17)**.

A few kilometres below Peer gali, and above the left bank of the Jadi nar, in a wide alp, is the large Aliabad Serai (2980 m) also known as Badshahi Sarai. It was built by Akbar during the latter part of his reign (1556 to 1605). Under orders of Shah Jahan it was improved by the talented courtier Ali Mardan Khan. The name Aliabad comes from Ali in the latter's name. Mughal emperors on their way to Kashmir would stay to drink deep of the silence and beauty here. After the Afghans controlled Kashmir from 1751 to 1819, this road was closed. This indifference continued during the Sikh and Dogra rules, and these stately serais crumbled. Most of their trellised windows are broken. Shepherds' campfires have blackened walls and roofs. The sacrilege is complete with ugly and insulting graffiti written on their still-standing walls.

In 1833, Baron Huegel describes in his book that this big serai was still in use. It had a team of soldiers under a corporal to look after it and privileged travellers could stay in it.[27] In 2010, when the tarred Mughal Road was through, a few people hoped that this noble serai would see better days. Nothing happened. Most don't notice the stupendous serai about 200 m below the road in a sloping bright lambent green treeless pasture with a couple of dokas standing respectfully at a distance.

Along the Rupri nala and its numerous tributaries are many shepherds' villages. They are only seasonal villages that see life for about three months annually.

Peer gali (3485 m) cuts the Pir Panjal range which runs in a north–south direction. This ridge, south of Peer gali, has several friendly peaks around 4200 m high. Below them, are a dozen lakes in typically Kashmiri ornamental settings *(Map 17)*.

On the western side in Reasi district of Jammu also are a few striking lakes. There may be around twenty lakes and tarns in all, but this region is called Sat sar (meaning seven lakes)! In Kashmir a few names are repeated several times. There is a group of lakes called Sat sar in the Haramukh region as mentioned earlier. Then in this region there are two Rupri passes (4095 m and 4075 m) and two Rupri villages!

Peer Gali, Sat Sar and Kounsarnag to Didam Gali I

From Bhag Sar the Pir Panjal starts to turn to the east harbouring galis, peaks, lakes and meadows as usual. Pir Panjal is a simple range to understand as it only has one crest with short subsidiary ridges and spurs flanking out from the main crest. One reason for Kashmir's unique and explosive beauty is the inumerable high-altitude lakes. To make the scene even more unbearably overwhelming, there are fine rock and snow peaks in the background. These lakes remain frozen for at least seven months every year.

On the Kashmir side, Peer gali (3494 m) has a rather large scree-strewn meadow. Out of it emerge several streams to form two larger streams called Hapat nar and Jadi nar. They meet south of Aliabad Serai and after passing it merge with Yanga nar *(Map 17)*. Two of its tributaries flow south-east from the Sunset Peak and passes quite high above the Aliabad Serai, a cross the Mughal Road, before plunging downhill to join Yanga nar.

Jadi nar flows out of Nandan sar, which lies at the base of a steep triangular crumbling rock peak. To its south begin a series of lakes more exotic than the most exquisite and daintiest setting of jewels that man could ever devise. Each gets its due reverence in an eight-day trek covering most of these lakes on the Kashmir side of Pir Panjal. The start could be from Peer gali or Aliabad. The route goes up the Jadi nar to Nandan sar, from where one can wend one's way south, visiting as many lakes as are possible till the last one—Dhaklar sar (3870 m)—and its two attendant tarns.

From here a pass is crossed towards the east followed by a gentle descent, passing some alps and ending on the left bank of the Harseni nar in a wide and friendly gorge that offers no obstacles. Halfway between this point and Kenawain village is an appealing and captivating inverted Y-shaped scree-filled depression about two tough kilometres up a small tributary on the right bank of the Harseni. Above the steep escarpment to the north of this depression is a volcanic crater lake near Prishi peak (4434 m) *(Map 17)*. Such topographical delightful surprises keep recurring in Kashmir. The Harseni nar rises below Budil Pir gali (4240 m) and collects more water from a short glacier to the west of the twin Parasing peaks (4575 m). A wide path criss-crosses the Harseni nar till the meadows of Kenawain village to the south of Chor gali (3200 m) *(Map 17)*. Aharbal used to be a few hours' walk from here, but now there is a road till Kenawain. All along this route are Gujjar dokas and temporary shelters and tents of Bakarwals and Kashmiri shepherds.

Nandan sar (3850 m) is the main source of Jadi nar. The wide well-trod path below Aliabad goes for a short distance along the Jadi nar till its confluence with Khushkidar nar. The way to Nandan sar criss-crosses the Jadi nar's normally wide bed above which are shepherd camping sites and Gujjar's dokas. A short distance before Nandan sar, a trickle flows in from Chandan sar (3910 m) and its two attendant tarns to the south to meet Jadi nar. From this fork, both these lakes are about an hour away. At the head of these two lakes are gentle passes called Khabhi ki gali (3970 m) and Barhal gali (3940 m) but descent to the west into Reasi is not easy.

Discovering all these passes must have taken aeons of explorations by shepherds. Time and experience helped them sift the manageable passes from the dangerous ones.

The next pass on the Pir Panjal is Rupri Gali but also called Sannan gali (4070 m) after Sannan sar, a lake to the west of Pir Panjal, in Reasi district. On its east is Bhag sar (3935 m). There is a Bahg sar on the Reasi side too *(Map 18)*. Between Sannan gali and Bhag sar and Barhal gali and Chandan sar to the north are an heart-pounding ornamentation of four large lakes. All are about one to two easy kilometres apart *(Map 17)*.

The largest is Laksukh sar (3990 m) about a kilometre long and half as wide at its broadest. It looks like a rectangle that is squashed in its middle. The smallest is Barani sar (3950 m). Between the two is a small spur about fifty to hundred metres higher. There is however not much of a view, as it is blocked by the 4000-plus peaks and ridges around the lakes.

To Laksukh sar's north-east, across a ridge of about 4000 m, is a roundish lake called Golio sar (3980 m). The Golio's effluent is one of the several sources of the Rupri nar.

South of Barani sar, the Pir Panjal turns sharply 90 degrees to the east at Rupri pass (4075 m). For perhaps 30 km till beyond Brahma Sakli peaks *(Map 17)* this range continues straight east. After the turn to the east is Rupri gali (4095 m). Around it, from north to south, is yet another string of more than half a dozen lakes and tarns, which remain frozen for most of the year. From Laksukh sar till Dhaklar sar (3940 m) is the extensive watershed of just one river, the Rupri nar. Midway down the wide bank of the Rupri is the seasonal village of Rupri on a spacious meadow, a little above the stream. And on a western tributary emerging from Golio sar is yet another village called Rupri! As expected, there are many shepherds' camps here.

After the sources of Harseni nar below Budilpir (4240 m) is the ridge of the twin Parsing peaks (4575 m and 4515 m). Beyond that towards east-south-east is another famous jewel of Kashmir—the large 2 km long Kounsarnag lake. It has three passes to its south and west. They are Kounsarnag gali (4120 m), Phuti Pansal gali (4030 m) and Gugumaran gali (4035 m) respectively. All of them lead to Reasi.

The most prominent of these is Kounsarnag gali (4120 m), to the east of which and beyond Kounsarnag are the stirring snow-speckled rocky summits of Brahma Sakli, which can be seen in their entirety from Shopian.

One would have thought that while completing the circuit of Kashmir's mountains, one had seen it all. Yet, there is one more glorious surprise lurking in the gorges to the south of Brahma Sakli (5076 m) peaks and Parasing (4575 m).

Between Peer gali and Kounsarnag are more than a dozen lakes on both sides of the Pir Panjal—Reasi to the west and Kashmir to the east. They are scarcely noticed these days except by some trekkers from Kashmir and Reasi. All the attention these days is on the Vishensar group of lakes in East Kashmir—known exaggeratedly as the Great Lakes. The latter are being mobbed so much every year that flowers that used to bloom in abundance in August along the path have visibly reduced and so have juniper bushes, I am informed.

Kounsarnag (3963 m) is shaped like an inverted isosceles triangle. It lies in a steep walled gorge of rock and snow in inscrutable solemn and solitary splendour. Around its base are stripes of snow fields dividing alps, scree and boulders. No fairer spot can be within two days of leaving a town. Nor any be so rugged and dainty at the same time. It has ice floes till late summer. In one incident on 30 June 2013, an ice floe drifted away along with some young men enjoying brunch. An IAF helicopter saved them.

Kounsarnag is also a Hindu pilgrimage spot. It is in such a stirringly haunting location; so much so that if there be some gods, they would naturally stay here. Kounsarnag's east and west shores have steep mountain slopes plunging into the lake. Its most comfortable approach is from the widest part in the north-west. Its narrowest portion points to the south-east. Kounsarnag is at the end of a long and narrow cwm.

Kounsarnag is an upside-down version of Italy's largest alpine lake, Lake Garda. Kounsarnag's narrowest portion points south, while Lake Garda's narrowest portion is in the north. Both have the shapes of typical moraine valleys. Both are stunning. Unlike Lake Garda, there are no islands in Kounsarnag.

At the eastern edge of this cwm is the third highest of the Brahma Sakli peaks as the Pir Panjal ridge starts ascending from here to the highest (4630 m) of four Brahma Sakli peaks. These peaks hold at least three glaciers. The one clinging to Brahma Sakli I (4630 m) is separated from others by a bare rock and scree craggy spur. The Brahma Sakli I glacier feeds a small lake called Kishir sar (3490 m) and the other peaks feed the slightly larger Brahm sar (3595 m).

Near the end of the craggy spur jutting from Brahma I to the north is a pretty tarn called Indra sar (3820 m) *(Map 17)*. Below it is an enormous undulating scree and knoll dotted meadow called Astaanmarg. Astaan refers to a sacred place where some holy men meditated. There are several Astaanmargs in Kashmir, each one in an exquisite setting, which must help meditation. The softness of the turf of this meadow is like that of Tosa Maidan. It delights shepherds and visitors. From the knolls can be seen peaks across the Valley and to the south the top of the Brahma Sakli peaks. The swathes of green entice an overnight halt to ooh and aah over a delightful sunrise and sunset that gilds every feature in sight *(Map 17)*.

Astaanmarg is a gradual climb high above to the east of the popular route from Aharbal to Kounsarnag, but a diversion after Kongwattan, not taken by many, is worth the effort. Kongwattan is a well-developed tourist friendly place. It is connected by an untarred road and has a well-furnished government run tourist guest house.

Below the Kishir and Brahm sar lakes is another large undulating green meadow. This is Zajimarg and ends in the substantial fir-forested hill (around 2500 m) of Kadalabal below. The Zaji nar flows out from these lakes and joins Kounsarnag, which after meeting the Harseni nar, hurtles over Aharbal's 19 m fall with a deafening rumble as the Veshav. Within 500 m of this cataract, the Veshav spreads itself out in the Valley and murmurs in the unfettered freedom of a more than a 500 m wide bed. It is one of Kashmir's most useful rivers as much of its waters are channelled to fields in Kulgam district. So much so that within 10 km of the falls it is so dry for about half the year that at places it is possible to motor across its wide bed. Zajimarg is yet another favourite of shepherds. In Kashmir, any patch of green, no matter how remote or small, has shepherds.

Brahma Sakli[28] rock peaks, as seen from the north, appear tough but there's a manageable route up Didam gali I (3810 m) according to old SOI maps and up Kali gali according to shepherds. The lowest of Brahma Sakli peaks—the thumb shaped 4282 m can be climbed from Didam or Kali gali (3810 m) which is at the head of another small glacier which is yet another source of Zaji nar.

One route to Brahm sar and flinty Brahma Sakli peaks is a circuitous one from Kongwattan through a pretty alp of Pachakul. The other one is from Damhal Hanzpur, near the confluence of Kandai kol and Veshav *(Map 17)*. It is two bus stops before Aharbal. A rough path used to lead up the Kandai kol till Kandimarg. Now there is a good road. From Kandimarg turn west over a well-beaten track to Khashrari gali

(3305 m) and thence to Gugalmarg. Roads have made approach treks shorter. Roads are reaching the smallest of villages bringing better health, education and modern facilities.

There are two roads to Aharbal falls, beyond which is Kounsarnag. One is from Kulgam and the other more scenic one is from Shopian that curves west and south through forests of pines and firs and creeps up behind the falls through a thick forest. In all the villages on either side of Veshav fewer and fewer traditional buildings remain. In Tangimarg, years ago was an impressive and attractive four-storeyed traditional house of a rich man. Concrete-based houses are fast replacing these traditional wood and clay structures which were cool in summer and warm in winter.

A shorter, less crowded, but slightly more strenuous path to Kounsarnag, is straight up from Manzgam, a bus stop before Aharbal. Manzgam *(Map 17)* is an interesting, widespread and pretty village above the right bank of the Veshav. For much more than a hundred years it has been known as a village of hazar (1000) cholas (houses). Above it, to its south-west, on a hillock, are a masjid and a temple with a dharamshala—at least they were there decades ago. A steep path goes through a forest to Abrupathri (Cloud Meadow) and thence to Kadalbal forest, amid which hides a seasonal Gujjar village in an alp. Follow the rivulet through the forest to the flower-flooded (only in August) vast Hawkwas meadow. Around and above stretching beyond what the eye can see are vast meadows and riveting views of Brahma Sakli peaks. And then there are several dokas attractively sprinkled around on several green pastures, and goats, sheep, horses and children milling around. The most immense and striking one is Zajimarg. To its north is a slightly smaller but equally arresting meadow called Gugalmarg, also drained by a fledgling tributary of Zaji nar, which is called Gugal nar till it reaches the marg of its name. From here, the sapphire-blue or jade-green circular lake Brahm sar is a couple of hours to the west.

18
Didam Gali I, Didam Gali II, Houen Heng to Banihal

THERE IS NO END TO KASHMIR'S VARIETY AND EXTRAORDINARY BEAUTY. You see Sheeshnag and you are overwhelmed by its solemn majesty. And you think there's nothing like it. Then you see the soaring rock peak of Haramukh above Gangabal lake or the Lidderwat or Bangus meadows, and again emotions are indescribable. At ice floes filled Kounsarnag mind and heart keep drumming till your eyes literally ache taking in so much of magnificent elegance.

If only conditions were peaceful, Kashmir would have had more nature lovers than it could have handled. Six decades ago, a stupendous fortnight-long trek from Drang on the Ferozepur nala to Kounsar and nearby nags (lakes) was popular amongst some students of St Stephen's College, Delhi in the autumn break. These days no one from the plains can even recollect such scintillating walks, but thanks to young Kashmiris these routes to Elysium are alive on YouTube.

Media-fanned uncertainty scares away people from the rest of the country. Then in areas close to the LOC army restrictions end any trysts with nature. While the eastern side of Kashmir Valley allows uninhibited trekking, the west is still subject to restrictions. During a particularly distressing time of over-reaction by the army after killing of an innocent in July 2010, I was trekking to Gangabal. On the path there were only foreigners and Kashmiris. The latter were escaping the army and the former the heat of north India's plains. Kashmiris were delighted to see me and were very friendly. They asked me to go back to 'India' and tell them how considerate and hospitable they were. Of that there is no doubt.

The Pir Panjal on its way east looses altitude and its threatening aspect of steep rock faces for a while. Even the pretty lakes that used to ornament its base are no more. There is yet another well-connected corner of southwest Kashmir that is still heavily forested but not often visited or even publicized as worth visiting. Kashmir is so blessed with appealing spots that all cannot be given equal attention or minimum facilities.

Nunkhel gali (3980 m), Pazmal gali (3045 m), Mandu peak (4010 m), Didam gali II (3930 m) and Nussu gali (3240 m) are almost the last passes before Banihal. Within their snowfields and springs are the sources of a few streams like Sikwas and Nunkel nar. They combine to form Kandai kol *(Maps 17 and 18)*. It's a tributary of the Veshav, which it meets at the village of Damhal Hanzpora near the pillars of an old bridge across Veshav. The forests above its course hide delightful bowls of meadows, doka-dotted alps and pretty villages. Another attraction of this picturesque corner is accessibility, with roads reaching quite far up the Kandai kol. These roads divert from the main ones along the Veshav river to Kulgam and Anantnag on the NH 44.

Beyond Nussu gali (3240 m) and before Banihal pass (2382 m) is an interesting pocket of a few villages in south Kashmir containing streams and small valleys that are to the north of the Pir Panjal range but are in Ramban district of Jammu to the south *(Map 19)*. The largest of these villages is Rujlu. Topographically, they ought to be in Kashmir. Nearly all these brooks become one large stream called Pachhagam and that flows into the Jhelum above Qazigund in the Valley. The villagers in this enclave find it easier to go to nearby Qazigund, and then take the train or bus to Ramban rather than go south over a high Pir Panjal ridge and after

Didam Gali I, Didam Gali II, Houen Heng to Banihal

a long torturous journey down the Mangat nala reach Banihal town and then the district headquarters at Ramban.

Before the Pir Panjal range descends to Banihal pass is a pass called Nyusu gali (3240 m) between two peaks called Sundartop (3880 m) and Houen Heng (3909 m). This pass was once called False Banihal by pilots flying in and out of the Valley fifty years ago. This pass has a deceptive similarity to Banihal Pass even though it is about 1000 m higher *(Map 19)* and is about 18 km west. This rough map shows how close they are. An error of a degree and—crash!

On the 7 February 1966 an Indian Airlines Fokker Friendship plane took off from Srinagar for Delhi in low clouds and about 15 minutes later crashed 100 m below Houen Heng peak killing all 37 people on board. The cause was navigational error due to inclement weather.[29]

This peak can be reached from Kulgam via Damhal Hanzpora and the road head at Iron Bridge within two days from Srinagar. As is usual in Kashmir, it's a satisfyingly pretty and exciting short trek along green valleys of the Kandai kol and its tributaries. This weekend trek is popular with youthful Kashmiris attracted not only to its myriad charms and extensive views but also by a desire to hunt for bits and pieces of the air crash. The view to the north from Sundartop and Houen Heng reveals the entire Valley and mountains girding it and beyond. To the south are the plains of Punjab and of Pakistan.

Houng Heng, which is 3909 m, is confused for the slightly higher Didam peak (4209 m), which is about 500 m to the south of it. Didam peak is to the east of Didam gali II (3930), and has a treacherous and steep climb from the north and a steep and easy descent on the Jammu side.

The Pir Panjal descends to Banihal pass (2832 m) and then steeply regains height to the sources of the Sandran and Bring rivers and beyond. Banihal means 'heavy snow'. And in winter this pass, despite the tunnels, remains cut off for days because of snow drifts and avalanches.

The Veshav meanders peacefully in the plains of Kulgam district with most of its water channelled through canals to fertilize innumerable fields and orchards. No more seeing a small ridge of a solitary peak. From many places in the karewa sprinkled Vale of Kashmir one sees expanse upon expanse of Pir Panjal's ridges and peaks from miles away—on a clear day naturally.

At Banihal ends the description of the mountains that girdle the Kashmir Valley. The circle is complete. Now to the Valley.

19
The Valley

THE KASHMIR VALLEY IS AN OVAL-SHAPED BASIN. IT IS ABOUT 140 KM long and 40 km wide. The Valley gently slopes towards the Jhelum. Its bewitching, elegant, exquisite, fertile, graceful, gorgeous, green, magnificent and stunning. At all times of the year, it is worth a visit. Now starts a gentler and softer Kashmir, sparkling with rivers and streams, orchards and fields of extensive plains, wide views, karewas and chinars.

The Valley was once a lake, geologists say. There was a natural narrow barrier before Baramulla at a time before history began. That eroded. The lake emptied quickly. Glacial moraine, together with silt from innumerable rivers and streams, filled the lake. Eventually the lake turned into the present fertile and exotic Valley we know. This action took ages.

During this process karewas were formed, as debris from the mountains was deposited by streams. Karewa in Kashmiri means elevated tableland. Godwin-Austin adopted this term in 1859 for the 50–100 m high plateaus that dot the Valley. They are packed and hardened with sand, gravel, silt and clay. These deposits are best for the cultivation of almond, walnut, apple and peach. And only in the karewa of Pampore, zafran grows. It is of such celebrated quality that zafran from Iran, for instance, is used to adulterate it.

Millions of years of continuous erosion have not done as much damage to these grand karewas jutting out of the Valley, as in the past two decades. A complicit state government is allowing the mining of fertile soil for landfills at construction sites and along highways. The karewas are the essence of Kashmir's beauty and its economy.[30] Srinagar's airport is on a karewa called Damudara, named after a Kashmiri king during the Mahabharata times.

Kashmir's mountains and Valley are administered through ten districts. About seven million people live here. Headquarters of all these districts are in the Valley. The districts are Anantnag, Budgam, Bandipora, Baramulla, Ganderbal, Kulgama, Kupwara, Pulwama, Shopian and Srinagar. Ancient Kashmir's administrative distribution was Kamraz (North Kashmir), Yamraz (Central Kashmir), Maraz (South Kashmir).[31]

All the districts have a slice of mountains in their jurisdiction. Demands for a better life keep increasing but haphazardly administered, according to the ability and clout of the elected representatives. The bureaucracy, most agro-industries and handicrafts, commercial and industrial activity are based exclusively in the Valley. Handicrafts, including silk and woollen textiles, which is the second most profitable industry after fruits, is concentrated in Srinagar, Ganderbal and Budgam districts. Another extremely profitable activity, but only for a few, is masterminded from the Valley but is concentrated in the mountainous part of every district. It is tree felling, an activity that illegal. The only progress in all the districts is road building. Perhaps because tree felling and road construction go hand in hand.

Anantnag (from Jhelum to Sind):

Area: 3574 sq. km; Population: 1,078,692; Density: 300 sq.km; Literacy: 64.32 per cent

Anantnag *(Map 20)*, formerly known as Islamabad, is the largest district and the second most populous town of Kashmir, with more than 200,000 crowding its largely narrow confines. It gets its name from a nearby spring called Anant nag. The district spreads from near Banihal in the south across East Kashmir till beyond Amarnath Cave far to the north-east.

This congested town spreads round the northern and western side of a partly wooded solitary hill about 160 m higher than the town. This hill has several longitudinal marks, which indicate the varying heights of the level of the Dal lake as it drained an eternity ago. There are several springs coming out from this hill. On the north-west side of the hill are three spring-fed ponds in a large geometric park, at the south of which is the 600-year-old Jamma Masjid or Masjid Baba Dawood Khaki. On the eastern side of the hill is a forested bowl, in which is the lovely and spacious garden campus of the University of Kashmir (South). The hill has a wide view of the Valley to the north and of the lower wooded and often bare hills to the south.

It is a large market and educational town and has many places to attract people keen to learn about Kashmir's past. Being a large town it hides terrorists easily. Working on this assumption, it has a large military and police presence. Despite restraints on trade imposed by the large army, police and paramilitary presence, this crowded and administratively neglected town is fairly prosperous.

It is also a dirty town—one of the many in the Valley. One keeps wondering why the government—state and district—has neglected sanitation.

Two of its urban clusters—Sangam and Bijbehara—have a flourishing cricket bat[32] making small scale industry. The bats are made from the many willows that are grown especially in this district and in Bandipora. The best willows are from Bandipora, as the Wular has plenty of water for seasoning the willow wood. But the Bijbehara–Sangam area has evolved as the best place to fashion them. At least 600,000 bats are sold every year. Cricket bats are made in the small factories along the NH 44 and in the villages to the east of Sangam.[33] Pangjam is one of the most prolific. Apart from the usual apple orchards innumerable willows grow here.

Bijbehara could have evolved from the words Vidya Vihara meaning Temple of Wisdom. A Mughal enlarged town, it was once more well known for its Mughal garden. It was called Padshahi Bagh and built by

Dara Shikoh (1615–1659), Shah Jahan's eldest son. He was an astronomer and mathematician, and had a tumultuous life that ended when he was executed by his brother Aurangzeb. Next to the Mughal garden are the ruins of an old Mughal bridge over the Jhelum, which was built by Dara Shikoh. It was 30 m long and 2 m wide. The bridge was washed away by heavy floods ages ago. There was a garden on the other side of the Jhelum too, but that has become an agricultural field.

Bijbehara has the second largest chinar tree in Kashmir. It is 18 m in circumference at ground level and is the handsomest of the twenty-four other chinars in the Padshahi Bagh. Guru Nanak (1469–1539) came to this town, and established a gurudwara called Shri Guru Nanak Dev Ji Pehli Padshahi Gurudwara Bijbehara, which is still in use.

Near the Padshahi Bagh is a road that crosses the Lidder to Pahalgam. It offers a more scenic, uncongested and enjoyable alternative route to crowded Pahalgam. The other one via Anantnag has traffic snarls for eight months of the year. The former road circuits the base of mountains to the east of Tral, leading to Pahalgam through quaint and pretty villages, dark forests and over rills. It has delightful views of the fields and orchards to the south especially at early morning or in the late afternoon sun *(Map 1 and 8)*. It is called the Sallar Kullar Road. It used to be a sublime leafy walking path once. The broad welcoming grins of thirty years ago have been replaced by worry-wrinkled foreheads. This is now an area of tensions and excesses.

Northwards from Bijbehara, the Jhelum becomes navigable and boats can be seen plying and parked at jetties.

A few kilometres later to the north an important hydrological point for Kashmir comes. This is the inverted tuning-fork-like confluence of Lidder with Jhelum. The Lidder in its journey till here has taken in the waters of Arapal, Arpat, Bring and Sandran rivers *(Map 5)*. The Jhelum has taken in the copious Veshav and Rambiara rivers *(Map 19)*. This point is known as Sangam. The new four-lane expressway crosses the Jhelum here. The railway goes along the left bank of the Jhelum.

The leaping foamy waters of the Lidder as soon as they escape from the claw-like confines of forested spurs of Ashidur Bal (2650 m) to the north and Tarwal (2360 m) to the south spread themselves far and wide in many branches in the Valley. Between them are more fruit orchards and agricultural fields.

Kashmir's highest and second highest peaks—Nichang (5444 m) and Kolahoi (5245 m)—are in this district.

Ganderbal:

Area: 1979 sq.km; Population: 297,446; Density: 150/ sq. km; Literacy: 59.98 per cent

Ganderbal *(Map 21)* on NH 1 starts from Baramulla and then passing through Srinagar ends in Leh. It straddles the Sind river. Fifty years ago, this highway passed through narrow lanes, from Nagbal through Ganderbal town till Wayil village. It does so today too. It was carved as a district from Srinagar in 2007. Improvements have been faster since then. Ganderbal is expanding rapidly on the right bank of the Sind as the left bank is congested.

There are more than fifty educational facilities, from schools to colleges to computer coaching centres, here. Yet literacy in this heavily financed district is much less than the national average. And like in the rest of the Valley, men are more literate than women by more than 20 per cent. There is a Central University in Ganderbal, built on a wide treeless expanse especially cleared for it. Around it are agricultural fields, majestic chinars and orchards. Above all rises Mt Haramukh (5148 m) and its neighbours in the north. This mountain is on the boundary with Bandipora. The east face is in Ganderbal, and the west face is in Bandipora.

Its fruit production is the third lowest in the Valley, but it produces the best grapes.

Ganderbal district has some of Kashmir's best known and easily accessible visual delights like Sonamarg, Thajiwas glacier, Krishansar, Vishensar and Gadsar lakes, Mt Haramukh's impressive east face and lakes below it, Zoji la and the source of the Kishenganga. A few kilometres to the north-west is the deep Manasbal lake, which on its northern bank has

Jharokha Bagh, designed by Jahangir's wife, Nur Jahan, but is now only a typical unimaginative municipal garden.

For some years now the NH 1 along the river Sind is going through throes of unprecedented activity like widening and tunnelling. Then there are three hydel projects, the oldest of which was started in 1955. Their installed capacity is 140 MW but because of old turbines and sometimes low water levels, only 70 MW is being produced. As in other parts of Kashmir, there is an embarrassingly large gap between promise and practice.

Across the national highway above Ganderbal town is Gutli Bagh. This is an exclusive Afghan village of about 700 houses. Their version of Pashtu is now laced with Kashmiri and Urdu. They were insular till two decades ago. With modern education being given in several schools, some of the young are giving up traditional rural lives and are administrators, engineers and doctors. Even marriages with Kashmiris have started. Afghans ruled over Kashmir from 1752 to 1819, when they were replaced by the Sikhs. Both rules were notorious for brutality and extortionate taxes.

Across the Sind river and about three kilometres from Ganderbal is Tulamulla village to the south of the Central University. Here is an ancient Hindu temple that was first mentioned by Kalhana in his twelfth-century *Rajatarangini*, a chronicle of the Kashmiri kings. It is still a popular pilgrimage spot. Till a few years ago, the caretakers of this temple used to be Muslims.

Bandipora:

Area: 3200 sq. km; Population: 4,706,708; Density: 1100/sq. km; Literacy: 57.98 per cent

Bandipora *(Map 22)* is the third largest district in the Valley, but only a tiny portion of its territory is in the Valley. It stretches from the impressive Himalayan sources of the Kishenganga at the foot of Kaobal gali (4150 m) in the north-west *(Map 11)* to the depressing sight of a decaying

The Valley

Wular—once the largest fresh-water lake in India—in the Valley. It became the district headquarters after Bandipora was carved out from Baramulla in 2007.

Before Independence, Bandipora town **(Map 12)** was on the main trading route to Gilgit, Chitral and Skardu. Beyond the town is Pahalwanpora village on the way to the varied and beautiful Kishenganga valley over the Razdhianangan pass (3560 m). Before Independence, there was a Customs and Immigration check post here as it was on a long trade route to Sinkiang and a shorter one to Punjab and Afghanistan. Now it is a forest check post. This was also a pilgrimage road to the eleventh-century ruins of a university and temple at Shardapeeth on the Kishenganga, but that is now in POK. Till World War II this was the preferred route for people trying to climb Nanga Parbat and the peaks in Chitral and around Skardu.

Bandipora is cradled in an inverted U formed by mountains that rise to a ridge around the 4000 m high to the north. It has the Wular to its south. It straddles the Madmati or Bot Kol river, which drains all the lakes, springs, snow fields and a few glaciers hanging off the west and northern side of Haramukh (5148 m). The western face of Haramukh is in Bandipora district. Another river, the Erin, meets the Wular at its north-east and below Madmati's mouth. Almost the entire river is diverted for agricultural use before Bandipora. The 47 km long canal, known as Zaingiri, meets the Pohru river of Kupwara at Wadoora **(Map 12)** after having irrigated at least 13,300 acres of land. The Pohru joins the Jhelum below Wular near Sopore.

Bandipora was once known for *aleem* (knowledge), *adab* (courtesy) and *aab* (water). These days courtesy is not widespread. After the closure of trade, pilgrimage and silting of the Wular, Bandipora for some years was neglected. With security, hydel dams, agro industries, expanding orchards, improved agriculture and roads reaching the farthest villages, Bandipora's future is improving. An attractive terraced Nishat Park, inspired by the Mughal Nishat Bagh in Srinagar, is here—sometimes well looked after and at other times neglected. It was designed in 1954 by the then Prime Minister of Jammu and Kashmir Bakshi Ghulam Mohammed. In a mohalla of Bandipora called Kaloosa is an ancient sycamore tree (locally known as bran). Next to it is an old temple called Sharda.

The sight of a dying Wular is a depressing one. It is shrunk to half its size and shrinking further still, all because of indifference. The river Jhelum, which flows through it and kept replenishing its fresh water, is unable to protect it any more now as it itself is polluted. Maybe the diverted waters of Kishenganga will help flush out its silt. Optimism is a good diversion but is of little use. Wular at 21 sq. km was once the largest fresh-water lake in the country. Not any more. In 1986, Wular was declared as a Wetland of National Ecological Importance. And the bureaucrats congratulated themselves for having achieved a victory. As with most bureaucratic successes, it was only a paper triumph.

The government still does not bother about conservation and protection. The rot continues in the ugly shape of sewage, siltation and weed infestation. On the way to Bandipora, the vast boundless clear blue of Wular's watery expanse used to hypnotize the viewer. This litter has nurtured plant growth that prevents sunlight from entering the lake and thus inhibits the growth of various planktons on which fish and birds feed. To make rejuvenation impossible are the plantations of willow trees on this silted Wular.

Wular has become the most devastated ecosystem in the Valley. About 60,000 fishermen used to depend on the lake for their living. Migratory birds like Brahmini ducks, red-crested pochard, tufted ducks and other waterfowl have reduced, and so have the resident birds like waterhen, lapwings, moorhen, coot and the little grabe. With half the lake gone, it may soon be time to say bye to the rest of its life too.

Kupwara:

Area: 2365 sq. km; Population: 870,354; Density: 537/sq. km: Literacy: 75.6 per cent

Kupwara *(Map 23)* is the second most productive district in fruits and dry fruit. Its haunting and contrasting beauty is unforgettable. Had conditions been peaceful and the state government more energetic in development, it would also have become a more popular tourist destination than it is now. It is only 100 km from Srinagar, but for visitors it may well be 1000 km away despite having a good road, for such are the irrational fears about security. The LOC at its northern and western borders does inhibit development, but a little more attention in less sensitive areas would have improved the plight of people in this extravagantly beautiful district. To Kupwara's north is the Shamsabari ridge, which separates the Kahmil river from the Kishenganga. It is pierced by several motorable passes.

The Kishenganga to the north and north-west separates the district from POK. To prevent infiltration, the central government has built roads in all sensitive forward areas. These roads, if and when the peace of pre-Independence times prevails, will become the infrastructure for development and a gift for tourism. Till that happens, the sensitive sectors on the LOC—Machil, Keran and Karnah—will also continue to depend on the army for education, health and employment.

In this Muslim-majority district, there are many Hindus and Sikhs too. In Kupwara there are a couple of temples next to mosques and there has never been any friction. There are two shrines—one Hindu and the other Muslim—that ought to be mentioned.

About 20 km to the east of the glamorous Bangus meadows is the dense fir forest of Watsar, covering a 2200 m high hill. On this hill and next to a spring is the ancient Badrakali temple. In 1981, the small black polished stone idol of Ma Badrakali *(Map 14)* was stolen, recovered mysteriously in 1983 and for security reasons, sent to Jammu. The temple was burnt by insurgents in 1994 and a new all-marble temple built in 2004. The idol was reinstalled in 2018.

About 5 km before Kupwara, to the right of the Srinagar–Kupwara road beyond Darugmul, is the village of Muqam Shah Wali at the foot of a hill. Here is the ziarat of Saint Zaiti Shah Wali. He was once a general in the army of Ali Shah Chak, a late sixteenth-century king of Kashmir. Under the influence of Hazrat Hamza Makdoomi he became an ascetic. His brother and sister are also buried near his shrine, which is near Jamma Masjid. Next to it is a clear water spring which is supposed to have healing properties. It certainly has an unusual and welcome taste. Mid May, every year, a mela is held here and all communities join.

Kupwara has many eye-riveting spots: Bangus, Drangyari, Reshwari, Keran, Machil and to a lesser extent Jabri before Tangdhar. Lolab and Bangus valleys are its prized attractions for the present. The Jammu-Kashmir Government had built some tourist homes in the Lolab valley near Kupwara. They were being used till insurgents burnt at least one of them down a couple of years ago. With a road having being built from Bandipora to Lolab over the Nagmarg ridge, visitors can increase if politics allows. Trekking to these places makes one wonder at the never-ending feast of beauty that Kashmir is. One never gets the same sense of overwhelming continuous divine glamour elsewhere in other mountainous regions as one does in Kashmir. Whether one is in the narrow confines of Kishenganga or by the wide valley of Mawar at Reshwari, the magnetic grip that Kashmir has on one's senses is never ever loosened.

Baramulla:

Area: 3353 sq. km; Population: 1,008,039; Density: 305/sq. km; Literacy: 71.2 per cent

Baramulla *(Map 24)* is the second largest district in the Valley. It is the largest producer of apples in Kashmir. It was on the ancient trade route into the Valley from Punjab and Afghanistan. Late in the nineteenth century, the British made a cart road from Muzaffarabad through Baramulla to Srinagar, but it was so uncomfortable that from Baramulla onwards many preferred to take a houseboat up the Jhelum to Srinagar. In the late nineteenth century, the then Dogra Maharaja had a way surveyed along the Jhelum for a railway track but the colonials found it too expensive to support this enterprise. In the early forties, a motor road was made. Baramulla is now connected by rail with Banihal in

Jammu through Srinagar and has a stable all-weather road till the LOC at Salamabad. Salamabad has a large on-again off-again trading centre for business with POK.

There were ruins of an early nineteenth-century bridge at the east of Baramulla as well as of a fort on the west. All these and nearly all of Baramulla were destroyed in the 1885 earthquake.

Baramulla town, despite its development and its beautiful places, is still remembered for the horrors it experienced in October 1947. Pashtuns from the Afghan border were brought by the Pakistani Army along with Pathans to invade Kashmir but dallied in Baramulla, pillaging and raping. St Joseph's Convent and Hospital, where the unspeakable was common in those two horrible days, has forgotten those terrible times and moved on to do good. The narrow entrance passage through a red wall gives no inkling of the vast spaces and clean buildings inside the convent. Or the terrible times it went through seven decades ago. The assassinated president of Afghanistan, Mohammed Najibullah, finished his schooling here. Before Partition it had attracted students from present-day Pakistan. There's a popular story here of a major in the Pakistan Army who prevented the further loot of the convent and rape of the nuns here in 1948 as he had studied in this convent.

By the fifteenth century, Baramulla was an important caravan stop and had a revenue check post. In 1421 Syed Janbaz Wali, a saint from Isfahan, Iran, settled down at the present Janbazpora, above the right bank of the Jhelum, to preach and started a school here. He was buried on the left bank of the Jhelum in a tree-studded meadow in what is today called Khanpora. There is a ziarat here to which people come to pray from all over Kashmir.

Across the Jhelum from this ziarat is the impressive all-white Gurudwara Shri Chatti Patshahi Sahib that was made in memory of Guru Hargobind Singh's visit to Baramulla in 1620. It is built on a bend in the river and thus is visible in its commanding entirety for many kilometres from the road to Uri. A little to the south of the Baramulla railway station is a sweet water spring near which Guru Hargobind Singh meditated for some time. There's a simple and attractive gurudwara called Sri Thara Sahab at Singhpura here.

Baramulla has expanded on both sides of the Jhelum, which has four bridges over it. It has forested hills above both banks of the Jhelum. It was not always so. A certain Charles Ellison Bates, writing in the Kashmir Gazetteer published in the late nineteenth century, describes the hills above Baramulla as being bare. Baramulla has developed impressively in the past two decades, but with the LOC hanging sometimes merely a few kilometres away, development is still to cover its farthest villages.

Baramulla is supposed to have been founded about 2000 BC by a king called Bhimsina. Mid-nineteenth century excavations uncovered ruins of Buddhist stupas here. It is an important Sikh, Hindu and Muslim pilgrimage centre. In Baramulla, Hindus, Muslims, Buddhists and Sikhs live in harmony and contributed to its culture. There is also a small but significant presence of Christians here with St Joseph's Convent being an important and large centre of education.

Budgam:

Area: 1370 sq. km; Population: 753,745; Density: 537/sq. km; Literacy: 57.98 per cent

Budgam *(Map 25)* is so close to Srinagar that the only civilian airport in the Valley is in Budgam. So is Srinagar's railway station.

In Budgam, on the Srinagar–Gulmarg, road is Kanihama. This is where the famous Kani shawls are made. Kani shawls are made from either silk or wool and the work on them is so fine that they look like delicate and precision crafted paintings. The state government has given the copyright of these shawls to Kanihama. So, only shawls made in Kanihama can be called Kani shawls. It is an ancient craft but was encouraged by the Mughals. In 1776 Napoleon presented a Kani shawl to his wife Josephine, and with that started its popularity in Europe. These days they range from Rs 80,000 to Rs 2.5 crores.

The district's natural attractions are the meadows of Tosha Maidan, Yusmarg and Dudhpathri; hot and cold springs of Khag; and the Pir Panjal. An ugly artificial reservoir before Yusmarg, Nilnag, has been attracting the undiscerning, as it is near the road. One of Kashmir's most revered shrine, that of Sheikh Noor-ud-din Wali at Charar-e-Sharief is here. It was completely destroyed in a ham-handed security operation to free it of terrorists but has been rebuilt.

Budgam has another treasure too. The oldest and largest chinar in Kashmir is at Chattergam in Budgam and only a few kilometres from Srinagar. M.S. Wadoo in *The Trees of Our Heritage* reverentially writes, 'The circumference of this chinar is 31.85 metres and its height is 14.78 metres.' This chinar is in the garden of Sufi Saint Syed Qasim Shah in Chattergam.

Shopian:

Population: 266,215; Area: 613 sq. km; Density: 430 per sq. km; Literacy: 63 per cent

Shopian **(Map 26)** is the second largest producer of apples and the third largest of walnuts in Kashmir. Industrial activity is almost nil. It was carved out as a district from Pulwama in 2007. There is economic discontent, and thus it is a popular place for insurgents. 'The fear of arms and the fragrance of apples'[34] co-exist. It's a small town that becomes smaller and quieter in the non-apple season when fear stalks the town. Its first college started in 1988 only.

Shopian's most prominent landmark is the Jamia Masjid in the heart of Shopian and near a large park. It was built during the Mughal reign and resembles the Jamia Masjid of Srinagar. The famous Aasar-i-Sharief Dargah at Pinjura attracts thousands of devotees on the occasion of Eid-i-Milad-un-Nabi and Shab-i-Mehraj.

Shopian has always been a shelter for pro-Pakistan insurgents. At the height of insurgency in the early nineties, it used to be called India by day and Pakistan by night. Even now there are incidents where soldiers, insurgents and innocent people are killed—nearly every second month.

Apples in season are plenty but so is corruption. I have seen apple trucks (as in other apple growing areas) being stopped at paramilitary check posts and crates of apples off loaded. No payment naturally. Our soldiers could easily win hearts but prefer to add to their wallets and break hearts. Many of the apples are from small orchards.

The Pir Panjal, from Sunset Peak and Peer gali till Brahma Sakli peaks, is in Shopian district. Rambiara river and Harseni nar—the rivers and their tributaries that run down to the east from these and other peaks—are its northern and southern boundaries *(Map 17)*. Half of this district is mountainous, but 95 per cent of its population is in the Valley. The most remarkable attribute of the crowded Shopian town is the impressive view of the Pir Panjal peaks, towering 3000 m above the town. Shopian is above the right bank of Rambiara river.

The road from Shopian to Kulgam is pleasant to drive on, especially in an autumnal evening. Through the dark tree-lined road, the rice fields glow, as if bathed in gold. These fields are interspersed with apple orchards.

Kulgam:

Area: 1067 sq. km; Population: 424,483; Density: 925/sq.km; Literacy: 60.3 per cent

Kulgam district *(Map 27)* is the rice bowl of Kashmir and also a hefty producer of apples. Kulgam is on a karewa. Kulgam town has about 25,000 people living in it. Apple orchards adjoin the small district town. Surrounding the karewas are miles and miles of rice fields.

Kashmir produces about 70 per cent of apples in the country. On 1,46,327 lakh hectares about 2,00,000 metric tonnes of apples are produced. Out of these 1,91,300 metric tonnes were sent outside Kashmir in 2018.[35] Kulgam produces about 21,000 tonnes of apples.

The Valley

Kulgam was founded by a saint, Syed Simnan from Iran, in the fifteenth century. He liked the view from a high bank of the Veshav and the forested hills across it to the south and settled down here. He was buried at the place he liked the view from. His ziarat has a stone foundation and the mazaar is made of deodars—which must have been got from the hills as they don't grow in the Valley. In peaceful days of old, both Hindus and Muslims used to revere him. To the north can be seen the Haramukh (5148 m) peak and to the south, 3000 m above the forests, are the Pir Panjal peaks. Sheikh Noor-ud-din, Kashmir's most revered saint, also known as Nund Rishi, was from Quimoh nearby. Pandit Jawaharlal Nehru's ancestors were from Nadi Marg, a village in Kulgam.

The Valley plains are at a height of around 1650 m, and the karewas or plateaus on which almonds grow are about 150 m higher. In a karewa at Kutbal an archaeological excavation has found first-century tools and stamped tiles from the reigns of Kushan kings.

The old Kulgam town is situated above the banks of Veshav and at the point where the man-made Kawal kol carries water out of the Veshav. There are many ancient man-made kols flowing out of Veshav and its tributaries. These are the reasons for Kulgam's fecundity and why the Veshav has little water beyond Kulgam.

At Kulgam, there is a kilometre-long bridge over the Veshav, after crossing which the road goes along the right bank of the Veshav, skirting forested foothills to the south towards Anantnag. Three more bridges on the Veshav have made trading and movement easy. From the Aharbal Falls till Sangam, where it meets the Jhelum, the Veshav is about 60 km long.

Kols are an ancient—some say as old as the Kashmiri language—way of irrigation. Channels draw out water from rivers to distant fields and orchards. Some have even taken water to the orchards and fields on karewas 100 m higher than the Valley plain by an ancient lift irrigation system.

Qazigund on NH 44 is Kulgam's busiest town. Fifty-two years ago, four of us on motorcycles, reached Qazigund in Kulgama district from

Jammu late one October night. Qazigund was dark. Going ahead was impossible as we were tired. Only a small lamp flickered in one of the less than humble huts along the road. This was a tea shop. We spent the night in it. In 2019, Qazigund has a railway station and a bus stand as big as the whole village was then, and around the clock electricity. It is such a busy place that now it has a road by-passing it. Qazigund is firmly in the Valley. As one descends from the tunnel one sees the green poplar-strewn and apple orchards-dotted villages around the Sandran to the right of the road, with attractive and durable A-shaped roofs of houses. After a snowfall, the view is peaceful with snow stifling, momentarily, the never-ending roars of trucks.

Pulwama:

Area: 1398 sq. km.; Population: 560,440; Density: 598 per sq. km; Literacy rate: 63.48 per cent

Pulwama **(Map 28)** is a large producer of milk, rice, zafran (saffron) and cement. It is known best for the zafran that is produced in Pampore. Pampore is on a large karewa, on which grows the famous purple zafran, which when dried becomes dark red. The zafran flower comes before the leaves—an unusual phenomenon that has puzzled visitors since Jahangir's time.

Most of Pulwama is in the Valley. The town is crowded, unkempt and littered with pill boxes, barbed wire and sandbags. To the east and across the NH 44 is the prettiest part of the district—a mountainous area. Though their base is scarred and polluted with cement plants. Between Khrew and Wuyan, in the foothills, are all the cement plants in Kashmir. The gashed hillsides show where limestone is being mined. As a result of all this pollution, Khrew has the highest death rate in the district. It is an unhappy district. Insurgents and soldiers also interrupt life's routine.

Along the NH 44 are Pulwama's better known towns Tral, Khrew and Avantipore. Avantipore has ruins of graceful tenth- and eleventh-century temples. Despite suffering restrictions and lack of facilities, many young from all over India are roughing it here and liking it, as they are well received by the people here.

Near Tral, in the east, at Shikargah is an optimistic and successful conservation project to protect the rare Kashmir stag called hangul. A little to its south in a karewa is Gufkar, which has caves where implements of Neolithic people were discovered in 1981 *(Map 8).*

Near Khrew, in the village of Loduv, stands an ancient Hindu temple where a flame used to burn and was thus also called Jwalaji. After hundreds of years of being smothered in vines and vegetation it was discovered atop a hillock by the British archaeologist Sir Aurel Stein in 1891. It has been rebuilt so many times since then that the old Gandhara style architecture is hidden.

The new NH 44 crosses the Jhelum further south of Pampore's zafran fields to go alongside the even newer Banihal–Srinagar–Baramulla railway.

20
Srinagar

Area: 1979 sq. km; Population: 1,269,751; Density: 640/sq. km; Literacy: 71.2%

About 10 km north of Shalamar Bagh, by Dal lake in Srinagar ***(Maps 29 and 30)***, a country road lined with poplars winds its way through fields to the village of Burzahom above the right bank of Ara nar. To the east of this village rises a vast lambent green karewa about 20 m higher than the rural road which carries on to Ganderbal. Below the karewa are homes, fields and orchards. Close by, to its north, is the 3450 m high Harawar peak on a slightly lower ridge that has a few lower peaks. Across its ridge are thick forests and the Sind valley. To its south beyond the village is Dal lake and Srinagar ***(Maps 19 and 30)***. On the Burzahom karewa are several cricket fields, where heedless of the ancient ruins children play.

The site is thousands of years old. Excavations began in the 1930s and are continuing. This karewa had been inhabited from the time people lived underground thousands of years ago and then above ground inside stone slab structures (megaliths) that dot this plateau. Its first residents were hunters, then food gatherers and later farmers. There are a few large menhirs here and it seems that they were dragged down here from high up the mountain to the north that form an impressive backdrop to the cricket and football fields.

Burz refers to birch trees which grow on the leeward side of the 3000 m high ridge behind Burzahom. These were used to make roofs for the homes of the pre-Neolithic (12000 to 6500 BC) inhabitants of this karewa. Excavated pottery from sites here shows similarities with excavations in Swat (POK) and Central Asia. Srinagar is that old. These excavations also show trade links with Central Asia and north India. Srinagar was that well connected even then.

King Pravarsena II established the present Srinagar at the beginning of the sixth century, but it had not expanded much even a century later. In AD 631, the Chinese pilgrim Huen Tsang described the ancient capital as being small and spread around the Pandrethan temple.

Only from AD 960 did Srinagar explode as an administrative and trading centre. Historian and traveller Charles Girdlestone in his *Memorandum from Kashmir* (1871) describes the long arms of Srinagar's trade links. Turks brought tea, silver and horses; Chinese brought earthenware, shawl wool and the 'produce of trans-Himalayan looms'; Baltistanis brought dry fruits; 'Hindustanis' brought chintzes, brocades; Russians brought guns, vessels and tea urns. They took away pashmina, iron, zafran and rice. Many would stay in Yarkand Serai,[36] which today is also called Safa Kadal Serai and is on the left bank of the Jhelum before the new Nawab Bazar bridge. This historic emblem of ancient trade is in tatters **(Map 30)**. The market used to be held in a large ground outside the serai. This is now a congested colony, and the Safa Kadal Serai has since 1960 been a shelter for Tibetan Muslim refugees, some of whom have opened shops in the ground floor.

Srinagar is the political, trading, cultural and handicraft centre of Kashmir. It has been its heart from at least the seventh century, according to the British explorer Aurel Stein who came to this conclusion after he studied coins and old texts including Kalhan's twelfth-century *Rajatarangini*.

Before the broad new NH 44 that connects Jammu to Srinagar, there was an old road that went by the karewa on which Pampore's zafran fields are. The road descended to a plain below the karewa. At the end of a descent was the spot where a skeleton of an elephant was found.

Mughals used to bring elephants to the Valley from Delhi. This skeleton was of one of those elephants. In a spectacular accident involving Aurangzeb's caravan in 1665, on the climb to Peer gali fourteen elephants and four ladies in waiting were killed. The French traveller Francois Bernier describes this accident in *Beyond the Three Seas: Travellers' Tales of Mughal India*. He felt more regret for the anguish of the elephants than for the humans.

As the Jhelum nears Srinagar it twists and turns and makes several S bends. The new four-lane NH 44 crosses the Jhelum on two bridges. Gone is the charm of the old, congested road that was separated from the Jhelum by a 3 m high embankment, which kept Jhelum's flood waters off the road sometimes. The old two-laned crowded road passed by fields, through bazaars and under chinars. The suburbs of Srinagar start from Pampore.

The black of the new NH 44 contrasts glaringly with the dark green of vegetable fields and bright green of paddy as it slashes above them. If there's snow, the contrast could be considered by some to be even attractive. Avoiding contact with crowds, it often runs parallel to the rail track for a while before entering the congestion at Pantha Chowk.

Pantha Chowk is on the outskirts of Srinagar. To the east of Jhelum, from Pantha Chowk onwards, Srinagar sprawls around the base of Zabarwan (2916 m) mountain. *Zabar* means beautiful and useful and *wan* means forest. Its northern spur ends at Harwan reservoir in the Dachigam Reserve Forest. On its southern face, symmetrically arranged military and paramilitary camps are crawling up.

There are two ways into Srinagar from Pantha Chowk. One goes west as a kind of a ring road to Nowgam and beyond, with roads branching into the heart of Srinagar. The other road goes straight skirting the large, geometrically laid out, tree-lined Badami Bagh Cantonment.

Near the entrance to the cantonment is an army stadium. To its south is a tenth-century stone temple called Pandrethan, also known as Pani Mandir. It has a pyramidal roof and was open on all four sides. It is partially and artisitically immersed at the edge of a spring-fed pool surrounded by giant chinars. Alexander Cunningham started restoration of the temple around 1848. Pandrethan is at the foot of the Zabarwan mountain.

Zabarwan looms over Srinagar. It has seven, peaks from about 2035 to 2900 m in height. The lowest one is above the forest behind the Grand Palace Hotel. There are springs all over the mountain. Under its northern forested face are the Mughal Gardens, the sprawling Indra Gandhi Tulip Garden, Raj Bhavan, the Boulevard on the eastern bank of the Dal and the unnecessary golf course. The wind-lashed eastern and southern faces are quite bare but dotted here and there with scrub. The more prominent feature of this face are the roads that weave up its sides from the army cantonment at Badami Bagh and paramilitary camps at Pantha Chowk. After snow, this mountain, when seen from Char Chinar on the Dal together with its reflection, creates a fantasy world of perfect symmetry. To its south are Khrew and Pampore and some minor streams that flow in from the south-east. At its south-west snakes the Jhelum **(Map 19)**. The north is circumscribed by the Dachigam stream and its tributaries, which rise from its north-east. The Zabarwan range is about 25 km long. The northern side of this mountain is forested, has Pari Mahal, a college built in 1650 by Dara Shikoh, and the Chashmashahi Garden.

Srinagar in the nineteenth century was built on both sides of the Jhelum as it is now. It was easier to go by boat to shop or visit than walk on the rough cobblestoned or dusty paths. Today it is a carpet of congestion flung all around the looping Jhelum. The Dal lake is silted, Anchar lake is finished and 1.4 sq. km of Nageen lake's northern neck is now fields. The Jhelum, from Iqbal Park near the once stately Sher Garhi fort (now an untidy police station) till Safa Kadal, is filthy and even has islands of trash-covered sediment.

From ancient times, Srinagar had canals to tap the overflow of Jhelum and of the Dal lake. These canals, like at Barzulla, had worked in the past but with concrete invasion of the banks, floods are frequent and destructive. There has always been a problem of silt in Srinagar stretching to more than 500 years ago when the population of Srinagar was too small to pollute the lake and river. The Dal had marshes from hundreds of years ago. The Mughals tried to reclaim some and desilt the lake and Jhelum. Even before they came in the sixteenth century, earlier rulers had made lagoons and canals and periodically desilted the Dal to refresh it. Their efforts were more successful then than now—if such an effort is made at all. The silt removed had been used to form embankments (bunds) and islands (Sona Lank and Char Chinar) for recreation and agriculture. One of these canals was built by Zain-ul-Abideen (1418–1470), lovingly known as Bud Shah (the Great King). This canal is the present one that leads straight upto the Shalamar Garden, which had been a garden for eight centuries. The Dal once had a 6 km long bund with nine bridges to connect the western portion of the Dal with the eastern one. It's gone now. Only an arched bridge, now known as Unt Kadal, remains stranded in its water to the east.

By medieval times, houses and bazaars were increasing on both sides of the Jhelum in Srinagar. Attractive wooden bridges were built. One, Fateh Kadal, first built in the sixteenth century, had homes and shops too.[37] There are now fourteen new bridges, seven old and historic bridges and a couple of foot bridges that span the Jhelum in Srinagar. Some of the new bridges are on the sites where ferries used to ply. When Srinagar had only the medieval kadals (bridges), there was leisurely pedestrian and horse-driven traffic. Now there are so many vehicles that stronger new bridges have had to be built. From Shadipora in the north of Srinagar to Pantha Chowk in the south, fourteen new bridges have been built. There are several more on the spill channels of the Dal and the Jhelum. The old wooden bridges were picturesque but are being replaced as their life is almost over.[38]

Srinagar has large swathes of crowded localities interspersed with generous sweeps of green. Some of the still surviving popular old spots are

Srinagar

the five Mughal gardens, Pari Mahal, Pandrethan temple, Pathar Masjid, Hari Parbat, the mausoleum of Zain-ul-Abideen and Shankarcharya hill. During Mughal times, there were about 300 gardens.

Near the northeastern extremity of Srinagar is Harwan, which is the entrance to the Dachigam Reserve Forest. Here the waters of the Dachigam nala are collected in a reservoir. A canal called the Sharab kol is drawn from this artificial lake to provide water for the fountains of Shalamar and Nishat Mughal gardens and for a part of Srinagar.

The highest point of Dachigam Forest is Mahadeo (4000 m) which can be seen from the western end of the Dal in its entirety. North of Mahadeo are a couple of peaks (3900 m and 3440 m). Within these peaks and a couple of smaller ones are the sources of the Mahadeo nar and Dara *(Map 30)*.

Dara is a village, above Srinagar, with many fields and walnut orchards, and a spectacular view of the capital city. It is connected by a good road that continues to climb past it and the long village of Fakir Goojree to yet another craggy and rather bare slope called Astaanmarg above. This is the fourth Astaanmarg in Kashmir and is the driest of them all. The reason why there are so many Astaanmargs in Kashmir lies in its name *(Map 30)*. Astaan means a holy place where a shrine is or where a pir or a sadhu meditated. They are always in supremely picturesque locations, which must have helped in meditation, reflection and revelation. The view of the Valley and the snows of Pir Panjal behind it is intoxicating, especially at sunset. It must have been difficult to meditate with so much arresting scenery spread at one's feet.

This point is about 30 km from Srinagar. Above it is a forested peak 3140 m high. From here, there is a formidable and stunning 300 degree view of the Valley in the south and the Sind valley to the north. Above the Sind can be seen Haramukh and Kolahoi and other peaks. All this can be had within half a day of leaving Srinagar.

This ridge carries on to west-north-west and then plummets to Ganderbal and Woyil. There are several 3000 m high peaks on this ridge. From each, a similar view can be had, though all are not easily reached.

The westernmost peak of this ridge is Harwar (3451 m) and north of it, on a gentle slope, is the serene meadow of Khudmarg (2760 m). The easiest approach to it is from the Afghan village of Gutlibagh above Ganderbal *(Map 30)*. The peak is reached after a pretty walk through a thick fir forest.

Srinagar has a couple of old temples and several mosques. The most singular of these is the Pathar Masjid, designed and made by Nur Jahan in 1623. It is on the left bank of the Jhelum and diagonally opposite to the revered Shah Hamdan mosque. The entrance to the grey-stone Pathar Masjid is from the river, up a flight of large stone steps. There is a classical garden of four squares divided by stone footpaths. Within each square was a garden with chinar trees, the descendants of which are still there giving shade.

At the head of the square garden and pointing east is the nine-arched Pathar Masjid. The central arch is twice the size of the others. There are eighteen massive stone pillars that hold up the mosque. Unlike other Kashmiri mosques, it was made only of stone. Instead of the usual pyramidal roof is a dome which was destroyed during the Sikh invasion of 1819. Each arch including the central one leads to a 60 m long gallery. Above this are nine domes that have delicate elliptical leaves carved on each of them. On the pillars and inside of the arches along the gallery are 10 cm deep arched niches. The whole mosque is of grim, stern grey. Except in an inner sanctum, where the morose walls have been framed in colourful and marvellous bands of gold, blue and red mosaic patterns.

This austere and spacious Pathar Masjid had been converted into a stable during the Dogra Pratap Singh's rule (1885–1925). One Austrian carpet trader, C.M. Hadow, based in Srinagar and Lt Col J. Manners furiously objected and convinced the Maharaja to reconvert it into a mosque. This was done in 1919. C.M. Hadow helped establish the Tyndale Biscoe Boys School and a dispensary, which is now the SMHS Hospital. He is still fondly referred to as Hadwun saab, as he paid fair wages to his workers. These were much higher than what other carpet manufactory owners paid.

Amongst Srinagar's many mosques, monuments, shrines and temples is the unusual shrine of Rozabal (roza means tomb and bal means place).

Srinagar

It is a modest tin-roofed structure on the Rozabal Khaniyar road, in congested Khaniyar just north-east of the stagnating Baba Dem lake. It has two graves. One is of a Shia saint called Mullah Mir Sayyid Nasiruddin, who is a descendant of the eighth imam of the Shias, Musa Raza, buried in Meshed, Iran. The other is supposed to be the controversial one, of Jesus Christ. Many books have been written about this grave despite there being no historical evidence at all.

There are legends that suggest Kashmir's links with Jesus Christ. Apart from the exquisite valley of Yusmarg, said to be named after Jesus (Yus), Srinagar too is rumoured to have had one such link. There is a Government of India's Films Division documentary (2010) called *A Search for the Historical Jesus* by Prof. Fida Hassnain. Many Kashmiris, though, dismiss this myth as a tourism ploy.

Near the Tyndale Biscoe Boys and Malinson Girls schools is Lal Chowk, the old Christian cemetery, where apart from soldiers, bureaucrats, doctors and surveyors, some unusual people are buried. One of them is Lt Robert Thorpe of the British Army. His father was also an officer in the British Army and his mother a Kashmiri. He was brought up on stories of Kashmir's beauty and the tyrannical rule of the Dogras. In 1865, he visited his mother's homeland. In those days, British Army officers could not stay for more than two months in Kashmir without prior permission. The young Lt Thorpe stayed there for three years, studying the exploitation of Kashmiri peasants and writing a book[39] and also for British newspapers, highlighting the vicious misrule of the Maharaja. Among other things, he highlighted the 'capitation tax on every individual practicing any labour, trade, profession or employment, [which] was collected daily'.[40] On 22 November 1868, he was poisoned in Srinagar and buried in this cemetery. He is considered to be the first prominent aggressive and articulate supporter of justice for the Kashmiris. Every year, on 22 November, Kashmiris gather at his grave to remember him.[41]

There was a time when dongahs and even houseboats could float against the current to the jetty near the Jamma Masjid at Ganderbal from the Dal lake. There was so much water. They would go up the Sind from Shadipora till Ganderbal, and inspite of mosquitos in summer, the four-hour journey was delightful. It was a leafy float past the forest, houses and fields of Shalabug and then the Haran forest and village. Further upstream, the Sind has no depth and is tempestuous.

Shadipora village is at the confluence of the Sind and Jhelum. It was a quiet, hydrographically important corner. In his book *Kashmir*, Sir Francis Younghusband—a Resident of Kashmir in 1908—had written, 'At Shadipur, at the junction of the Sind River with the Jhelum River, there is a charming grassy camping ground under chinar trees …' W. Wakefield, an English visitor in 1877, wrote that there were ruins and the foundation of an old temple amid the chinar-clad meadow.[42] Shadipora these days is a large and hectic place with many buildings and offices and bridges over the Sind and Jhelum *(Maps 19 and 30)*.

Water bodies of Srinagar:

Many lakes, streams and rivers have made Kashmir unusually fertile *(Map 19)*. Many streams join the Dal lake or the Jhelum river near Srinagar, forming water bodies in and near the crowded city. All these are in a sorry state.

In less than fifty years, every water body in Srinagar has been polluted, silted or killed for lack of dredging. Even the Jhelum needs frequent dredging.

The Dal is the largest water body in Srinagar. In 1907, the Dal was 22 sq. km. And now it is less than 11 sq. km.[43] The Dal had two contiguous lakes, Gagribal and Nagin. Gagribal has been dry for decades.

According to Tarikh-e-Hassan, the Dal was once an arid wasteland called Vitalin Marg. During King Durlab Vardhan's reign (AD 625–661) it became a lake. Sultan Sikandar (AD 1389–1413) built an embankment from the west of Rainawari to Isherwari on the east bank of the Dal. This embankment divided the lake into two parts, Bod (Bigger) Dal and Lokut (Smaller) Dal. It is now a well laid out broad path carrying a pipeline

(Map 30) from the water works near Isherwari to Mir Behri on the western side of the Dal. On the western part of Bod Dal are vegetable and flower gardens—floating as well as stable ones made on silt. The floating gardens, known as 'Rad' in Kashmiri, also have lotuses blooming in July and August. From dawn, they teem with boats selling vegetables and flowers.

A path from this Isherwari embankment was made in the sixteenth century. It once was an enchanting path with willows and poplars lining it. Erosion and lack of maintenance reduced it to a few metres of tree-covered path on either side of the bridge in the early sixties. Now only a sorry ruin of a much painted and photographed arched bridge in front of Nishat Bagh remains.

In every season the Dal is different. In spring, the green of the chinars, poplars and willows around its periphery are reflected in its murky waters. In summer, boats laden with flowers dart between houseboats dodging tourist-laden shikaras to offload their fragrance at jetties. By late autumn the chinars turn warm red and then glowing crimson. The bare poplars look like measuring poles. After winter's snow each dark twig of these trees is crested with white.

Once the Dal was called the jewel of Kashmir, now it's the garbage dump of Srinagar. Seen from distant Astaanmarg, the reduced Dal looks serene and magnificent. Seen from atop Shankarcharya, algae and muck can be seen. Boat on it and weeds will be seen growing less than a metre below the often-placid surface in the downright unhealthy lake. One can't even drown in this lake now.

The Dal had exit channels that were crucial for reducing the Dal's overflow during floods and for its survival. One such channel was Nallah Mar. It was built by Zain-ul-Abidin (reign 1418 to 1470) to drain the Dal and take the waters to Anchar lake *(Map 30)* through Baba Dem and Khushal sar lakes. This pretty and useful channel remained intact for centuries. It was also used as a waterway to shop and visit other parts of Srinagar and was ecstatically described by many travellers. Then, by 1978, it was filled and a road made from Baba Dem till Khushal sar. This road has been called Nallah Mar (Channel Killed), reflecting cynical wit.

The result is that Khushal sar and Anchar are swamps in some parts and dry in others. The trapped sewage flows back and forth between the Dal and Baba Dem.

Earlier kings had looked after the Dal as best as they could in those days. They had had bunds and spill channels made for the Dal as well as for the Jhelum. Some of these, like Nallah Mar, have been built up, and some like the Chunt Kol that used to be clean enough for a swim and flowed through Chinar Bagh, Babarshah, Nai Sarak and Gaw Kadal now stink. From the reign of those kings till Maharaja Hari Singh's time the water bodies and forests of Srinagar were preserved.

From the 1970s the rot started. In the twenty-first century, despite unlimited resources and scientific expertise, the Dal is ruined because of indifference. It will be dead in a few decades, unless encroachment and construction are undone. The warning is there in the form of the worst species of red algae blooming in the lake. They kill fish and can also make the surrounding air nauseous.

'Just 80 years more and Dal will be no more' was the headline on 20 June 2004 in the *Greater Kashmir* newspaper. This and several other articles described how hundreds of tonnes of waste and sewage clog the Dal every year; how the increase of houseboats, especially those without septic tanks—from 400 in 1975 to the present 1400—has meant more garbage dumped into the Dal; how floating vegetable and flower gardens, though traditional and attractive, are shrinking the lake; how Jogilankar, a fresh water stream flowing out of the Dal, is now yellow, festering and smelly; how at the height of the tourist season at least 120,000 plastic bottles and 200,000 plastic bags are tossed into the Jhelum and the Dal each year. The list goes on becoming more nauseating.

The attractive row of fountains on the Dal, near the Sher-e-Kashmir International Centre, which enthrall people on the Boulevard were installed to increase oxygen levels, which were depleting because of the dumping of waste. These fountains kill the algae. That they extract admiration is incidental.

In the early nineties, portions of the Dal turned red. Not because of insurgency-related dark deeds but because of Euglena, an organism that sometimes forms a green or red scum on the lake's surface. Prof. Mohammad Rashiduddin Kundnagar from Srinagar, Kashmir's most experienced limnologist, has been studying Kashmir's marshes and lakes for thirty years and had warned about their imminent decline. There were futile gestures like fitful dredging made by the government, but decay continues.

The Dal is just one of the two dozen or so imperiled water bodies in and around Srinagar,[44] which have been ruined by a bumbling and indifferent bureaucracy.

Consider the large Hokersar Wetland about 10 km west of Srinagar *(Map 30)*. This former lake, fed by the Dudhganga and Sukhnag and the flood waters spilling from Jhelum, is now largely dry land. Unchecked encroachment and siltation has reduced its size from 13 sq. km to less than 1 sq. km.

No one seems keen to stop this rot.

In the north of the vast Idgah grounds, in one corner of which is the Martyr's Cemetery, stands the second largest mosque in Kashmir, Aali Masjid. It is built of stone and has the unusual sloping red wooden roof common to most mosques and ziarats in Kashmir. From across the road, to the north-east of this mosque, stretched the Khushal sar, which was about a kilometre and a half long and half a kilometre wide. That was thirty years ago. Now, across the road from this mosque are houses built on reclaimed land. Beyond them are fields and only a small part of it has some stagnant water. Khushal sar is connected to Gil sar by a narrow channel, which has an ancient bridge called Gil Kadal. If one stands on it and looks in both directions one will see plastic and other waste in the dirty waters which are so fouled and filled with silt that they are closing around the bridge, which will eventually not be necessary to cross over.

Gil sar was connected to Anchar lake, which has no water now. It covered about 700 hectares, of which more than 600 are now fields and weeds. The rest is silted and marshy. Its eastern shore near the Sher-e-Kashmir Institute of Medical Sciences has even radioactive waste dumped into it. From Nageen lake's south-west corner an old channel called Nallah Amir Khan flows to meet an almost dead Gil. Nageen is in turn connected to the Dal by a narrow canal that passes under Ashal Kadal. Till the late seventies, there was a large and wide twisting canal that connected the two lakes. At some places south of Hazratbal, it was so wide that it enclosed the large vegetable and flower gardens of Asha Bagh. These days, the broad swathes of water have been replaced with festering marshes, and soon another inimitable tradition of Kashmir will vanish.

The Nageen has considerably reduced in size, but its blue water has not been sullied much yet. Its southern portion is clogging both sides of the new four-lane Ashal Kadal. Its northern shore has disappeared to sedimentation and then landfills. On a part of it, a large multi-storey public school has been constructed. The process is ingenious and evil. First silting is allowed, then rubbish piles up followed by the land filling up with mud collected from karewas. This land is then sold by the government.

The waters of all the lakes in Srinagar were linked through canals and spill channels with each other and then with the Jhelum. Today, the main link for Bod Dal to the Jhelum is through Dal Gate which is across a channel from Nowhatta Golf Course. It splits into two canals to meet the Jhelum. In the eighteenth century, the people of Srinagar, till then living along the Jhelum, started to occupy land near these lakes. That's when embankments and spill canals were made—of earth, not stone or concrete, which deoxygenates water.

If those visitors who had seen these lakes and canals in their untarnished glory of the sixties feel pained by the disintegration of the waters of Srinagar, imagine how much more must be the agony of those who live here. They are witnessing their beloved waterways in their final death throes because of criminal indifference.

Islands in Dal lake

There are two man-made islands in the Dal that cannot be ignored. Char Chinar (Rupa or Silver) Lank and Sona (Gold) Lank. They existed before the Mughals, who refashioned Char Chinar into a well-crafted miniature garden. Char Chinar is in the Bod Dal or larger part of the lake. Sultan Hassan Shah (reigned AD 1475–1478) was the ruler who had this island made.

In 1630, Shah Jahan improved it. He had a square embankment and a jetty made and planted chinars at each corner of this square island and a classical rose garden in between. The jetty at the north of the island looks colourful because of the red, yellow, blue, violet, purple and cream of shikaras berthed there. The old chinars are decaying now. Char Chinar was called Rupa Lank or silver island. Baron Huegel and G.T. Vigne who were there in 1833 describe that in the middle of the rose garden was a marble-pillared tower that had a silver roof.[45] Hence the name.

Many years ago, the silence here was broken by the rhythmical slap slap of waves and twitter of birds. Now it is shattered by police motor boats and others dragging water skiers. Houseboats are moored here, vendors prowl the island and there is a seasonal restaurant too.

Sona Lank is on the northern side of the Dal called Lokut or smaller lake. Kashmir's legendary King Sultan Zain-ul-Abidin (reigned 1420–1470) had the square island of Sona Lank made for the shelter of boatmen and fishermen in 1421. It can be seen from Hazratbal in the west and Shalamar Bagh in the east. It has two old chinars and three new ones and a beguiling myth surrounding it. There's a belief among the old Kashmiris that this island is moving towards Hazratbal at the speed of a single mustard seed a year. Once it touches Hazratbal, the world will end! A CRPF camp has taken over the island.

Chinars:

The Valley has another magnificent feature that complements the beauty of its girdling mountains, its waterways and lakes. It is the towering tree called chinar. The local Kashmiri name is booni. A legend credits Jahangir for coining the word chinar. He saw these grand trees in autumn when they were crimson and declared that they resemble a chinar—blaze, fire!

In Srinagar, they are on many roads where chinars cover them with shade in summer and colour in autumn. They are around the Dal, in its islands, hanging over the Jhelum and its canals, in the Mughal gardens, in the university and in most places where people dwell. Tall and stately, they compel awe. On the grounds of an old serai in Rambagh, Barzulla in Srinagar are many of these grand and imposing trees.

These deciduous trees have an average height of about 30 m and a girth of 15 m. Some are taller and larger. Chinar, which is the same tree as the plane of Europe, sycamore of US and maple of Canada, but larger than all the others, is so much a part of Kashmiri tradition and culture that its palm-shaped leaves are a motif in all handicrafts.

Its sacred status has not protected it from decimation. In 1972, there were 42,000 chinars, but by 2004 only 17,394 were left.[46] The state government, alarmed at last, has numbered and registered all the existing trees, and more are being planted—about 14,000 till 2019. The largest of all chinars has a circumference of 19.70 m. It was planted by the Sufi saint Syed Qasim Shah in 1374 in Chattergam near Srinagar and is now in his ziarat.

21
Mughal Gardens of Kashmir

KASHMIR'S NATURAL CHARMS ARE VAST, HEADY, SERENE AND CHAOTICALLY beautiful as only nature can arrange. Next are the attractions of its Mughal gardens, which are strictly classical and geometrical in design.

The Mughals added flowing waters to the gardens they built in India and especially in Kashmir. Their canals bisected gardens and were tastefully and thoughtfully designed to wreathe, embellish and frame Kashmir's graceful beauty in symmetry. On either side of the running water were flower beds and pergolas covered with rose bushes. The remaining gardens are now as much a part of Kashmir as its lakes, springs, mountains and valleys. To improve nature is impossible, but the Mughals provided pavilions and arches in their classical gardens to admire it from.

In the middle of a large square or a rectangular garden, chinar-shaded straight water channels cross at right angles to divide the garden into four quarters—forming Char Bagh, which was a classical Persian concept. Each square was different from the other in the plants that were cultivated in it. The Mughal Gardens in Kashmir were arranged on sloping hillside terraces. On the highest terraces, arched and pillared pavilions looked out over the shining green fertile countryside, bordered by forests and surrounded by distant blue hills, some topped with snow.

The highest terrace in each garden had a secluded zenana (women's suite), suitably protected from prying eyes. Each had dramatic views from raised gazebos in the corners. Through their soaring, ornate arches mountains, lake, trees, gardens and fields were dramatically framed.

A characteristic of every Mughal garden is the majesty of numerous tall chinar trees. They give shade, colour, depth and background to the gardens. They are green in summer, rust-coloured in late October and golden by early November. In winter, their dark, bare bulky trunks are snow speckled and their branches snow covered, forming a stately and magical foreground.

If anything could enhance Kashmir's beauty, it was the gardens that the inspired Mughals tastefully made. Only five Mughal gardens are left in Srinagar: Nishat, Shalamar, Chashma Shahi, Pari Mahal and Naseem Bagh. In the Dal is the island of Char Chinar, improved by Jahangir.

Spectacular natural waterfalls of Kashmir inspired the cascades in the Mughal gardens, 'while existing springs, at Nishat, Chashmashahi, Achhabal and Verinag, became the focal points round which captivating new gardens were developed'.[47]

In Jahangir's time (1569–1627) the eastern bank of the Dal had a cluster of classical style geometric patterned gardens. Now, there are only three—Shalamar, Nishat and Chashma Shahi.

Pari Mahal and Chashma Shahi are higher on the northern spurs of the Zabarwan. The former was built by Dara Shikoh (1615–1659), the astronomer/mathematician son of Shah Jahan, mainly to study the stars and teach mathematics, and he also had gardens on each of its five terraces.

Chashma Shahi *(Maps 31 and 32)* (Spring of Kings) is the only Mughal garden on a hill. Unlike all others, it is high above the Dal and not next to it. The longer road starts from the Shikara Ghat and goes between the Grand Palace Hotel and the red-roofed Hari Niwas. Next on this road comes an immense eighteen-hole golf course that has taken over public land for the private pleasure of the influential class. It stretches down till the Boulevard Road along the Dal. To make this golf course, several old gardens had been taken over, trees cut, green grass laid and artificial ponds made so that a few could hit funny white balls around.

An inscription at the gate to Chashma Shahi reads that it was made by Shah Jahan. It is shaped around the contour of a spur from a forested north face of Zabarwan. The spring is supposed to have healing qualities for some ailments and is sweet to taste. A local legend insists that Indira Gandhi used to get her drinking water from here.

It's a small garden by Mughal standards. On its east is a hill and to the west is a large expanse of the mountain-ringed Dal below it. There are few trees but topiary has carved out juniper trees in eye-catching patterns that make attractive posts to see the Dal.

Chashma Shahi is the largest spring in, around and above Srinagar. It is a hearty, bustling spring, bubbling up under a Kashmiri-roofed Mughal-designed high and spacious pavilion built in 1632 by Ali Mardan Khan under orders of Shah Jahan. Ali Mardan Khan was a governor of Kashmir and is credited with building the serais along the Peer gali route to Kashmir from Delhi. The blue mountains to the north are framed by the tall rectangular frames of the pavilion where the spring is.

Out of the pavillion the spring waters go through pretty and minor cascades to a channel, which flows into a rectangular pool with a fountain in its centre. In this is reflected the main vine-covered double-storeyed pavilion, which also had a zenana. The channel goes through it, and the waters ripple down a stone chadar (water chute) with minute ridges designed especially to give this effect. Another rectangular tank interrupts the flow in such a way that the water in it seems still. Then come some fountains spraying thin streaks of water. At the end, there's the small, canopied stone entrance gate facing a mountainside and not the Dal.

Any time and every season is the best time to visit Chashma Shahi and other Mughal gardens. But late afternoon in mellow autumn and snow-filled winter is more gratifying. The colours hit your heart and mind—the shining green of the grass, the gleaming blue of water and sky, the deep yellow of the dahlias, the blood reds of the rose, coxcomb and the salvia. Even when the white of winter's snow buries all colour, the view is electrifying. This minor (by Mughal standards) garden of the senses has square and rectangular patches of cobblestones, green and flower beds all along the water course.

There are several springs near and at some distance from Chashma Shahi on both the northern and the arid southern face of Zabarwan. The closest springs are four kilometres or so to the north, across a ridge of the higher Zabarwan peak (2839 m). One is above the village of Takinizam, and the other is a place of pilgrimage called Baba Gulamudin Sahib. These springs are not far from the Dal and are reached from Brein, a colony east of the Dal.

Chashma Shahi is close to a VIP Guest House and the Governor's House and thus has security breathing down on it. Yet it is worth suffering the offensiveness of suspicious uniforms to carry on ahead to the nearby Pari Mahal.

Pari Mahal (Fairy Palace) is not really a garden. It was an observatory and a college built in 1640 and set in a five-terraced garden. The builder was the unfortunate Dara Shikoh, the multi-talented and unworldly but unfortunate eldest son of Shah Jahan. He was assassinated by his younger brother, the cruel ambitious Aurangzeb. Dara made two gardens in Kashmir, Pari Mahal and the one in Bijbehara where nothing else but great chinars and some ruins remain. Pari Mahal is on a lower slope of the Zabarwan ridge.

The canopied entrance is small. Looking from this main pavilion, one understands why the entrances of the Mughal gardens here were not made large in usual Mughal flourish. Had this gate been any larger, it would have blocked a part of the view of the Dal from the terraces.

Once inside, there are manicured lawns with flower beds bordering them. The buildings are arranged on four other terraces. Each structure's outer walls have a number of arched, metre-deep alcoves. These could have been for students to study or as perches to admire the terraced gardens and the Dal far below. Fifty years ago, there were traces of fountains and tanks, but these have disappeared in the renovation of later decades. The hills behind Pari Mahal that were once bare now have pines and firs.

Dara Shikoh stayed in it sometimes. It was used for teaching astronomy and mathematics mainly. In the seventeenth century, it was the highest building in Srinagar, but now there are army camps on the ridge above. The view from the balcony is dramatic when framed in its arch. Beyond the green of the lawns within the fort walls, the Dal is spread out lavishly. To the north and west is the blue wall of sometimes snow-buried mountains stretching from Mohand marg (2710 m), including Safopora (3138 m), at the foot of which is the unseen Manasbal lake. The colour and grandeur of nature is spectacular in all seasons.

The arches-lined retaining walls and the gate have been renovated just as the garden and a water tank. Adjacent to the entrance are living quarters for uniforms. From the patio in front of the gate, the view of the Dal, Hari Parbat, Hazrat Bal mosque and Naseem Bagh and the Chinar Bagh of the university is uplifting.

The fountains that once ornamented the five-terraced buildings and gardens are no more. Inside the central and highest building are large roomy corridors, galleries, halls and alcoves that were once classrooms.

The highest terrace has a building decorated with deeply recessed arches at its massive and solid base. Perhaps they were used for guards, but from the ground it is not easy to get to them unless there were steps. There are a couple of arched halls that open to magnificent views of the Dal. Each terrace's walls are wide enough to saunter on and drink in the spectacular views on all sides.

Pari Mahal, whenever it is flood lit, can be seen from many parts of Srinagar.

Nishat Bagh (Garden of Happiness) is the first and the largest of the gardens that is on Dal lake, heading north from Dal Gate *(Map 33)*. The Nishat and the Shalamar gardens are at the foot of the sprawling Zabarwan ridge and are separated from the Dal by a road.

The most scenic way of reaching Nishat Bagh is slowly by shikara, even though the waters are no longer clear and have weeds and moss floating on top. All of Nishat Bagh can be seen from here. The old jetty has chinars, shops, restaurants, a bus stop and a taxi stand.

In the days of the Mughals, this approach by water at dusk was a unique fairytale experience. The last waterfall below the first terrace was called chini khana. This referred to exquisitely carved pigeonholes, in which were kept lanterns to shimmer behind the waterfall. These sconces were a favourite pattern of Nur Jahan and it is also seen in Shalamar and Achabal gardens. This unrivalled ornamentation would have hypnotized even the coarsest human approaching the Nishat.

When seen from the Dal, its enormous terraced conception thrills one as every single square metre blends with the rest of the 173,900 sq. m of the luscious garden spread over eleven ascending terraces. There were twelve previously but the lowest one has been dismembered by the Dal road, and the waters flow under it into the Dal. In late summer, all the beds are aflame with red, blue, yellow, white and purple flowers. In late autumn and the stately chinars light up the garden with their yellowing leaves. After all the leaves have fallen, in late autumn's late afternoon ethereal sunshine, more of this long garden is seen. And when wreathed in snow, the view is divine and even a shout is muffled.

The entrance is a 4 m high red stone wall pierced by two modest, covered staircases and two lion mouths, from which gush steady streams.

The two-storeyed attractive wooden trellised pavilion, called baradiri, was built around a pond with fountains. In an act of unforgiveable madness, this pavilion was removed in the sixties. There is no doubt that it existed. Its broad foundation is still there. Tantalizing photographs and paintings of the glorious views inside and outside this pavilion can be seen in several books.[48]

Nishat is the only surviving Mughal garden that was made by a non-royal. A brother of Nur Jahan—Asaf Khan—had built it. It is the only one of the existing gardens that does not have demi palaces, though it did have a pavilion at the lowest terrace and a zenana at the highest terrace. Nur Jahan had influenced the construction of this garden. Her precise and exquisite touch can be seen everywhere from the time-polished stone benches bridging gurgling water channels, to the diamond-patterned chadars (water chutes).

The view from the lake down the canal is of a tiered-garden, but without the grand structures that decorate Shalamar and Chashma Shahi. Unlike the Shalamar, only a few chinars line the pavement along the canal.

The highest terrace, where the zenana was, has the most scintillating view—especially at sunset—from the three-storeyed gazebos on either side. In the middle of the large ground are eleven rectangular, paved terraces divided by a fountain-strewn canal sweeping down to the Dal. On either side of the pavements are numerous flower beds. Waterfalls connect each terrace and rows of sparkling fountains trap sunlight. Over some waterfalls are stone slabs to sit on and admire at leisure the dainty beauty of mountains and water. A couple of waterfalls are guided to ripple and whisper over diamond-patterned inclined chadars. The effect of this bewitching scene is increased by the single-arched decaying bridge, seemingly floating in the Dal.

The whole length of the central canal running down the terraces till it meets the Dal is pleasing. The gardens, the central paths, the canals, waterfalls and water chutes, two square ponds and all the fountains complement each other. There are a few chinars towering above two pools. On either side of the classical terraced garden are large stretches of lawns, more flower beds and thickets of chinars. In Mughal times, fruit trees were grown here.

In any season, from white winter, wet spring and lush summer to the colours of autumn, this garden is a joy to be in. In early winter, yellow chinar leaves cover the garden. Under the uniform white of snow, it is incredibly touching and eerily quiet. Nishat, as does the Shalamar, gets its waters from a canal called Sharab kol, which branches out from Harwan reservoir *(Map 30)*.

The zenana and its garden at the end have a 6 m high retaining wall decorated with plain arches and is as wide as the whole of Nishat Bagh, which extends far beyond on either side of the canal, pavements and flower beds. At each end in front is a three-storey spacious gazebo with satisfying views from the top two floors.

From Nishat two roads fork out. The right one leads to Shalamar Bagh and carries on to Burzahom and other villages circuiting the north end of the Dal to reach Srinagar's most revered mosque, the Hazratbal. The left road, a kind of a ring road, goes along the Dal's north-east bank filled with acres of dismal siltage and flotsam. The first bridge it crosses is over an ancient kilometre-long canal that even today leads to Shalamar's gates.

Shalamar is, according to visitors from Bernier (1665) to video-making ones of today, the grandest of all gardens *(Map 34)*. Francois Bernier was a French physician and traveller who worked as a doctor first with Dara Shikoh and after his assassination with Aurangzeb. He documented his impressions in his book *Travels in the Mughal Empire, 1656 to 1668*. He wrote, 'The most admirable of all these Gardens is that of the King, which is called Chahlimar.'

It was completed by 1619 mainly by Nur Jahan. Nur Jahan wielded most of the power while Jahangir was satisfied '…if I have a *ser* of wine and half a *ser* of meat' every day. One ser is almost a kilogram.

In early sixth century, King Pravarasena II had a small castle called Shalamar (Abode of Love) here. By the time the Mughals came to the Valley, only scattered ruins remained.

It covers a water-lined, chinar-shielded green expanse of 124,215 sq. m. In this garden, the varied use of water—running, still, falling and spraying—was raised to the level of exceptional, outstanding, superior and incomparable art. A well-known couplet by the thirteenth-century Indian poet Amir Khusro, who wrote it for some other place, is inscribed in many places, including Delhi's Red Fort, but nowhere does it fit the subject as it does in the Shalamar:

Agar Firdaus bar rōy-e zamin ast,
hamin ast-o hamin ast-o hamin ast.

It means 'If there's paradise on earth, it is this, it is this, it is this.'

The mammoth scale of conception is incomparable. There are over 500 fountains adorning symmetrical tanks, pools and channels. Some shoot up single jets of water, some plumes and some sprays. Water, till the Shalamar was built, was never manipulated in such sublime ways. Jahangir and Nur Jahan used the common Persian idea of a Char Bagh layout and converted it in Shalamar to paradise on earth.

Could anyone have imagined an Emperor's throne a metre above a channel before it becomes a murmuring waterfall? This has been done in the Diwan-e-Aam (the Hall of Public Audience) with such subtle grace that it is accepted without wonder at first sight.

The design of Shalamar is simple and daring. The rectangular layout is on three slightly raised levels pierced right down the middle from shoulder to toe by the broad chinar shrouded Shahi nahar (King's canal). These chinars spread out so far at the top that they touch each other, forming a canopy over the channels and the pavements on either side of them.

At the third and highest level, a few metres after the canal has been fed by a stream from the Harwan reservoir, is the most marvellous pavilion of all gardens. It's a large black marble pavilion under a pyramid-shaped roof added by Shah Jahan in 1630. The original roof—sloping too—was traditional burze pash, flower roof. Such roofs had packed earth on which grew flowers. The present-day tin roof was made[49] in the early twentieth century.

This is the zenana portion. This magnificent, now open, structure is called baradari, for it had twelve doorways—three on each side—to circulate the cool summer breeze. The doors had intricate and delicate lattice woodwork called pinjrakari. The front portico has four elaborately carved fluted black marble pillars of polygonal shape. They break the view of the entire garden in four decorated frames. The walls of the inside roof had gilded quotations. Amongst them was the famous one by Amir Khusro.

This majestic structure is in the midst of a large one-and-a-half-metre-deep tank which has about a hundred fountains. Causeways over this tank had arcades under them so that water could circulate easily, and the privileged could walk over the water and between the fountains. At the back of the pavilion are two waterfalls leading to the encircling tank. Here is a delicate ornamentation inspired by Nur Jahan's Achhabal garden. Behind each waterfall are two rows of chini khanas. In these, lamps were lit behind the cascades in the evening.

This part of the garden was named Faiz-Baksh (Bestower of Bounties) by Shah Jahan.

The second level had the Diwan-e-Khas, or the Hall for Special Audience, built by Jahangir, above the second cascade. All that remains now is the black marble base for the throne and the lofty chinars that surround it. The plinth is decorated with round lozenges, and the entire square is surrounded by fountains. From here onwards the channel is only ankle deep. On its way to the Dal, it flows between two gazebos with pyramidal roofs that are miniature versions of the Black Pavillion.

All along the channels course are waterfalls, which are so designed that they only murmur as they fall. Jahangir was so mesmerized by waterfalls that he would spend hours watching some of them on his way to and from the Valley. On the old Mughal Road from Rajouri, between Bahramgalla and Peer gali, is a waterfall near Chandimarh. Jahangir liked it immensely and so Nur Jahan had a terrace built to admire the fall and a secluded pool for her to bathe in. It is still called Nur-e-Chamb.

It is difficult to comprehend how the Mughals, capable of so much cruelty, could have designed such beautiful gardens and written passionate and tender poems about flowers, their gardens and Kashmir.

The first level, after the entrance, has the Diwan-e-Aam. This is where the Emperor sat to hear the grievances of common people. Between the throne and the gates was the garden meant for the public. The second level had the Emperor's garden and the third the zenana garden. Beyond the gates is the road and car park and then the kilometre-long canal, up which the royal barge and accompanying boats would come from the Dal. The waters flow under the road to the canal. At the end of this canal and between the Dal lake is a ring road that cuts the distance to the university, Hazratbal and to Ganderbal.

Francois Bernier, during his visit in 1665, writes about the many fruit trees in the gardens, which are now primarily large lawns with chinars and many flower beds. There were apples, almonds, peaches and walnuts. Baron Huegel described in 1833 how the grapes were trained on pretty pergolas.

The Shalamar is surrounded on three sides by congested tenements, from which rises a constant hum that disturbs slightly the silence of the grand garden protected by a thick leafy sound barrier.

Near the Shalamar, in the south-east, is the well laid out geometric and meticulously kept campus of an agricultural university which has expanded up the mountain behind the Shalamar.

Naseem Bagh (Garden of Morning Breeze) is the last of the Mughal gardens remaining around the Dal but was the one that was made first.

Akbar, in 1586, had made a garden with many chinars. It had a small palace and attendant buildings. These were in ruins by the time Jahangir took over. In his memoirs he mentions that he tried to restore them. He erected a high terrace '32 yards square' and planted a forest of geometrically arranged chinars. He called this garden 'Nur-afza' (Light Increasing). In at least one of these pavilions he had a burze pash roof made, it is said.

Jahangir is perhaps the first historian to notice burze pash, flowering roofs of Kashmir. From the terrace that he had made here, he could see the roof of the nearby Hazratbal mosque was full of colour from flowers. He writes, 'This year in the little gardens of the palace and on the roof of the chief mosque the tulips blossomed luxuriantly.'[50]

Flowers like irises and even of linseeds blossomed on the roofs of homes and on mosques, as they had a thick layer of fertile soil on them. Burz was birch wood that was got from higher than the fir-clad slopes of mountains around the Valley. From summer till early autumn, there would be an explosion of colours. As the poor usually had thatched roofs, only the rich could have birch wood and flowering roofs.[51] These roofs have been replaced with concrete or steep A-shaped tin ones, on which nothing can grow. Till a few years ago such burze pash could be seen on a couple of houses within the chinar splattered compound of Gurudwara Shaheed Bunga Baghat in Burzulla. They have also gone. Only one burze pash roof remains. It is on the roof of a mosque built by Sultan Zain-ul-Abideen (Bud Shah) in 1448 to commemorate his teacher Syed Mohammad Madani, who is buried nearby.

Shah Jahan also planted thousands of chinars at the same time in Naseem Bagh. Clumps of four chinars were arranged in each corner of rectangular plots. The saplings were fed water and milk! In 1833, when Baron Huagel visited this garden, he noted that the 1200 trees planted by Akbar were still thriving and had formed shady walks.[52]

Now about 700 grand chinars remain. They are in a rectangle of about 700 m by 300 m bordered by a wall and a road on the western side of Dal. It is no longer a garden with precise boundaries. For within this shrunken forest of noble ancient chinars and circling it are Kashmir University's buildings, homes and guest houses, making it the university with the prettiest campus in India.

In late autumn, when the chinar leaves turn red and then gold, the forest appears to be aflame, especially at sunrise and sunset. But the finest time is still to come. When the chinars shed their leaves, the ground is reddish gold and for the first time in the year more sunlight streams in to make the leaves glow. These leaves are dried and used as fuel for the kangris that Kashmiri's use to keep themselves warm under their pherans.

Nur Jahan was not only the power behind Jahangir's throne but was also a genius designer with a prodigious output of every kind—gardens, pavilions, tombs, mosques and even jewellery. She left her imprint more on the Valley than anywhere else in their demesne. There are two other gardens outside Srinagar that she designed.

Jharokha is in the middle of the north shore of Manasbal, a 3 sq. km lake. It is about 30 km north-north-west of Srinagar. One of the roads to it goes past the dead Anchar lake, and over the Sind river at Ganderbal. Jharokha means a trellised window. Nur Jahan had several oriel windows with trellises made here. Near it is a village called Zarogabal, which was the earliest known name of the three-acre terraced garden that was designed by Nur Jahan. Only a wall remains of the old palace. Little of the old glory of this exquisite garden is left. The present-day restoration is of routine municipal style embellishments—more convenient and ugly rather than restoring the charm of the past. Gone are the oriel windows that Nur Jahan had designed to see the lake through different frames. An idea of the delicate bay windows can be had from the orieles in Nur Mahal Serai designed by her at Nakodar near Ludhiana.

Since Kashmir's beauty is diverting, this garden is worth a visit. The view of the lake is unchanged *(Map 30)*.

From Jharokha can be seen the Safapora peak (3138 m) to the north. A motor road skirts its base. A happy development is that trees have again started advancing up the arid slope of Safapora. Fields, orchards, trees and houses are creeping up its sides. Jahangir in his memoirs describes the base of Safapora in autumn as having 'trees of all colours, such as the planes, the apricots and others reflected in the middle of the tank (Manasbal).'

In 1905, Manasbal lake had about 3 sq. km of pure water. Today, about 40 hectares have become marshy on its eastern side where Lar kul flows in. With a maximum depth of 12.5 m at a couple of places, it is the deepest lake in the Valley. Its water is still amongst the clearest and the cleanest of all lakes in the Valley. From Manasbal to Kundabal villages along the eastern curve of the lake, silting is increasing. The Jhelum flows close to it. To its south are two small spring-fed lakes worth visiting before they become fields in the near future; they are called Ahan sar and Waskur sar. Till a century ago Manasbal could be reached by boat from the Dal via the Sind river. Now this green watery route is silted up.

Achhabal *(Map 35)*

Achhabal is supposed to be the most powerful and voluminous spring in Kashmir. It is at the north-north-west base of a fir-covered hill called Achhabal Thang. The spring rushes out as a furious noisy waterfall that pours into a tank from which begins the Achhabal garden. The water feeds four pools through a central canal, which flows sometimes under a thick umbrella of chinars.

Akbar, Abul Fazl, Bernier and others down the ages have remarked on the excellent sweet taste of its water. It was an ancient spring called Akshavala, which Hindus had been visiting for centuries. It was founded by King Aksha, who reigned over Kashmir from 486–326 BC according to Kalhan's chronicles.

The garden was made by Nur Jahan in 1620. Sadly, only the stone foundations of the palace and pavilions remain. There is no record to show whether the structures were deliberately destroyed or decayed because of indifference. Over these bases Kashmiri-style fir and oak wood single-storyed and double-storeyed pavilions were made. This was done by the first Dogra ruler of Kashmir—Gulab Singh (1792–1857), to whom the British sold Kashmir under the Treaty of Amritsar (1846). He had fought on the side of the British against the Sikhs.

Fortunately, he left most of the fountains intact. Some of them shoot up just one jet of water while others form gossamer sprays in a circle as they descend. The best time to see their glory is in the evening, when seen against the setting sun's light, they seem to be shining golden threads.

The design is classical Mughal, spread over two terraces. There is a patterned chadar to control the flow of the water at its origin. Yet volume and pace are so muscular that all the ingenuity of Nur Jahan and her artisans could not subdue the roar and the foam. Two small nineteenth-century summer houses flank the waterfall. Behind this waterfall Nur Jahan had chini khanas made in which were kept lit lamps.

As the waters flow through a straight channel, they fill large tanks. On the first terrace is the main two-storey pavilion built on an archway through which the water glides into a channel, where fountains shoot jets of water. Next comes a tank in which are many more fountains spraying water. Beyond this and within a tank is an island hall with sloping wood roof and wide lattice windows that have flower-shaped corbels jutting out. The effect is pleasing but never close to the majesty of its original stone work, like in other Mughal gardens.

The original garden was much bigger. There were orchards that had a variety of fruit trees and large lawns further away from the water course. Here were also a palace and cottages. A large western portion is now a fish farm.

Verinag *(Map 36)*

Despite all the love and attention that Nur Jahan lavished on Achhabal, the spring at Verinag was her's and Jahangir's favourite spot in Kashmir. In 1620 he wrote '…in the whole of Kashmir there is no sight of such beauty and enchanting character.'[53] He would delay his departure for Delhi till snow started filling the passes. Some of the chinars that he had planted are still there—majestic and venerable. It is a small garden by Mughal standards, being only 5.3 hectares in area.

His last wish was to be buried here. Nur Jahan had other plans. He died near Behramgala on the Srinagar–Rajouri Mughal Road. To ensure a peaceful succession she delayed the news till his stuffed body got to Lahore. On the way she had secretly buried his intestines at a place near Rajouri, called Chingus, which already had a serai, and was then given a suitable fort and mosque.

Verinag spring was originally an irregular and shapeless pond, with water oozing out from different spots and spreading about to form a marsh. Emperor Jahangir, who decorated nature with marvellous architectural flourish, built the simple and striking large octagonal tank in 1620. All the springs were trapped first in the exact centre of the octagonal tank, with twenty-four arcaded recesses all around it. These alcoves are domed at the south and at the base of the hill. At the northern end is a three-arched red brick sloping roof building through which the waters exit in a series of cascades to a canal.

This spring is one of the sources of the Jhelum. Water from the spring flows through the central arch into a canal that is 305 m long and 3.5 m wide. All around it is a well-kept rectangular garden (460 m x 110 m) crowded with chinars. This garden was planted by Shah Jahan, Jahangir's son.

The canal meets the Naugam nar as soon as it leaves the garden.

Two tablets here commemorate, in Persian, the building of this tank and name one Haidar as the mason in charge. The simple and elegant structure was designed and built by architects and masons from Iran. The date on which this structure was completed is inscribed on a stone slab built into the southern enclosing wall.

A painting done in 1863 by British Army Captain Knight shows the main arcade through which the Jhelum flows out. It had balconied houses built on it. They are not there now.[54]

Mughals had made Kashmir well-known throughout India, Iran and Central Asia. The British made it known throughout the world. In 1817, a poem called *Lala Rukh* written by Irish poet Thomas Moore made Europe aware of Kashmir.[55] In 1908, an English woman Florence Tyzack Parbury wrote a book on Kashmir called *The Emerald set with Pearls*, packed with numerous watercolour paintings of Kashmir. By then the British were firmly in control of Kashmir through their puppet Dogra kings. In 1909 Francis Younghusband, a former Resident at the Dogra King's court, wrote his tribute to this garden of paradise. A hundred years later, nearly every part of Kashmir has been photographed.

My effort is to help people know where the splendour lies in Kashmir.

Maps

Map 0:

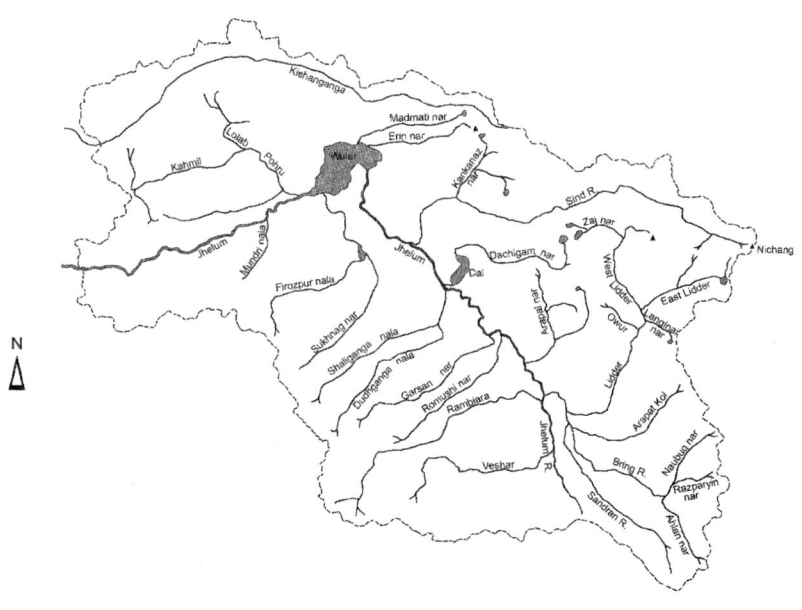

Map 1:

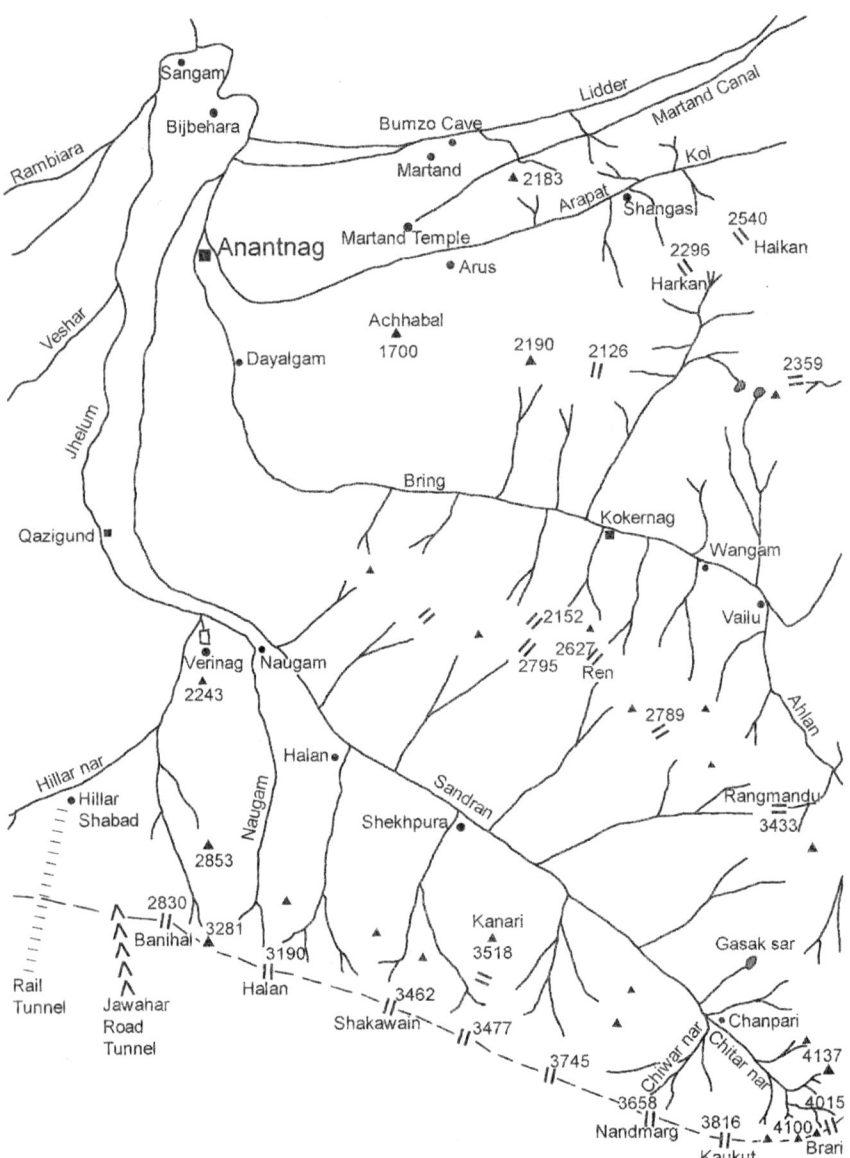

Map 2:

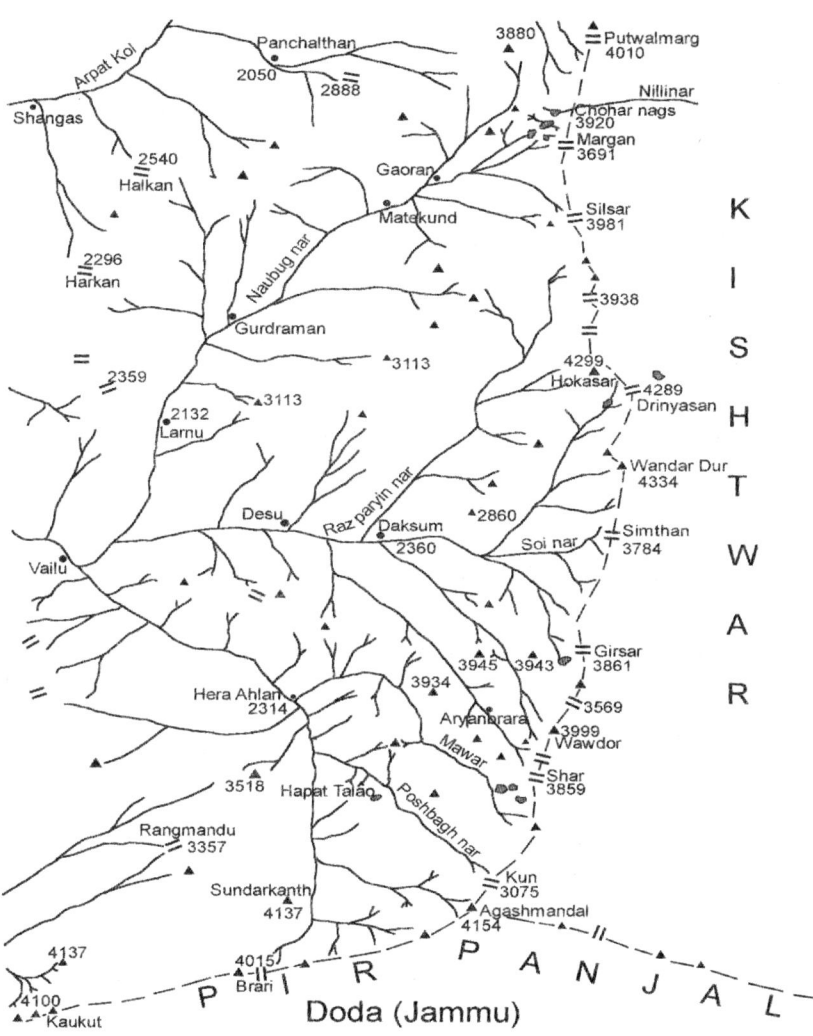

Map 3:

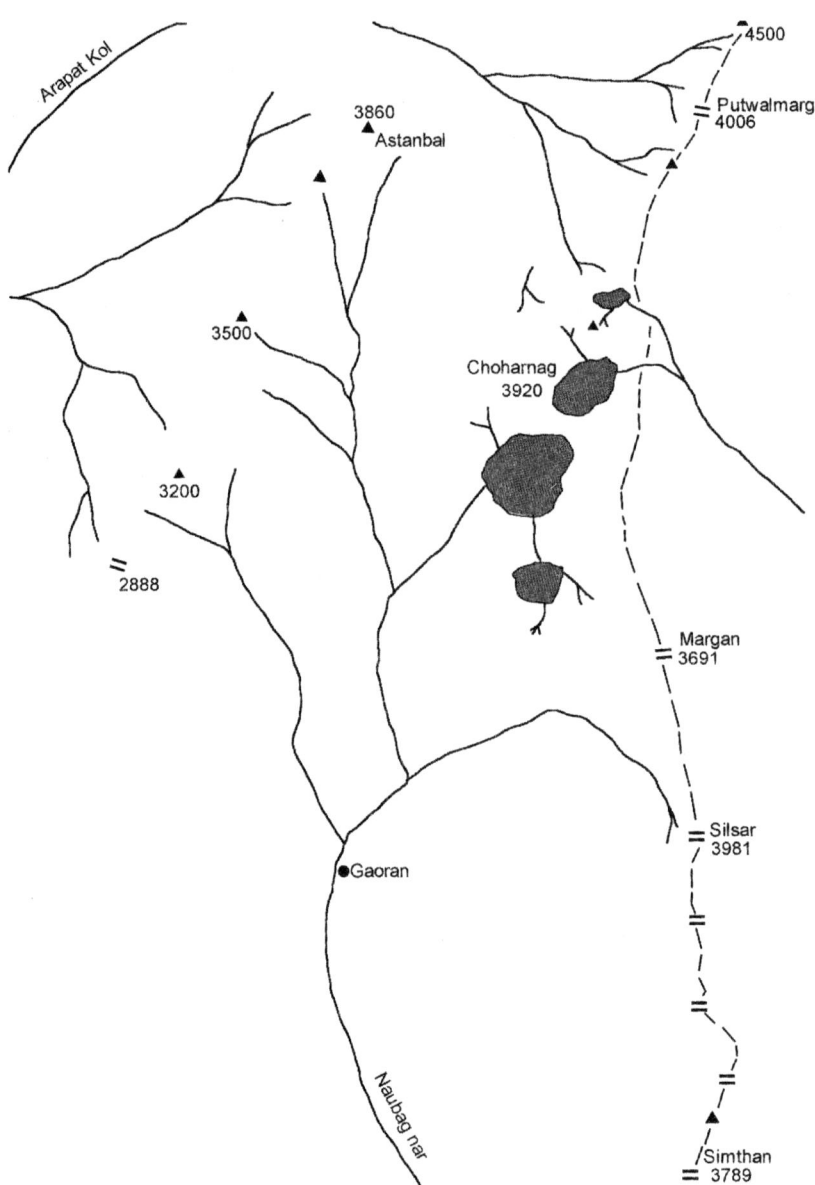

Map 4:

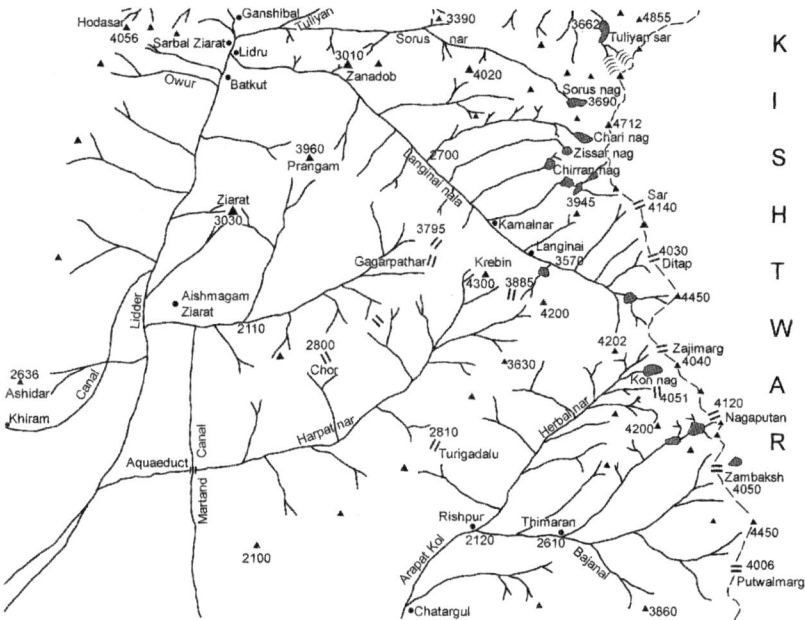

Map 5:

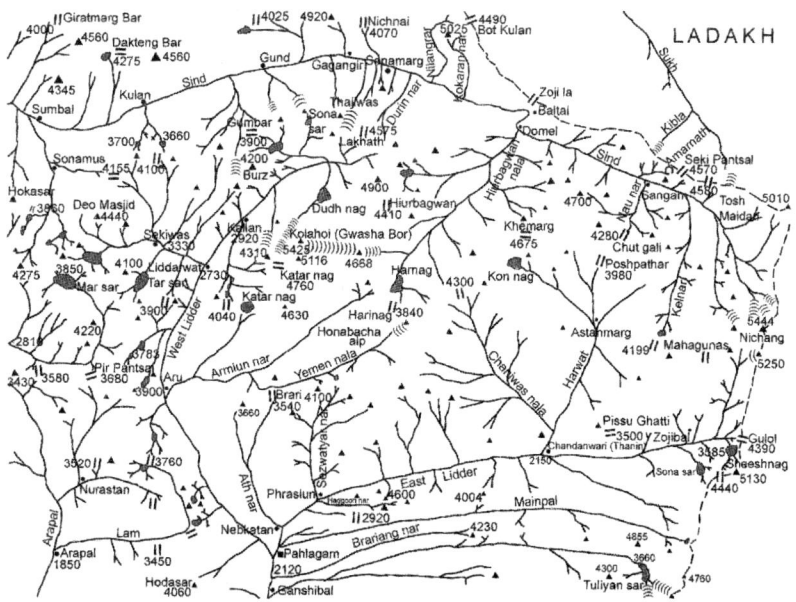

Map 6:

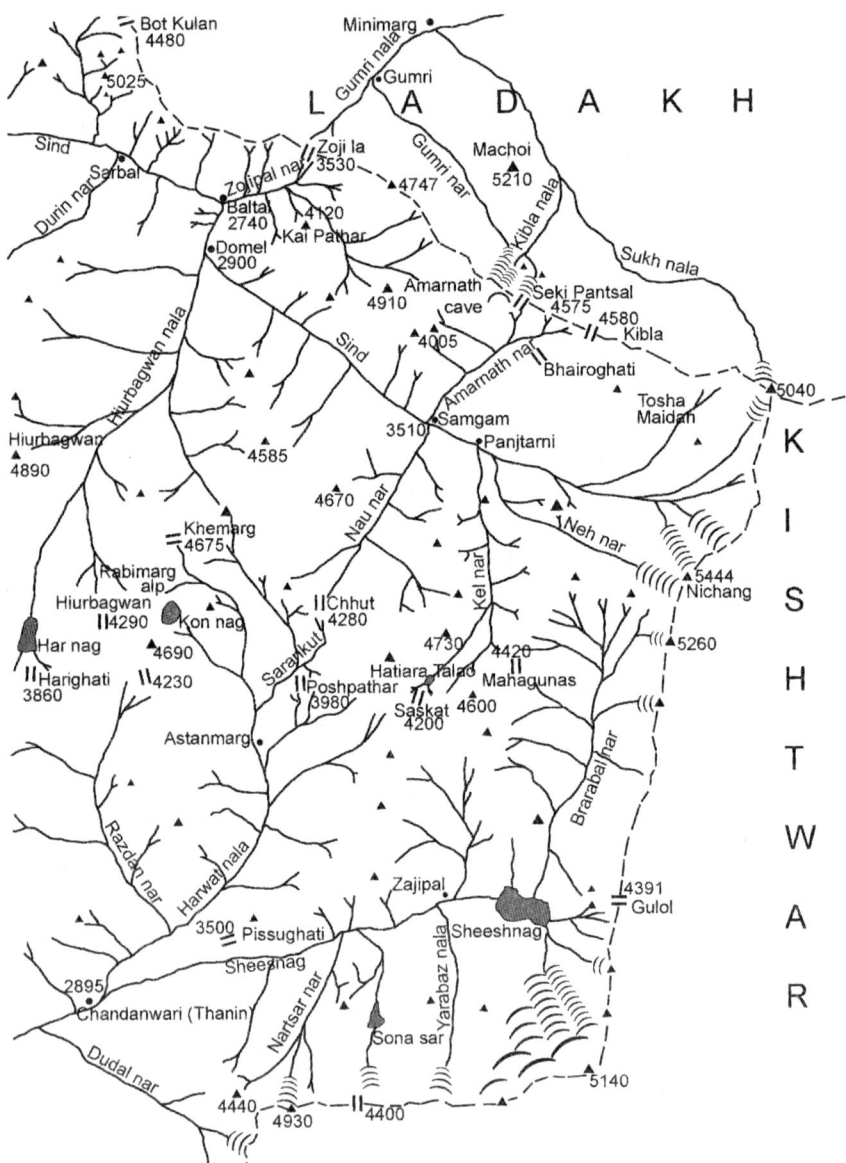

Map 7:

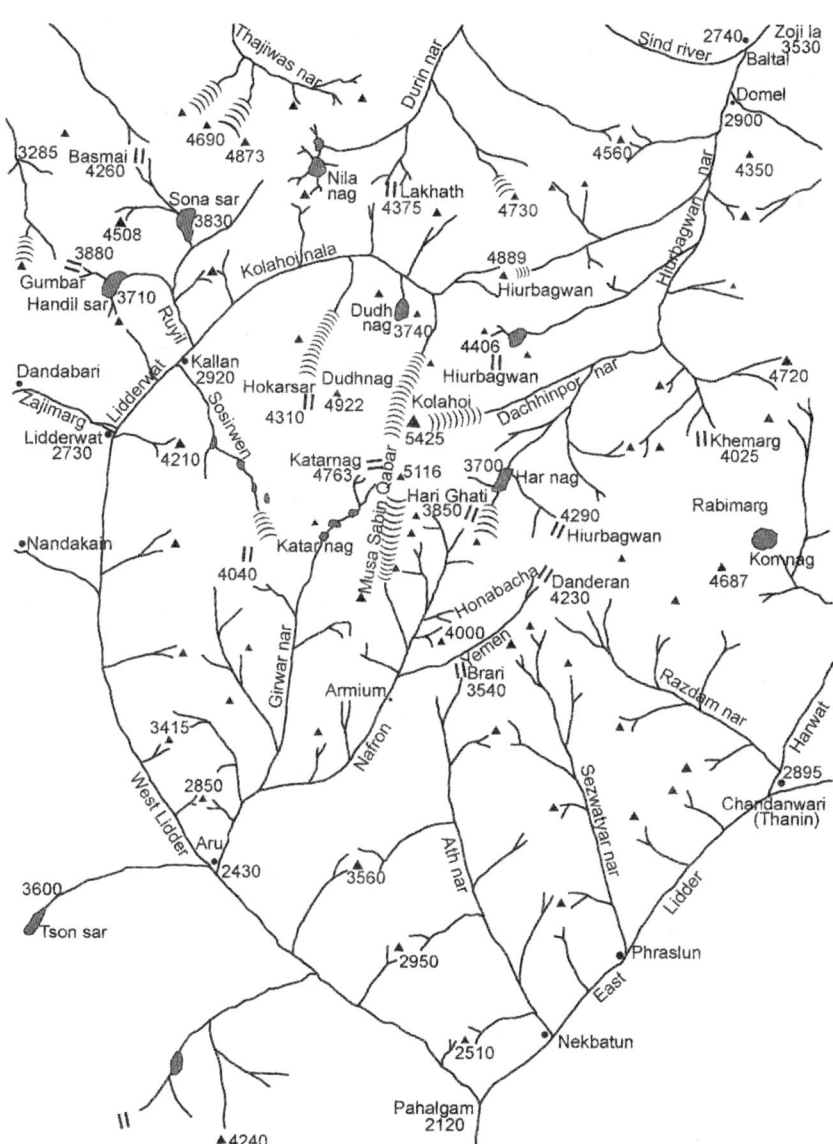

Map 8:

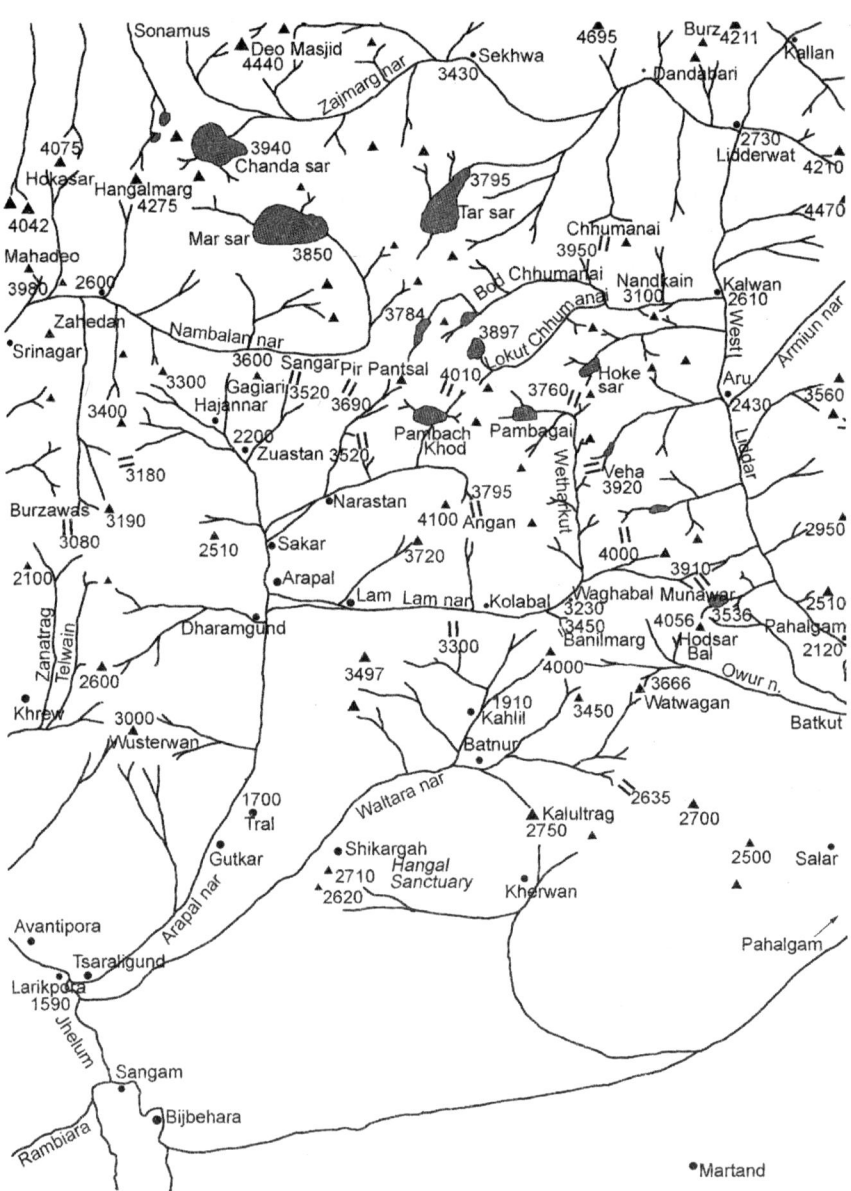

Map 9:

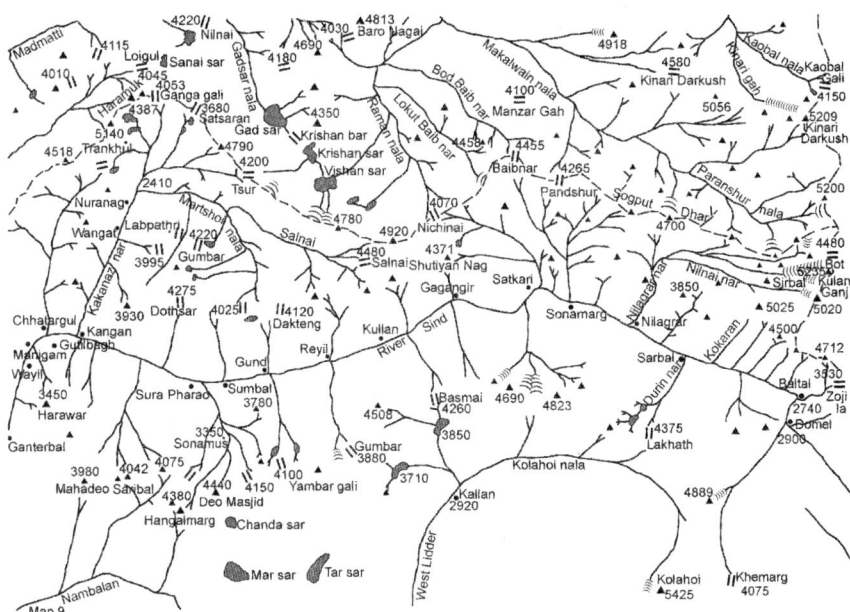

Map 10:

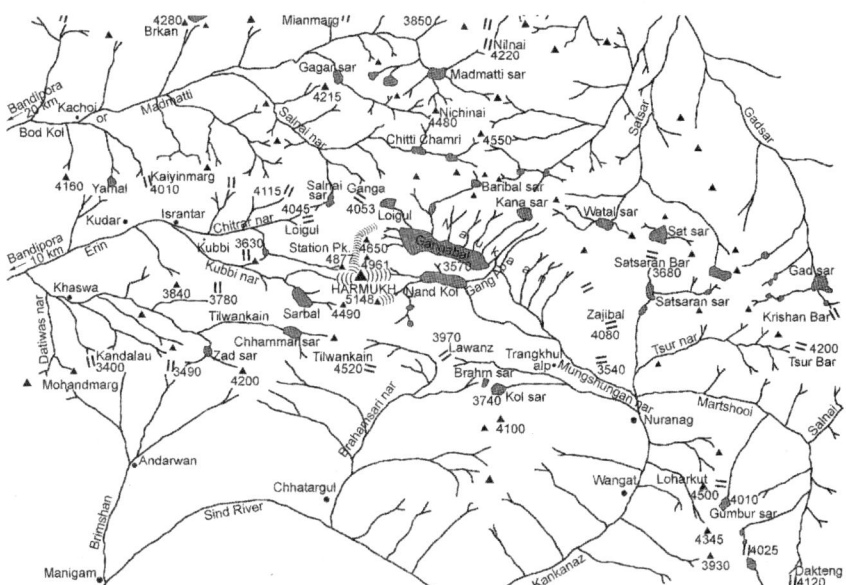

Map 11:

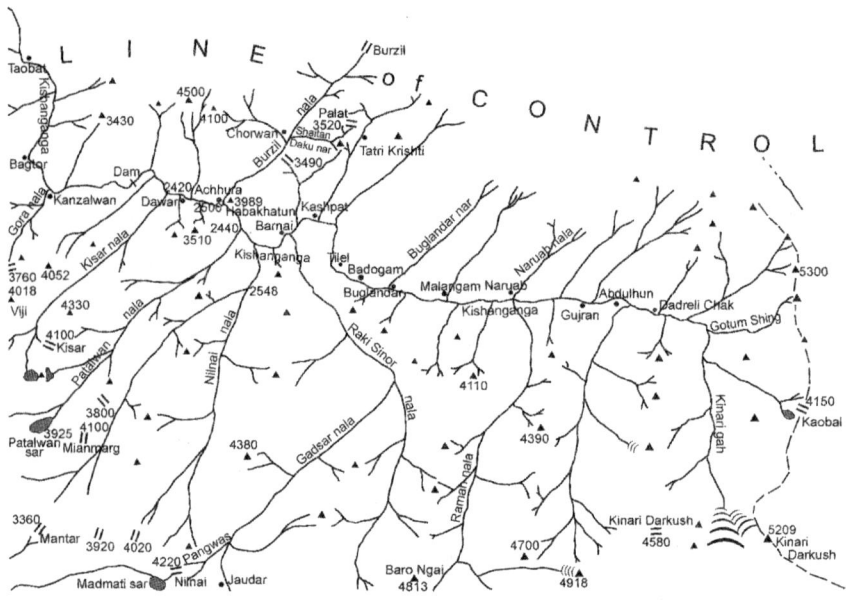

Map 12:

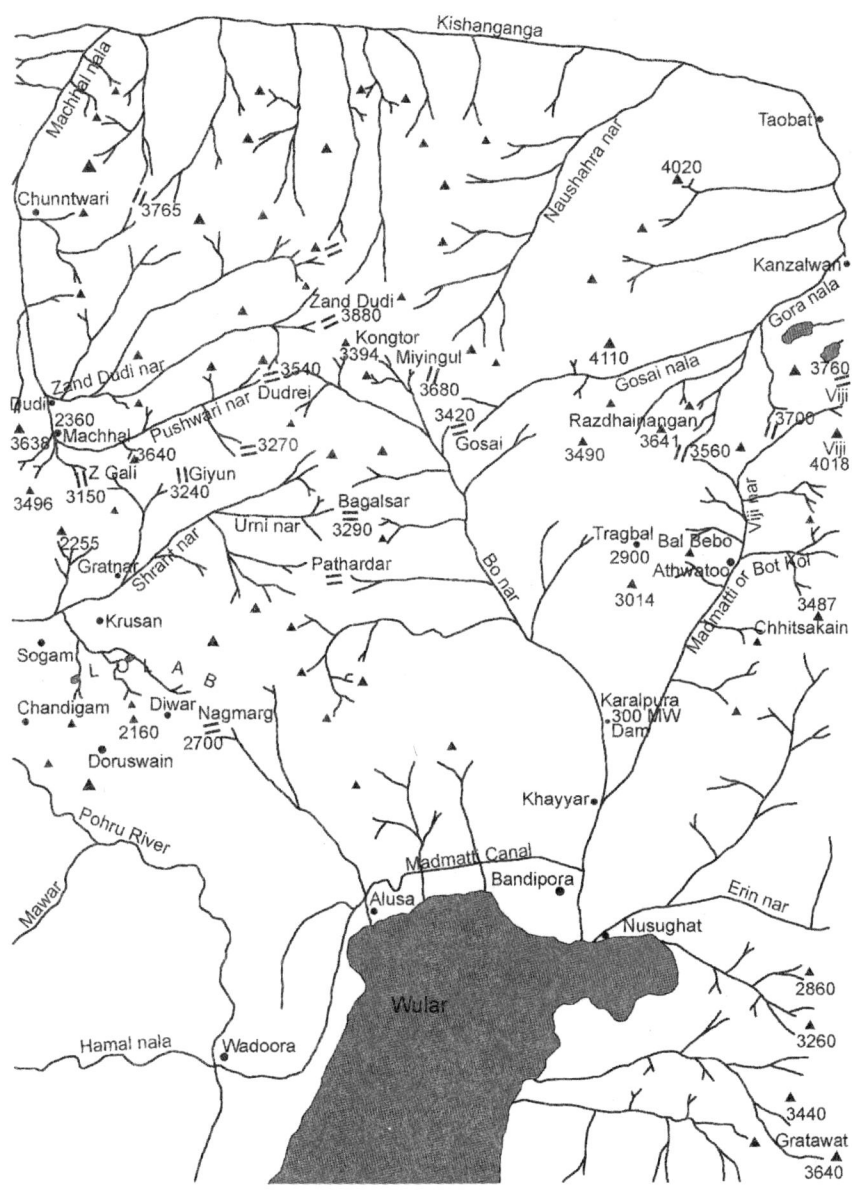

Map 13:

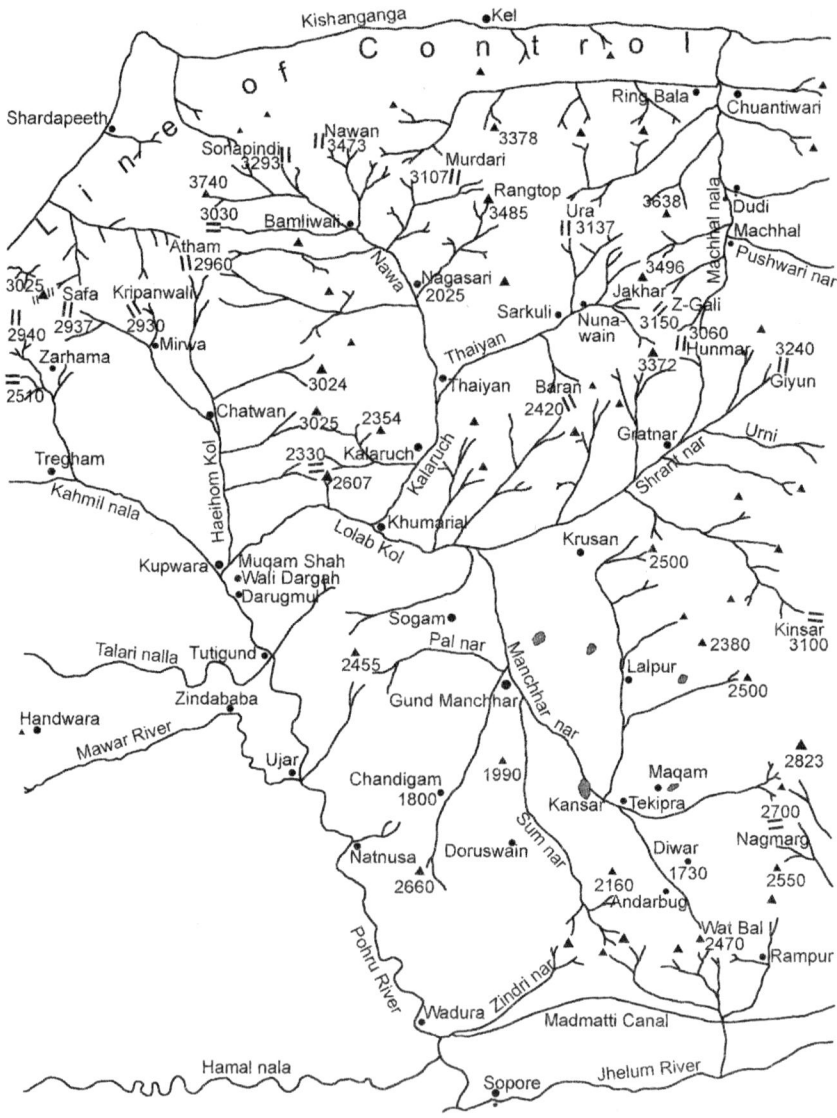

Map 14:

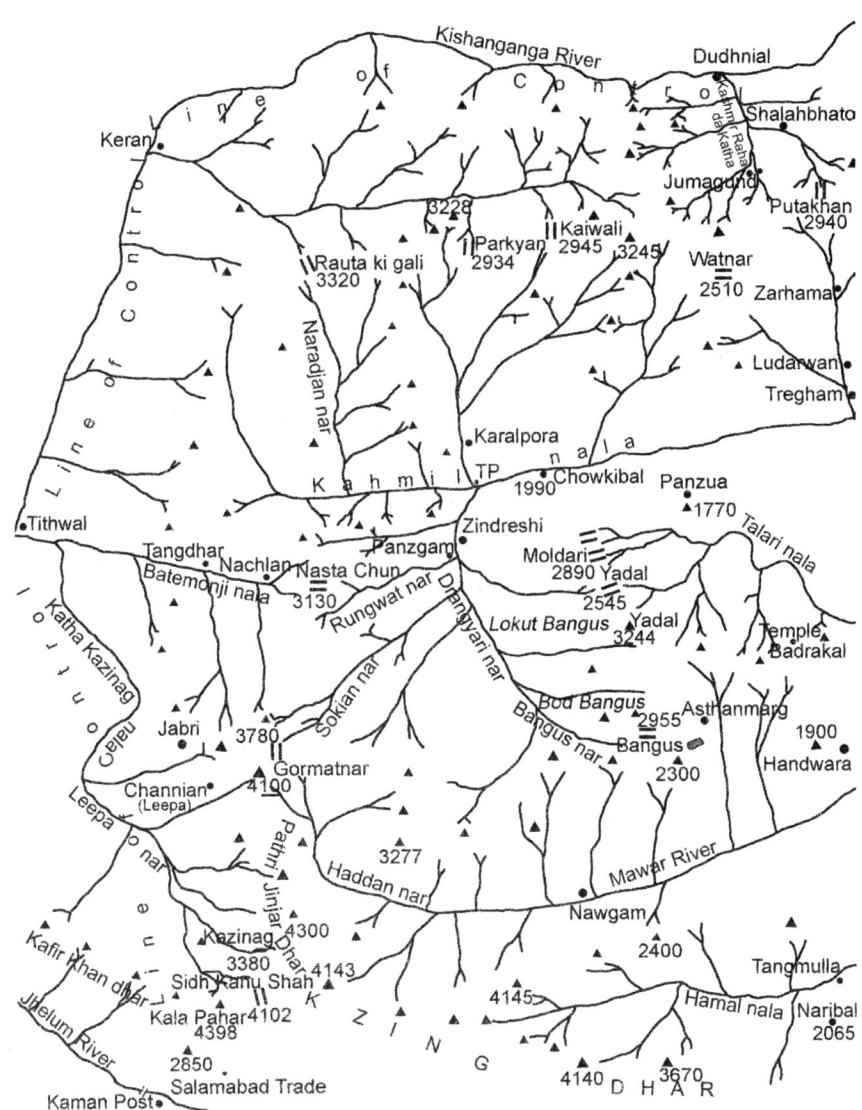

Map 15:

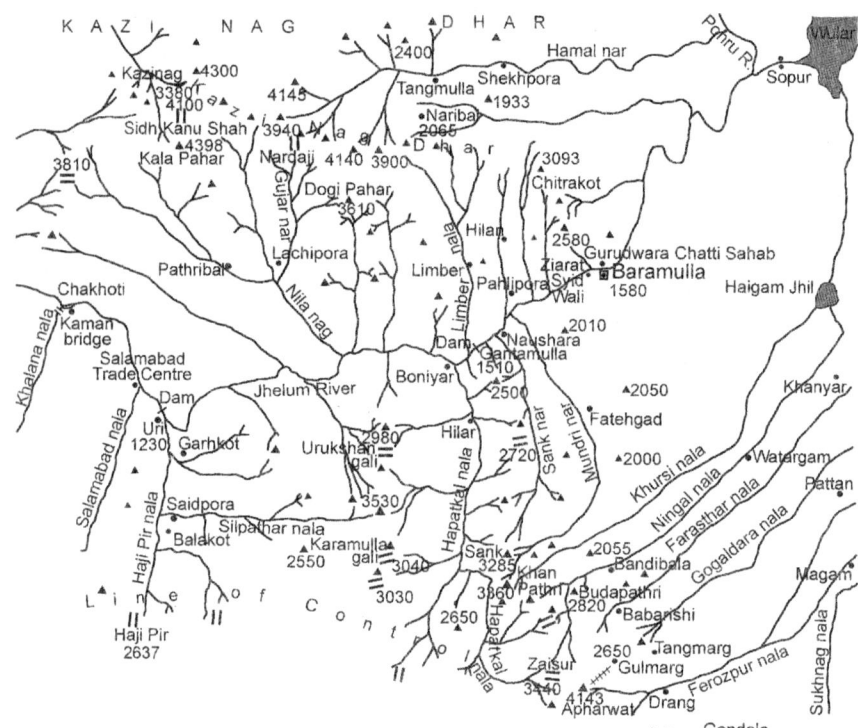

Map 16:

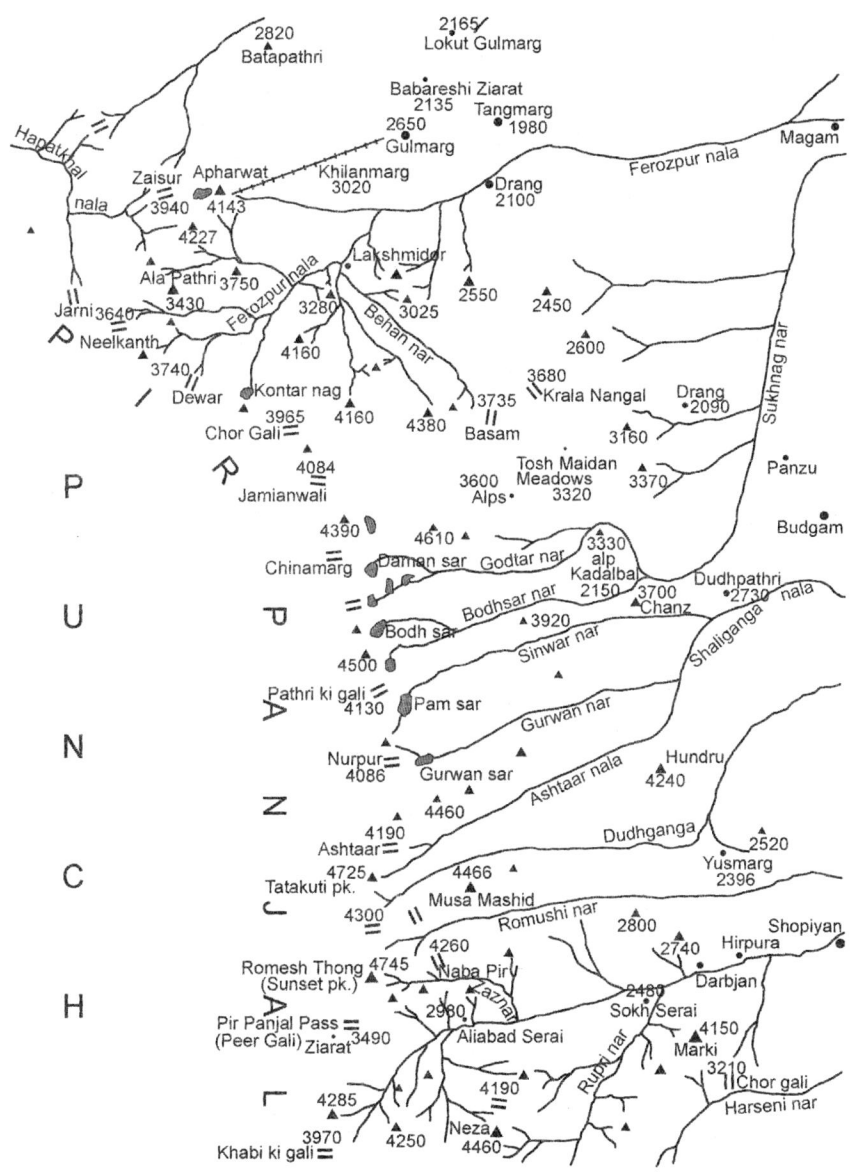

Map 17:

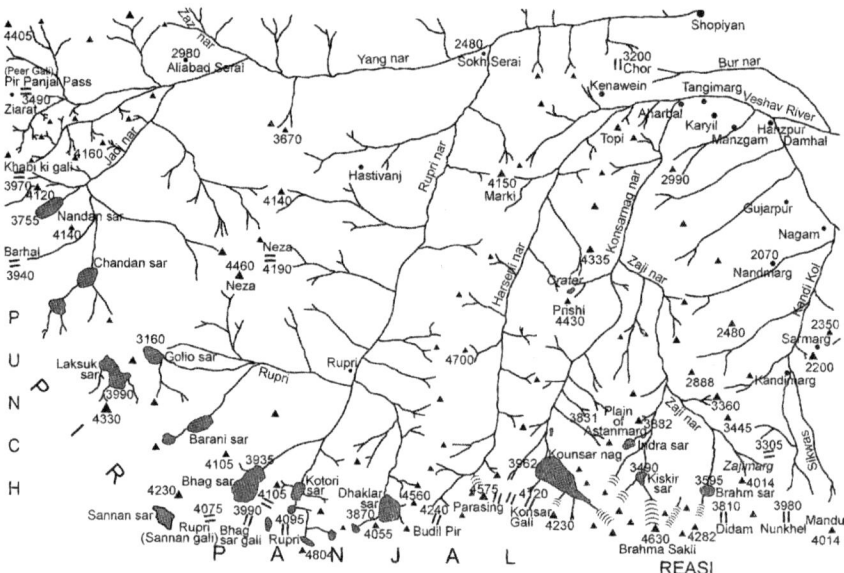

Map 18:

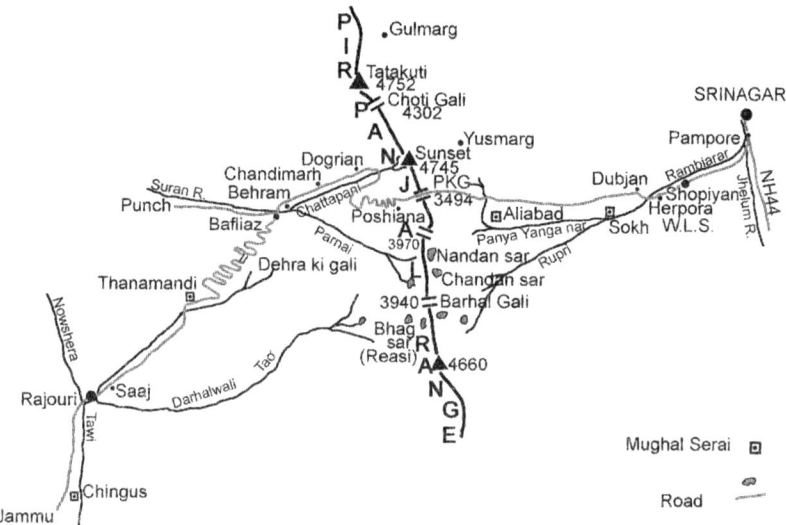

Map 19:

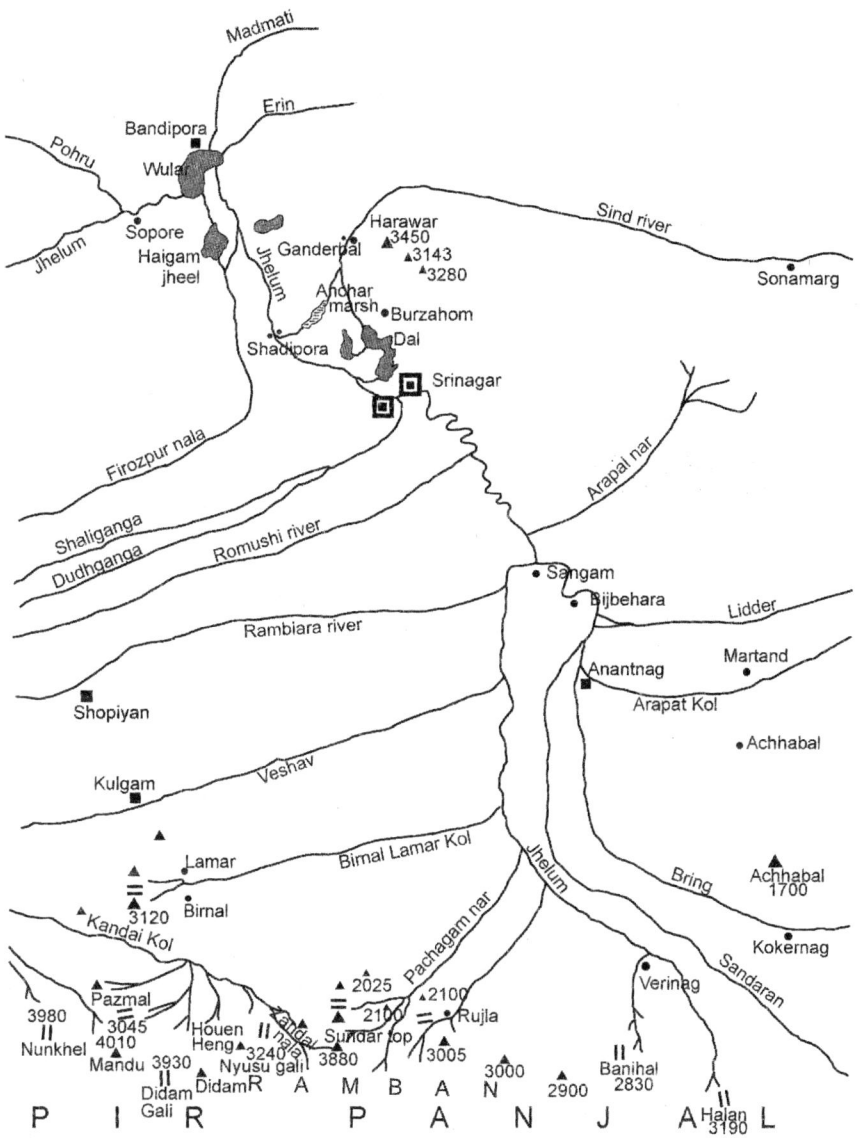

Map 20:

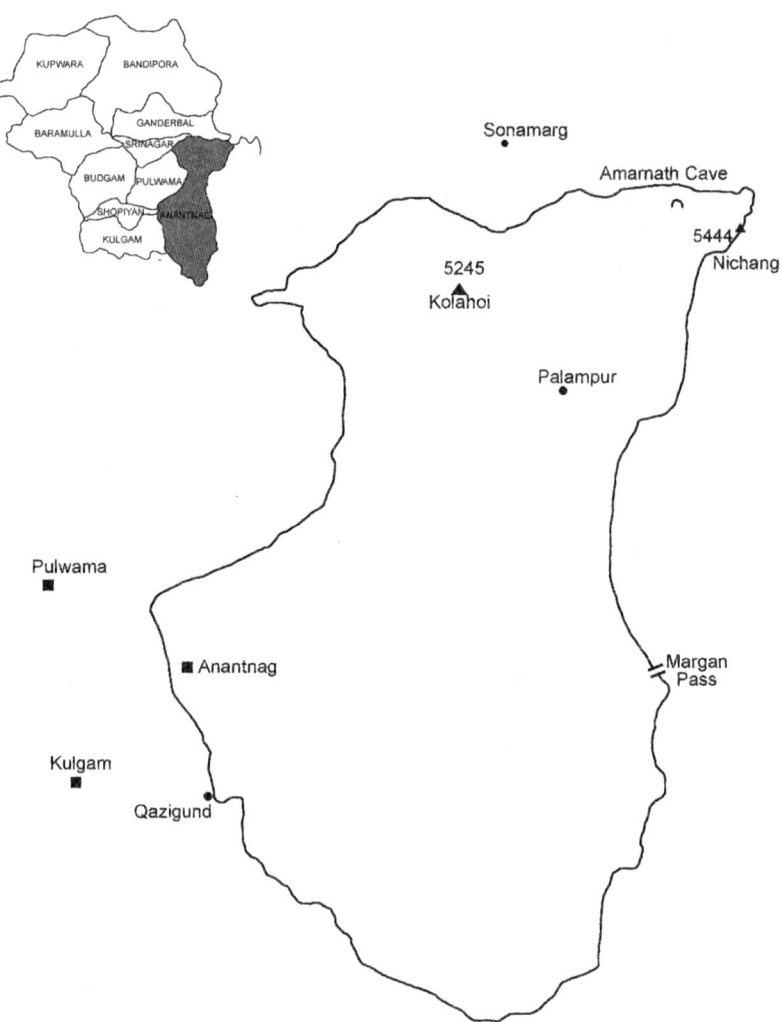

Map 21:

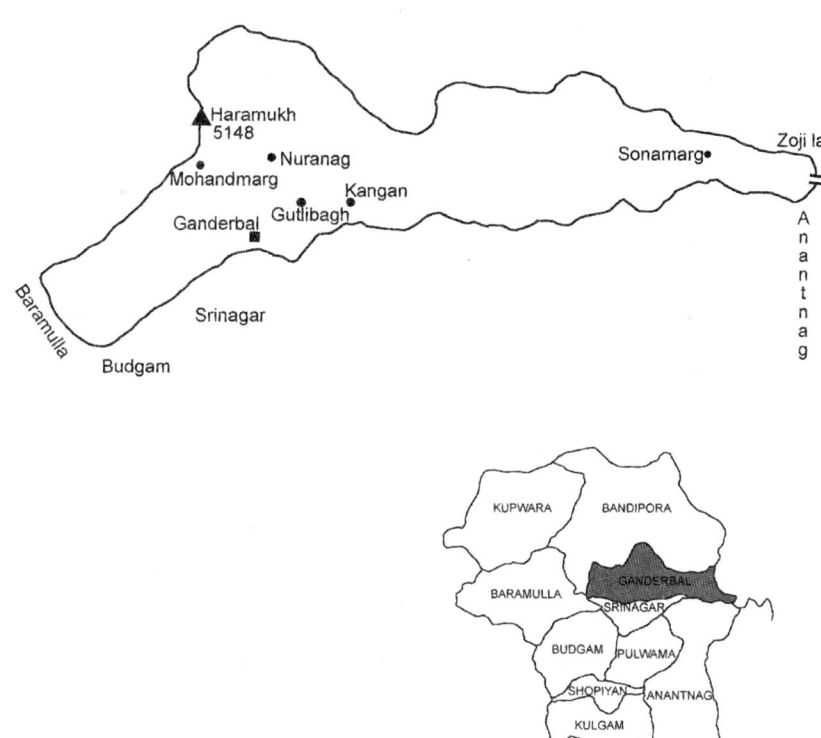

198 Maps

Map 22:

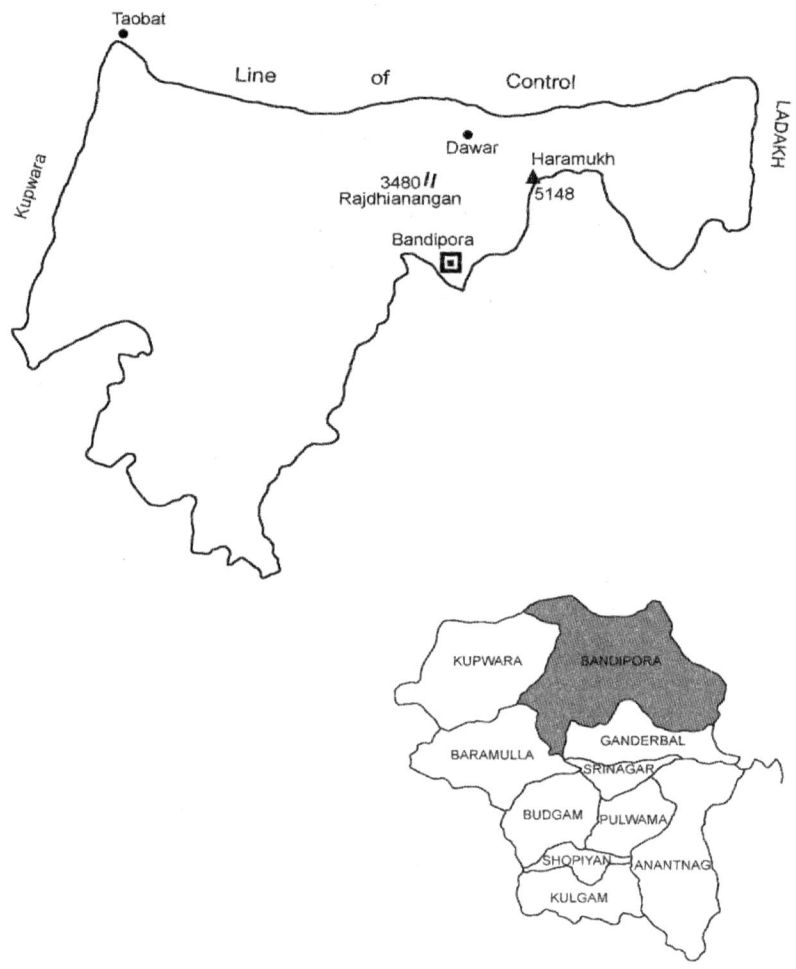

Map 23:

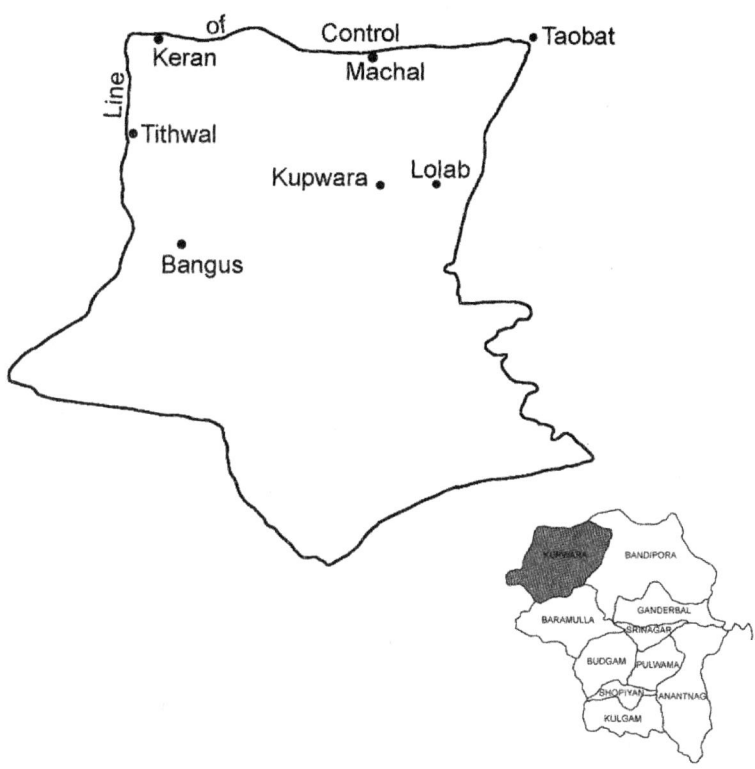

200   Maps

Map 24:

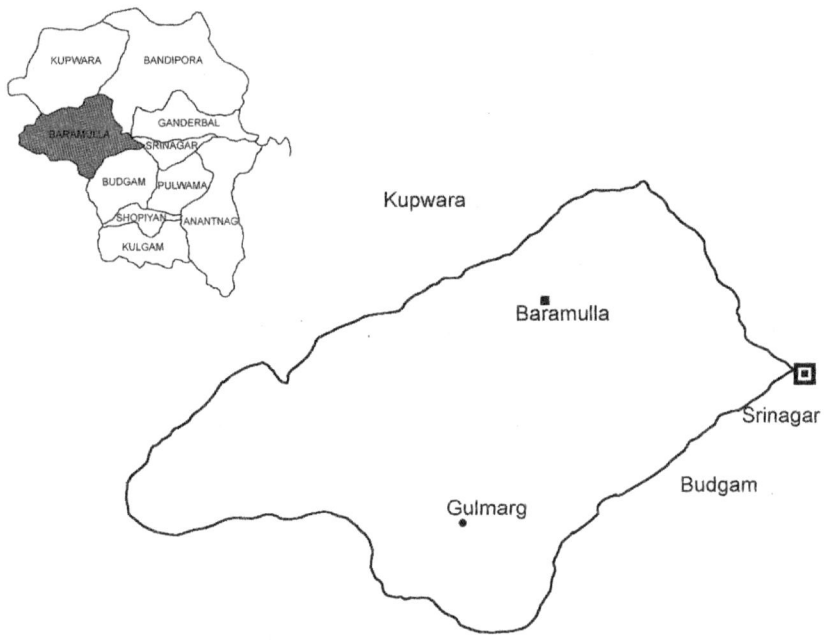

Map 25:

Map 26:

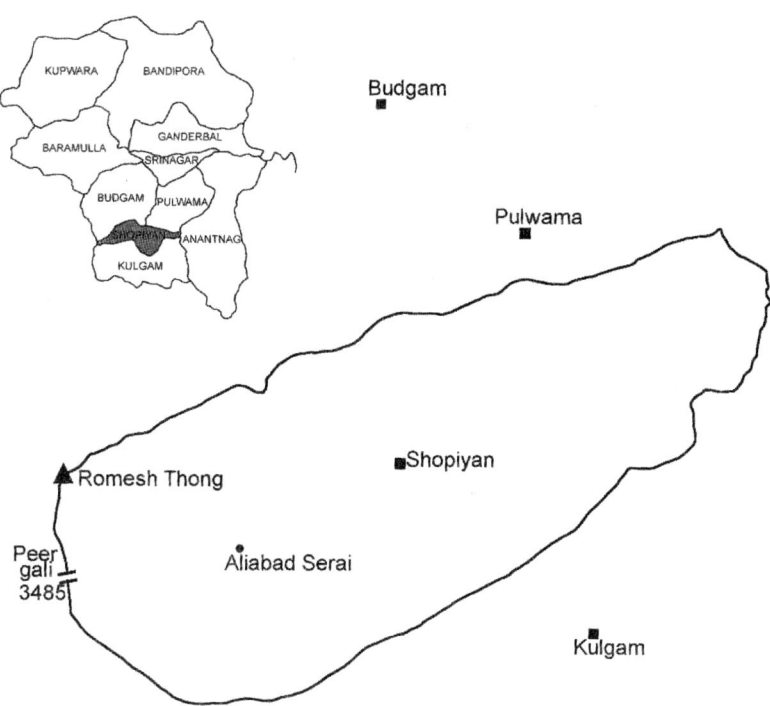

Map 27:

Maps

Map 28:

Map 29:

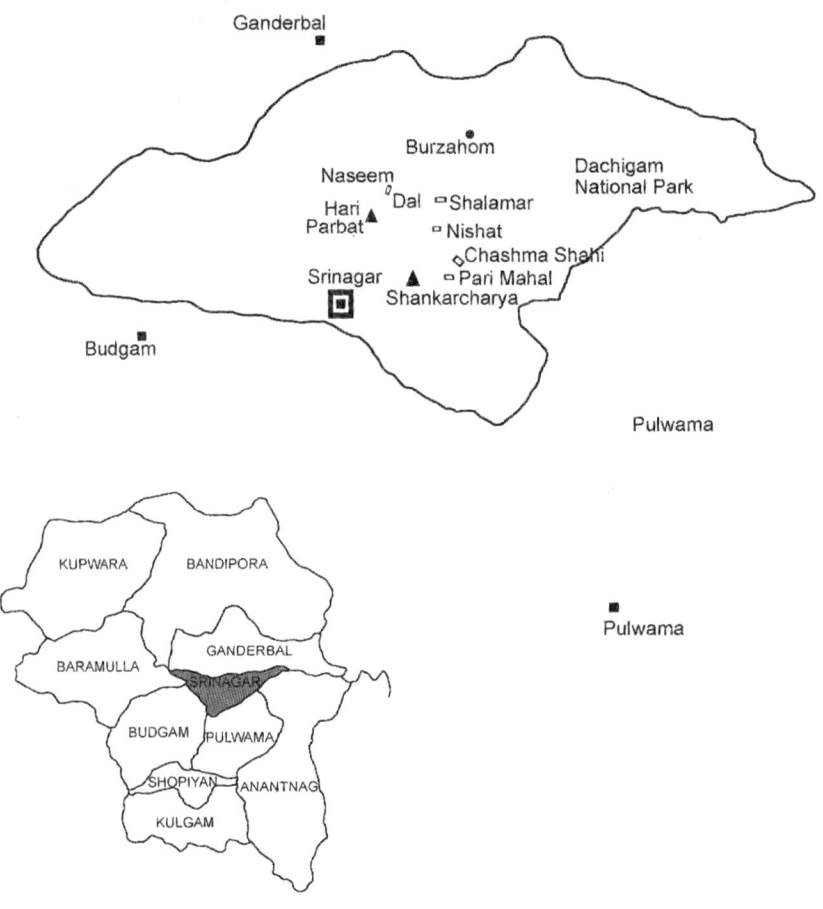

Map 30:

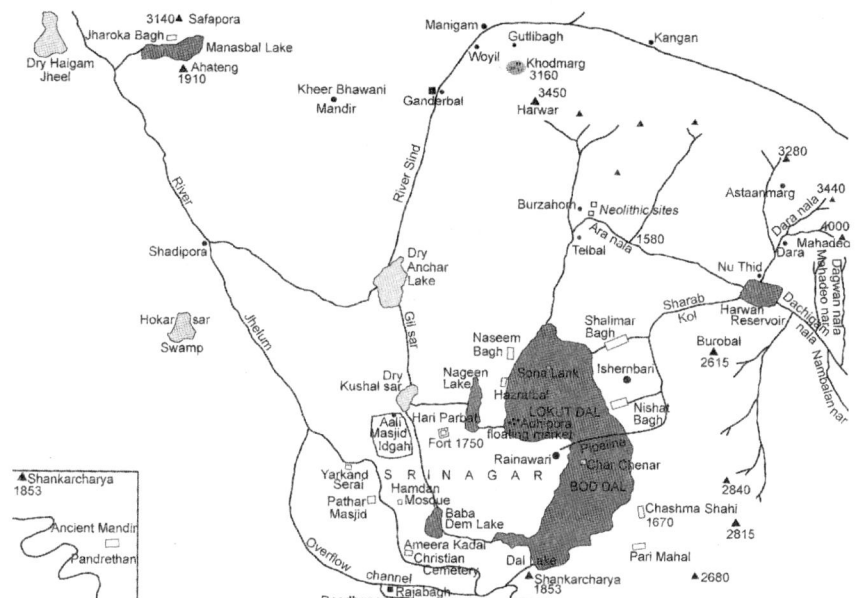

Map 31:

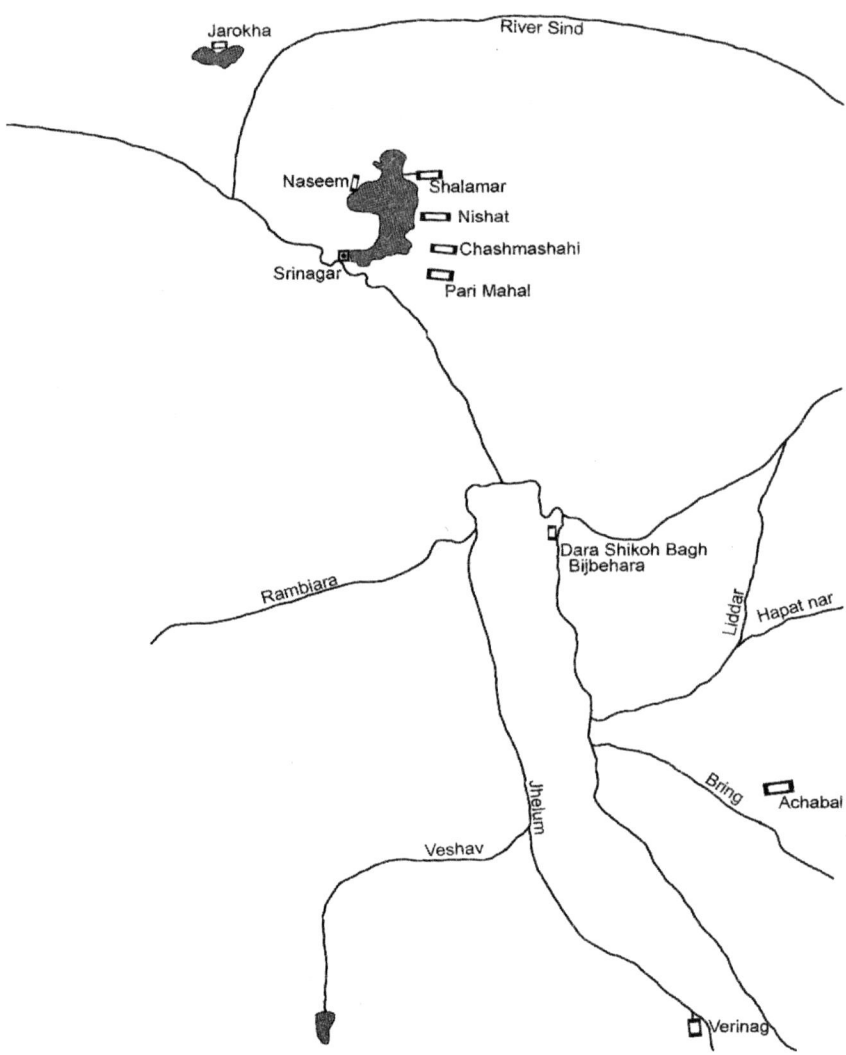

Maps 207

Map 32:

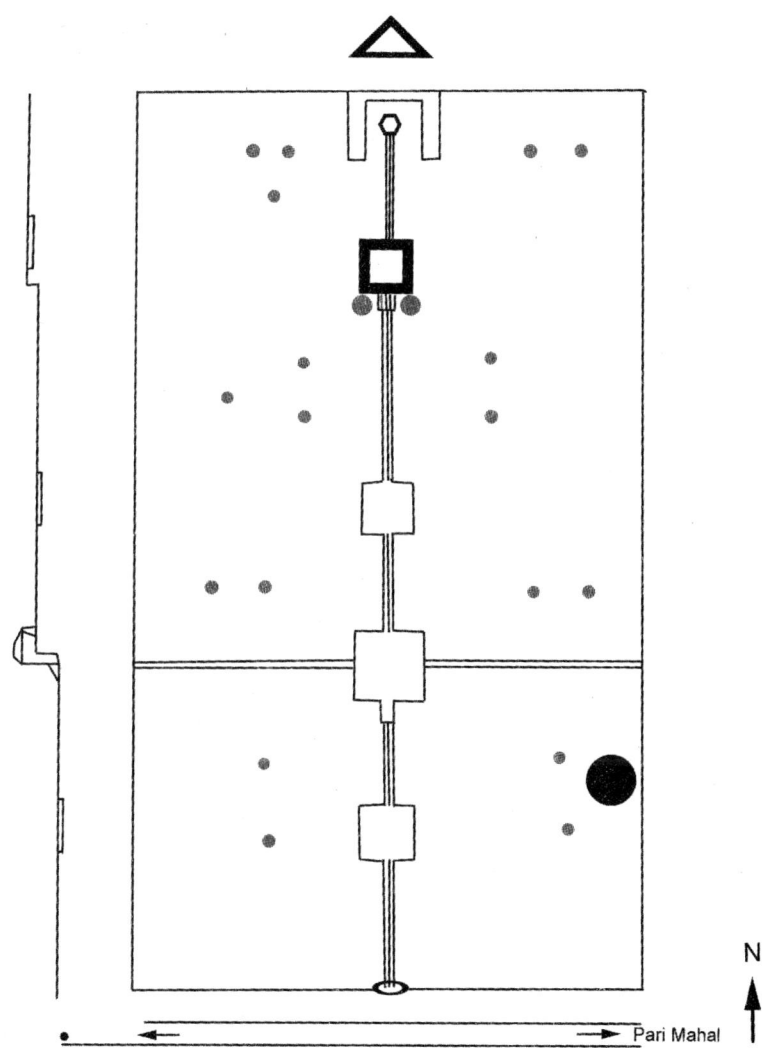

N

• ←————— ——→ Pari Mahal

Map 33:

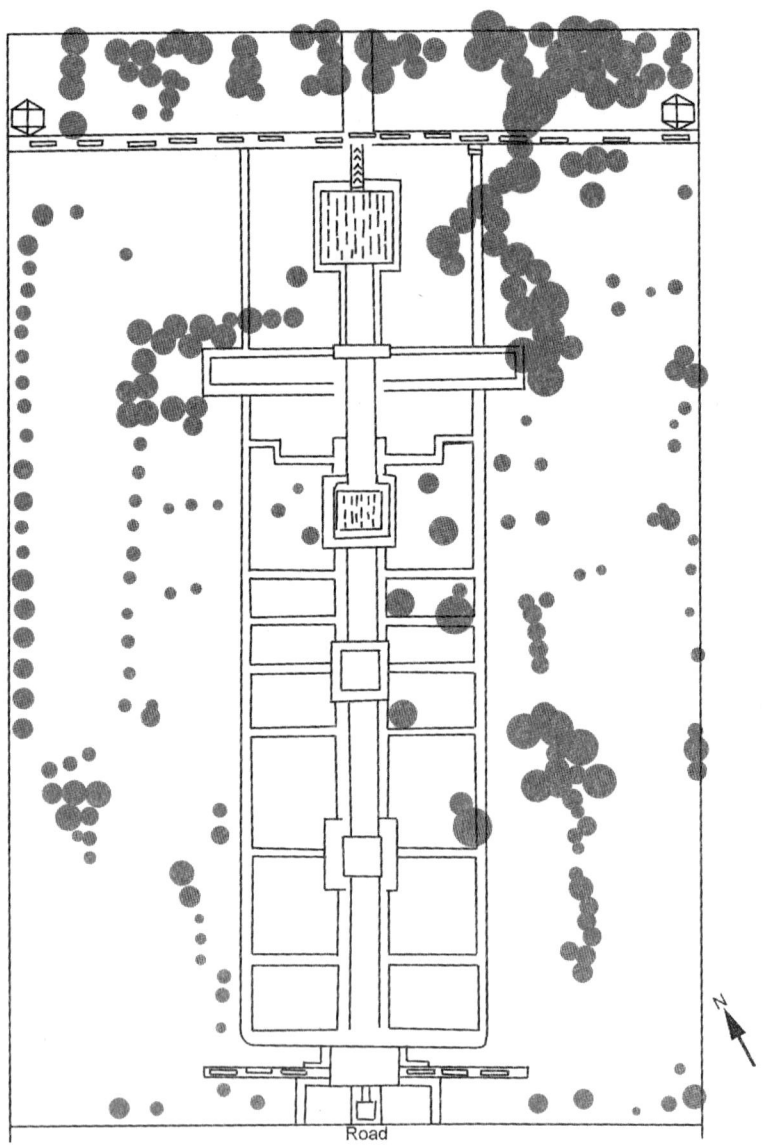

Map 34:

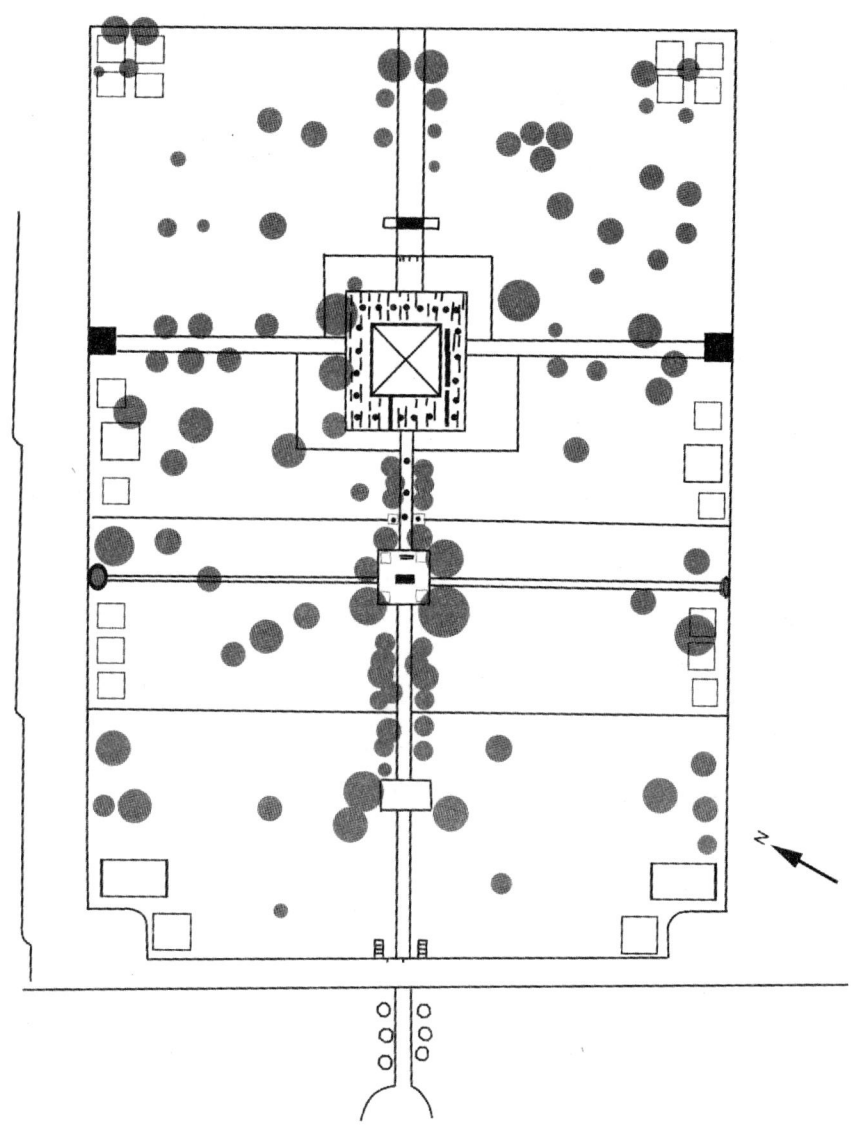

Map 35:

Maps 211

Map 36:

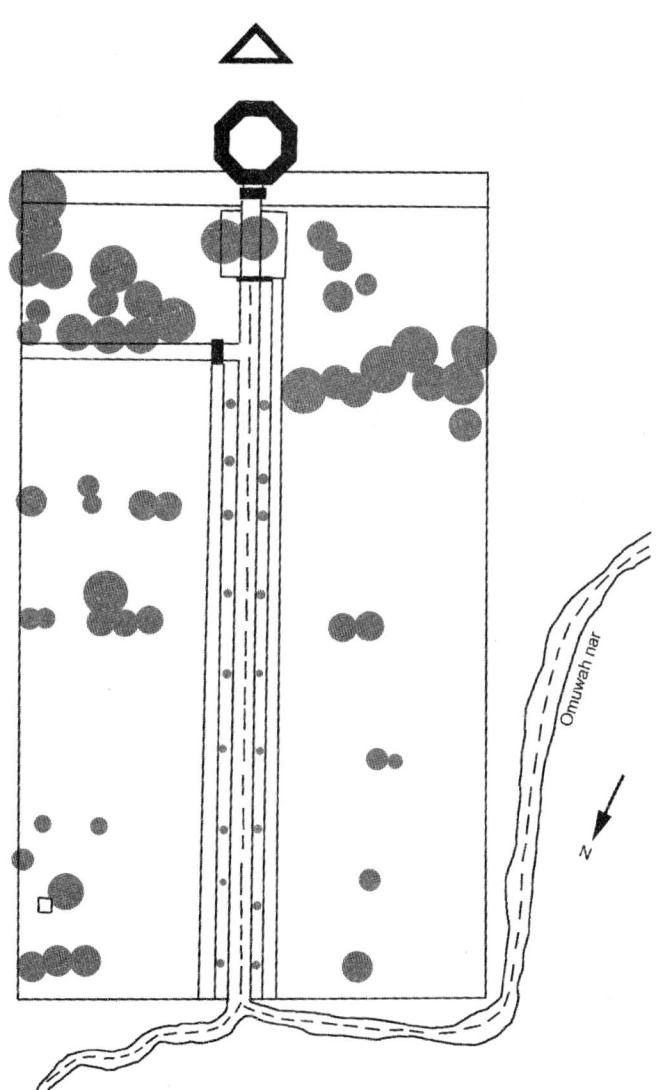

Glossary

Doka: Flat-roofed huts of Gujjars

Karewa: Plateaus formed by silt deposits brought by streams when the Valley was a lake during the Pleistocene period.

Pathar: Meadow

Marg: Meadow

Katha: stick

Kol: Usually a man-made canal or a stream

Nar and Nala: Stream

Nadi: River

Sar: Lake

Posh: Roof

Burj: Birch tree

Baihk: Meadow

Chak: Piece of land

Gali: Pass or saddle

Bar: Pass or saddle

Dhar: Ridge

Ziarat: Shrine

Bibliography

Kashmir, Francis Younghusband, A&C Black Ltd, London (1909)

Inside Kashmir, Prem Nath Bazaz, The Kashmir Publishing Co., Srinagar (1941)

Kashmir: Hindu, Buddhist and Muslim Architecture, Manohar Kaul, Sagar Publications, New Delhi (1971)

The Happy Valley: Sketches of Kashmir and the Kashmiris, W. Wakefield, Sampson Low, Marston, Searle & Rivington, London (1879)

Travels in Kashmir and Punjab, Baron Huegel (1845), reprinted by Oxford University Press, Karachi (2003)

The Valley of Kashmir, Walter R. Lawrence, reprinted by Gulshan Publishers, Srinagar, (2002)

Routes in Jammu and Kashmir, Maj. Gen. Le Marquis de Bourbel, Thacker, Spink & Co., Calcutta (1897)

Gazetteer of Kashmir and Ladakh, Government of India Central Printing Office, Calcutta (1888)

Himalayan Journals published for the Himalayan Club of India, by Oxford University Press, Delhi

The Gardens of Mughal India, Sylvia Crowe and Sheila Haywood, Vikas Publishing House, Delhi (1973)

Kashmir in Sunlight and Shade, Tyndale Biscoe (1921), reprinted by Dilpreet Publishing House, New Delhi (2002)

Curfewed Night, Basharat Peer, Random House India, NOIDA (2008)

Speaking Peace: Women's Voices from Kashmir, Urvashi Butalia (ed.), Kali for Women, Delhi (2002)

The Valley of Kashmir, Walter Lawrence, Oxford University Press, London (1895)

Notes

1 François Bernier, *Travels in the Mogul Empire*, http://www.columbia.edu/cu/lweb/digital/collections/cul/texts/ldpd_6093710_000/gallery/images/ldpd_6093710_000_00000471.jpg
2 'Who really wrote the lines "If there is Paradise on earth, it is this, it is this, it is this"?', Rana Safvi, Scroll, https://scroll.in/article/942273/who-really-wrote-the-lines-if-there-is-paradise-on-earth-it-is-this-it-is-this-it-is-this
3 This artistic impression was made by Christoph Horman and places detailed by Hermann Soldner.
4 'Chohar nag: An asset neglected', *Greater Kashmir*, https://www.greaterkashmir.com/news/gk-magazine/chohar-nag-an-asset-neglected/
5 Restored impression by J. Duguid (1870–73), https://en.wikipedia.org/wiki/Martand_Sun_Temple#/media/File:Restored_Martand_Sun_temple_India_1870.jpg
6 Surya temple at Martand, photographed by John Burke, 1868, https://en.wikipedia.org/wiki/M%C4%81rtanda#/media/File:Sun_temple_martand_indogreek.jpg
7 *The Lost Rebellion* by Manoj Joshi, Penguin India, Delhi, 1999.
8 'The History of Healthcare in Kashmir', JustJu, kashmirnetwork.com
9 'Memories of early Kashmir climbing', E. Neve, The Himalayan Club, https://www.himalayanclub.org/hj/12/10/memories-of-early-kashmir-climbing/

10 'Investigating changes in Himalayan glacier in warming environment: A case study of Kolahoi glacier', Mohammd Rafiq and Anoop Mishra, https://link.springer.com/article/10.1007%2Fs12665-016-6282-1
11 *Ibid.*
12 'Sonamarg as a climbing centre', E. Neve, The Himalayan Club, https://www.himalayanclub.org/hj/2/7/sonamarg-as-a-climbing-centre/
13 Zaji or Zoji is a name that is used often in Kashmir's geography. It is a Central Asian derivative of the word Shivji.
14 HJ/22/11 SURVEY OF KASHMIR AND JAMMU, 1855 TO 1865, himalayanclub.org
15 'Damaras: An Introduction', Kashmir Life, https://kashmirlife.net/damaras-an-introduction-issue-43-vol-12-257370/
16 '450 ton garbage thrown into Kahmil river every month in Kupwara', *Greater Kashmir*, 15 December 2018, https://www.greaterkashmir.com/kashmir/450-ton-garbage-thrown-into-kahmil-river-every-month-in-kupwara/
17 'Lolab: The Hidden Himalayan Valley', Brigadier Ashok Abbey, https://www.himalayanclub.org/hj/70/15/lolab-the-hidden-himalayan-valley/
18 'Impact of change in forest cover on soil status in Kahmil Watershed, J&K, using Geo-spatial tools', Pervez Ahmed, Earth Science India, http://www.earthscienceindia.info/pdfupload/tech_pdf-1288.pdf
19 2010 Machil encounter, https://en.wikipedia.org/wiki/2010_Machil_encounter
20 'Machil Moorings', Kashmir Life, https://kashmirlife.net/machil-moorings-issue-29-vol-12-249730/
21 India–Pakistan Borderline, Raashid Sarfaraz, https://www.facebook.com/watch/?v=802025931239380
22 'Understanding Karnah', Kashmir Life, https://kashmirlife.net/understanding-karnah-issue-34-vol-12-252535/
23 'Colonel, Major among 5 personnel killed in J&K's Handwara', *The Hindu*, 3 May 2020, https://www.thehindu.com/news/national/colonel-major-among-5-personnel-killed-in-jks-handwara/article31493302.ece
24 'Leepa Valley: The mini Kashmir', Rising Kashmir, http://risingkashmir.com/news/leepa-valley-the-mini-kashmir
25 Current World Environment Journal, Vol. 5, https://www.cwejournal.org/pdf/vol5no2/CWEVO5NO2P287-292.pdf
26 'Battle of Haji Pir Pass', Indian Defence Review, https://www.indiandefencereview.com/spotlights/battle-of-hajipir-pass-1965/

27 *Travels in Kashmir and the Punjab* by Baron Charles von Huegel. First published in 1845 by John Peterham and then by Oxford University Press, Karachi in 2003.
28 'Brahma Sakli Expedition, 1989', M. Amin, The Himalayan Club, https://www.himalayanclub. org/ hj/ 46 /11/brahma- sakli- expedition-1989/
29 'ASN Aircraft accident Fokker F-27 Friendship 200 PH-SAB Banihall Pass', aviation-safety.net
30 'Karewas: A treasure of Kashmir Soon to be lost forever', Kashmir Observer, https://kashmirobserver.net/2016/05/06/karewas-a-treasure-of- kashmir-soon-to-be-lost-forever/
31 Kashmir, https://www.google.com/search?q=Kashmir&stick=H4sIAA AAAAAA ONgVuLQz9U3SMlKL1nEyu6dWJyRm1kEANfVm_ 0WAAAA&sa= X&ved=2ahUKEwia-aqAy6vpAhWGbisKHUQDD BMQmxMoATAh egQIFxAD)
32 'The willow world of Sangam', *The Indian Express*, 24 January 2016, https://indianexpress.com/article/sports/cricket/cricket-kashmir-the-willow-world-of-sangam/
33 *Ibid.*
34 'Shopian: A for Apple, Arms too', *Greater Kashmir*, 15 September 2018, https://www.greaterkashmir.com/news/opinion/shopian-a-for-apple-arms-too/
35 'Kashmir produced 18 lakh mts of apple in 2018', Rising Kashmir, http://www.risingkashmir.com/news/kashmir-produced-18-lakh-mts-of-apple-in-2018
36 'When Safa Kadal Sarai was trade centre for Central Asia', *Greater Kashmir*, https://www.greaterkashmir.com/news/srinagar/when-safa-kadal-sarai- was-trade-centre-for-central-asia/
37 'Bridges of Srinagar', Kashmir Network, http://kashmirnetwork.com/justju/?page_id=180
38 'Bridges of Medieval Kashmir: An outline historical study based on construction and architectural work', Waseem Rashid, https://www.academia.edu/12080503/Bridges_of_Medieval_ Kashmir_An_outline_ historical_study_based_on_construction_and_ architectural_work
39 *Cashmere Misgovernment*, Robert Thorpe, Wyman Bros, Calcutta, 1868.
40 *The Jammu Fox: A Biography of Maharaj Gulab Singh of Kashmir, 1792–1857*, Bawa Satinder Singh, Heritage Publishers, New Delhi, 1988.
41 'Kashmir remembers Robert Thorpe on 149th death anniversary', Kashmir Life, https://kashmirlife.net/kashmir-remembers-robert-thorpe-on-149th-death- anniversary-156529/

42 *The Happy Valley*, W. Wakefield, Sampson Low, Marston, Searle & Rivington, London, 1879.
43 Greater Kashmir, 20 June 2004.
44 'Jammu and Kashmir floods: Rage of Jhelum submerges Paradise', *DNA*, 10 September 2014, https://www.dnaindia.com/india/report-jammu-and-kashmir-floods- rage-of-jhelum-submerges-paradise-2017449
45 *Travels in Kashmir and the Punjab*, Baron Charles von Huegel, John Petheram, 1845.
46 Greater Kashmir, 31 October 2004.
47 *The Gardens of Mughal India*, Sylvia Crowe and Shiela Haywood, Vikas Publishing House, Delhi, 1973.
48 *Ibid.* and *Gardens of the Great Mughal* by an English painter, Constance Villiers Stuart, Adam and Charles Black, 1913.
49 *The Gardens of Mughal India*, Sylvia Crowe and Shiela Haywood, Vikas Publishing House, Delhi, 1973.
50 *Ibid.*
51 Burza Pash: The rooftops that exploded with colours, *Greater Kashmir*, 17 August 2018, https://www.greaterkashmir.com/news/opinion/burza-pash-the- rooftops-that-exploded-with-colours/
52 *Travels in Kashmir and the Punjab*, Baron Charles von Huegel, John Petheram, 1845.
53 *The Gardens of Mughal India*, Sylvia Crowe and Shiela Haywood, Vikas Publishing House, Delhi, 1973.
54 *Ibid.*
55 'How an Irish poet's epic poem on Kashmir captivated the West, spawning operas, musicals and grandeur', Scroll, 10 September 2016, https://scroll.in/article/728492/how-an-irish-poets-epic-poem-on-kashmir-captivated-the-west-spawning-operas-musicals-and-grandeur?fbclid=IwAR38S6jhUg1zWSMZmXYhiQdoIxDA2h4GC4a2n5-QF654TPxRUKuMAW7UhD7Q

Index

Aali Masjid, 159
Aasar-i-Sharief Dargah, Pinjura, 143
Abdulhun, 69, 72
Abode of Snow, Mason, 21
Abrupathri (Cloud Meadow, *sea also* meadows), 126
Achhabal, 13, 164, 176–177; garden, 168, 172, 175
Achhabal Thang, 175
Achhura village, 71
Afghans, 117, 120; ruled over Kashmir, 136
Agashmandal, 7
agriculture, 15, 90, 152
Ahan sar, 175
Aharbal Falls, 103, 122, 125–126
Ahlan river, 6, 12; feeder streams of, 8; valleys, 4–5
Ain-i-Akbari, 13
Aishmuqam, 20
Akbar, 13, 71, 120, 173–174, 176
Aksha, King, 176

Akshavala spring, 176
algae, 58, 82, 157–158
Aliabad, 119–122
Aliabad Serai, 120–121
almonds, 82, 131, 145, 173
Alpathar, 108
alps, 3, 6, 8–10, 23, 26, 36, 38, 40, 45, 61, 109–111, 114–116, 118, 121, 124–126
Alusa post office, Bandipora, 83
Amarnath, 27–28, 30–33, 51; cave, 7, 23, 28, 30–31, 33, 54, 133; nala, 27, 30, 32; nar, 32; pilgrim route, 27; route to, 27; trek, 28
Amin, Mohammed, 41
Anantnag, 1–4, 12–13, 15, 19–20, 25, 42, 128, 132–135, 145
Anchar lake, 61, 151, 157–159, 174
Andarbug, 82–83
Andarwan village, 65
Angan gali, 44, 48
anti-insurgency camps, 109

Apharwat, 108, 110–111
apricots, 81–83, 104, 175
Arapal: kol, 45; nar, 42–43; river, 43–46; stream, 46; town, 46
Arcadia, 68
Armiun nar, 38, 42–46, 48, 134
army: camps, 76, 86, 92, 106, 167; roads, 90, 93, 98, 100, 110–111
Arpat kol, 12–13, 17–19, 21
Article 370, abrogation of, 100
Aru curves, 23, 37–41, 47
Aru– Lidderwat–Shekhwas–Tar sar–Mar sar–Chanda sar–Hoke sar–Sona sar–Sonamus to Sumbal route, 50
Aryanbra, 8
Asha Bagh, 160
Ashal Kadal, 160
Ashidur Bal, 134
Ashtaar: gali, 113–115; nala, 115
Astaan, 29, 124, 153; meaning of, 29
Astaanmarg, 29–30, 41, 124–125, 153
Atham gali, 81, 85
Ath nar, 25, 41
Athwatoo, 78
Aurangzeb, 134, 166, 170; caravan accident of, 150
Aurel Stein Museum, 66
avalanches, 41, 72, 76, 129
Avantipore, 42, 74, 146

Baal Bebo, 78
Baba Dem lake, 157–158
Baba Gulamudin Sahib, 166
Babarshah, 158
Babnar, 57
Babul, 14
Badami Bagh, Cantonment, 150; Pantha Chowk, 151

Badrakali temple, 139
Badre gali, 18
Badroni nar, 99
Badshahi Sarai, 120
Bahg sar, 122
Bahramgalla, 172
Baib nar bar, 69
Baihak Sangam, 61
Bajnal, 17
Bakkarwals/ Bakarwals/ Bakerwals, 26, 36, 44, 99, 122
Baltal, 33, 39, 51, 55; tax collecting station, 31
Bandipora, 65–66, 72, 74, 77–78, 80, 83, 132–133, 135–140
Bangus, 97–100, 140; nar, 98–99; valleys, 94–95, 98, 140
Banihal, 1, 13, 127–130, 133, 140, 147; Pass, xix, 2, 128–129; town, 129
Banilmarg: gali, 45; peak, 45; ridge, 48
Banmir village, 43
baradiri, 168
Baramulla, 86, 94–95, 99, 101–109, 131–132, 135, 137, 140–142, 147; to Srinagar by houseboats, 107
Baramulla–Uri–Salamabad road, 103
Barani sar, 122–123
Barhal gali, 122
Barnai, 70–71; gah, 70–71; village, 59
Barzulla, 152, 162
Basam gali, 112–113, 115
Basmai: gali, 35–36, 60; nar, 60
Batemoj (Rice Mother) nala, 94; nar, 94, 100
Batkut, 20–21, 47; rest house, 48
bazaars, 13, 150, 152
Behan nar, 112
Bernier, Francois, 150, 170, 173, 176
Betaab (1983), 26

Index

Betul nala, 106
Beyond the Three Seas, Bernier, 150
Bhag Sar, 121–122
Bhimsina, 142
Bijbehara, 15, 47, 133–134, 166
Bijbehara–Sangam, 133
Bimar Nursar, 17
birch forest, 3, 9–10, 27, 29, 36, 40, 44, 50, 52, 67, 69, 112, 117
Bod (big) Chhumanai nar, 47
Bod (Bigger) Dal, 156–157, 160–161
Bod Angan, 115
Bo nar, 76–77
Boniyar, 103, 105; ancient Shiv temple in, 105; Datta temple near, 104; nala, 105
Bot Kol river, 77–78, 137
Bot Kul or Madmatti, 67, 77–78; gali, 52
Bot Kul or Madmatti Ganj pass, 55, 68
Brahamsari nar, 65
Brahma I, 124
Brahma Sakli, 123–125; peaks, 123–126, 144
Brahm sar, 65, 124–126
Brarbaz, 79
Brari, 5
Brariangan: nar, 46, 48; valleys, 48
Brari gali, 6; nar, 6
Brarimarg, 25; gali, 41; ridge, 25
Bratabal nar, 27–28
Bring river, 3, 5, 8, 12, 129
Brithwari gali, 101
British Army, 155
Budapathri, 109
Buddhist stupas, 142
Budgam, 112, 114–115, 132, 142–143
Budil Pir, 122–123
Bumzo caves, 23

Buniyar, 74
Burke, Jim, 15
Burz, 149, 173
Burzahom, 148–149, 170
Burzil: nala, 69, 71–72; pass, 55, 71–72
Buttress peak, 29, 41
Byari, 33

canals, 14, 20, 129, 152–153, 160, 162–163, 169, 171–172, 177–178; at Barzulla, 152
Cariappa, General, 55, 75
cattle, 9, 38, 88, *see also* shepherds
Central University in Ganderbal, 135–136
Chahlimar, 170
Chak, Ali Shah, 139
Chak, Yusuf, 71
Chammar sar, 65
Chandan sar, 122
Chandanwari, 27–30; shepherd track, 29
Chanda sar lake, 36–37, 40, 44–47, 49–50, 60
Chandigam, 82–83, 85
Chanpari, 4, 6
Charar-e-Sharief, 143; Bimar Nursar, 17
Char Bagh, 163, 171
Char Chinar (Rupa Lank or Silver island), 151–152, 160–161, 164
Chari nag, 21
Chashmashahi Garden, 151, 164–166, 169
Chattargul, 65
Chattergam, 143, 162
Chattergul, 61
check posts, 6, 58, 73, 144

Index

Chhang peak, 114
Chhatargul, 18
Chhiti Chhamri sar, 67
Chhuhumanai sar, 44
Chhumahai, 42–43, 45, 47, 49; gali, 47; lake, 42, 47; sar, 44, 47
Chhumanani lake, 42–43, 45, 47, 49
Chhut gali, 29–30
Chinamarg: gali, 113; peak, 113
Chinar Bagh, 158, 167
chinars, 15, 90, 131, 134, 143, 150, 154, 156–157, 161–162, 164, 166–167, 169, 171, 173–174, 176–178
Chingus, 177
Chirran nag, 21
Chitar nar, 4
Chitral, 137
Chitrar nar, 66
Chiwar nar, 4
Chor Panjal pass, 111
Chorwan village, 71
Chowkibal forest, 97
Christians, 142
Christ, Jesus, 116, 155
Chugom, 18
Chunt Kol, 158
Chuntwari, 87–88; village, 86; Bala, 87
Chut gali, 39
civilians, 6, 73, 86, 90, 106, 111
construction, 2, 4, 14, 53, 118, 158, 168
craggy peaks, 2
crops, 73, 82; Maize, 90
CRPF camp, 161
Cunningham, Alexander, 151

Dachigam (Harwan), 48; nala, 44, 46, 153; nar, 153; stream, 48, 151

Dachigam Reserve Forest, 45, 49, 150, 153
Dachigam Sanctuary, 43
Dadreli Chak, 70, 74
Daksum, 8–10
Dakteng bar pass, 61
Dal Gate, 160
Dal lake, 44, 48–49, 109, 133, 148, 151–152, 156, 167, 172; Islands in, 160–161; as jewel of Kashmir, 157; Tarikh-e-Hassan on,
Daman sar, 113
Damhal Hanzpora, 128–129
dams, 73–74, 104
Damudara, 132
Dandabari, 36, 46–47, 49
Dara stream, 153, 166
Dardapur, 17
Dards, 70, 73
Dariyadar forests, 39
Darugmul, 80, 139
Dawar, 67, 69–73; Juma Masjid, 73; shepherds, 73
deforestation, 4, 84
Delhi, 93, 103, 129, 150, 165, 177
deodars, 8, 23, 84, 95, 105, 107, 110, 119, 145
Deo Masjid, 36–37, 45, 50; peaks, 50
Deo Mir (now Diamir), 37
Deo Tibba, 7
Dewar: gali, 111; pass, 111
dhabas, 112, 114
Dhaklar sar, 123
Dhanwas forest, 111
Didam Gali I, 118–119, 121, 123, 1251 27; peak, 129
Didam Gali II, 127–129
Diwan-e-Aam, 171–172
Diwan-e-Khas, 172

Index

Diwar, 82
Doda, 6–7; sar lake, 60
Dogras, 15, 20, 117, 155
dokas, 6–7, 11, 24, 26, 37, 41, 59, 64, 66, 107, 109, 114
Domel, 7, 33, 39, 51, 54, 95, 102
Drang, 110–113, 127
Drangyari, 140; nala, 97–98
Dras, 72–73
Dringyan: gali, 9; sar, 10
Dubjan, 113, 117, 119; forest, 119; gazebo, 119; Mughal Road at, 119
Dudhganga, 114–116, 159
Dudhmarg nar, 44
Dudh nag, 39
Dudhnial, 89, 93
Dudhpathri, 113–115, 143
Dudrei, 75
Duguid, J., 14
Durin: nar, 40, 51–52; river, 52

earthquake, 1885, 141
Earth Science India, 84
East Kashmir, 7, 12–13, 15, 21, 32, 104, 123, 133
East Lidder, 23–34, 41, 48
Eidi-Milad-un-Nabi, 143
election of 1988, 24
Elysian, 37
Elysium, 82, 127
Erin, 67, 137; nala, 66, 78; tributaries of, 66
Euglena, 158
excavations, 104, 148–149; Swat (POK), 149

Faiz-Baksh, 172
Fakir Goojree village, 153
False Banihal, 129

Farkyangali, 92, 94
Fateh Kadal, 152
Fazl, Abul, 176
Ferozepur Nala, 110–113, 127
fir forests, 4, 8, 36, 38, 48, 50, 53, 60, 69, 117, 125; of Watsar, 139
fishermen, 138, 161
flora and fauna, 67
flowers, 23, 28, 34, 41, 50, 54, 58, 63, 69, 114, 171–173; Honabacha (puppy), 38
Forest Rest Houses, 7, 12, 40, 53, 72, 93
forests, 3, 8–9, 18, 26, 43–45, 60–61, 64–65, 79, 83–84, 104–107, 110–112, 114, 119, 126, 150–151, 173–174; deodar, 99; firs, 2, 4–6, 9–10, 12, 17, 19, 21, 24, 26–27, 29, 36–37, 44–46, 52, 65, 69, 104–105; of Israntar, 66
fountains, 158, 165–168, 171–172, 176; of Shalamar, 153
fruits, 82, 132, 138; apples, 8, 43, 81–83, 102, 104, 116, 131, 140, 143–144, 146, 173; cherries, 8, 82, 102, 104; peaches, 8, 82, 131, 173; pears, 8, 82, 102; trees, 20, 169, 173, 177
Furkiyan gali, 92

Gadar nar, 116
Gadsar: lake (fish lake), 57–59, 68, 135; nala, 59, 67–68
Gagangir gorge, 52–54
Gagan sar, 6
Gagarpathar: gali, 20; nar, 16, 20; river, 20
Gagiari peak, 45
Gagribal lake, 156

Index

Ganderbal, 51, 53, 55, 61, 132, 135–136, 148, 153–156, 172, 174
Ganderbal town, 135–136
Gandhi, Indira, 82, 165
Gandpathar lake, 47
Gangabal lake, 56, 59–65, 127–128; ridge and passes, 62; sedgy bank, 64
Gang Ab stream, 63
Ganshibal, villages, 21, 23
Gantamulla barrage, 103
Gaoran, 10, 12
Garden of Eden, 37, 113
gardens, 2, 12–13, 37, 113, 134, 143, 152–154, 161–178; geometric patterned, 164
Gaw Kadal, 158
Ghazi, Sultan Sajjad Khan/Daulat Beg, 55
Gilgit, 93, 137
Gil Kadal, 159
Gil sar, 159
Girdlestone, Charles, 149
Girsar: gali, 9–10; lake, 10
Girwar, 38; nar, 38
Giyun, 75, 88
glaciers, 6–7, 19, 21, 26–27, 31–32, 35, 38, 41, 53–54, 58, 68–69, 124; western, 24, 40
Godtar, 114; nala, 113
Godwin-Austen, H.H., 107, 131
Golio sar, 122–123
Gorkha troops, 74–75
Gormantar gali, 99–100
Gosai, 75
Gotum Shing stream, 69
Government Chest Diseases Hospital, 31
Governor's House, 166

grazing ground, 29, 47, *see also* shepherds
Great Bend, 32; of Tsangpo, 32
Greater Kashmir, 11, 158
Great Himalayan Crest, 7, 19, 21, 32, 39, 51, 55, 66, 68
Great Lakes Trek, 58
Gufkral, 43
Gugalmarg, 125–126
Gugal nar, 126
Gugumaran gali, 123
guides, 56, 85
Gujjars (nomadic shepherds), 6, 9–10, 26, 41, 44, 99; 6; camping, 24; dokas, 18, 26, 36, 122; hamlet, 26; paths, 18; settlements, 114; village, 114, 126
Gulmarg, 66, 85, 100, 102, 107–111, 142; ridge, 94
Gulol, 28; gali, 28
Gumbar gali, 36, 60
Gumri river on NH, 31
Gumur glacier, 31
Gund Circuit, 61
Gund nar, 60–61
Gurdali, 109
Gurdari gali, 109
Gurez valley, 71–72, 74
Gurudwara Shaheed Bunga Baghat, Burzulla, 174
Gurudwara Shri Chatti Patshahi Sahib, 141
Gutli Bagh, 136
Gwasha Bor, 39–40

Habakhatun, 71–72
Haddan nar, 99
Hadow, C.M., 154

Index

Haehom, 81; kol, 81; nar, 81; valley, 94
Hagoon, 26; nar, 26; rivulet, 26; valley, 26
Haidar, 178
Haji Pir, 105–106; nala, 105–106; pass, 106
Halan: gali, 4; village, 3
Halkan nar, 18
handicrafts, 132, 162
Handil sar lake, 60
Handwara, 85, 94, 99–100, 106; Bhadrakali temple, 80
Hangalmarg, 50
Hapathkhal nalas, 103, 105–106
Hapat Talao, 6–7
Haramukh, 4, 59, 62–64, 66–67, 71, 75, 77, 93, 108, 127, 135, 137, 145, 153; peak, 68, 111; region, 120
Haramukh III /station peak, 62–63
Harawat river, 41
Hari Ghati gali, 38
Hari Niwas, 164
Hari Parbat, 153, 167
Haramukh, 63
Harnag, 39, 41
Harpat: kol, 18; nar, 19–20
Harseni nar, 121–123, 125, 144
Harwan: nala, 45; nar, 49; reservoir, 150, 169, 171
Harwan Forest Sanctuary, 37, 49
Harwat, 27, 29; nala, 29
Hassnain, Fida, 155
Hatiara, 30
Hazratbal mosque, 167, 173
Hera Ahlan, 6, 8
Herbal, 17
Himachal Pradesh, 95, 103
Himalayan: ridges, 55, 68, 79; view, 7

Himalayan Club, 64
Himalayan Journal, 32, 64
Hindu: pilgrim route, 101; temples, 13, 136, 147
Hindus, 139, 142, 145, 176
Hirpora, 117, 119
Hiurbagwan, 25, 33; gali, 39; lake, 25; nag, 39; nar, 33, 51; peak, 51
Hodsar Bal peak, 47
Hoi Bal, 87
Hokersar Wetland, 159
Hoka sar, 37, 45, 47
Holdsworth, R.L., 64
homestays, 72, 74, 91, *see also* guest houses
Honabacha, 38, 41
hotels, 9, 20, 25, 52–53, 91, 107–108, 110
Houen Heng peak, 129
houseboats, 107, 140, 155, 158, 161
Huegel, Baron, 104, 120, 161, 173–174
Hunmar gali, 86

ice lingam, 28
Indian Airlines Fokker Friendship, 129
Indian Army, 76, 106
Indo-Pakistan trade, 103
Indra Gandhi Tulip Garden, Raj Bhavan, 151
Indrasan, 7
Indra sar, 124
Indus, 31–32, 59
infiltrations, 73, 91–92, 139
Inner Line Permits, 90, 95
Inshan village, 11
insurgency, 6, 9, 12, 44, 75, 79, 83–84, 86, 88, 91, 100, 143–144, 146

intrusion, 75
Iqbal Park, 151
Isherwari, 156–157

Jabri village, 95, 140
Jadi nar, 120–122
Jahangir, Emperor, xvii, 2, 161, 164, 170–175, 177
Jamma Masjid or Masjid Baba Dawood Khaki, 133, 140, 155
Jammu, 6, 9, 11, 36, 103, 106, 113, 118, 120, 137, 139–140, 146, 150
Jammu–Anantnag–Srinagar highway, 42
Jammu and Kashmir Tourism Development Corporation (JKTDC), 99
Janbazpora, 141
Jatti gali, 99
Jawahar Tunnel, xix, 1–2
jetties, 134, 155, 157, 161
Jharokha Bagh, 136, 174–175
Jhelum, xvii, 2–5, 12–13, 15–16, 59, 68–69, 94–95, 100–107, 131–132, 134, 137–138, 140–142, 149–152, 156, 158–160; hydel projects on, 103; river, 78, 156, 175, 178; valley, 68, 99, 101
J&K Police Training College, 65
Josephine, 142
Jumagund stream, 93

Kachhama Melyal, 79
Kadalbal, 114, 125; forest, 126
Kafir Khan range, 101
Kahlil village, 44
Kahmil, 80–81, 93–94, 97; nala, 85, 92, 97; river, 80, 84, 93, 139; valley, 92, 97

Kahuta, 106
Kain nar, 81
Kainthawali, 93
Kaiwal gali, 92
Kajpathar, 32–33; nar, 32–33; peaks, 33
Kala Pahar, 100
Kalaruch, 84–85; nala, 84; valley, 85
Kalhana, 65, 136, 176
Kali gali, 125
Kallan, 36; grazing grounds, 35
Kaloosa (bran tree), 137–138
Kalultrag, 43
Kaman bridge, 103
Kamraz (North Kashmir), 132
Kanari peak, 3
Kandai kol, 125, 128–129
Kandalou gali, 65
Kandi: forest, 85; marg, 125
Kangan, 14, 57, 60–61
Kanihama, 142
Kani shawls, 142
Kankanaz nala, 60–61
Kanzalwan, 73–75, 89
Kaobal, 73; gali, 68, 72, 75, 79, 136; pass, 70, 73–74; road, 72; sar lake, 68
Karakoram, 62–63, 99
Karalapora, 77
Karamulla gali, 105
Karapora, 90
karewas, 43, 130–132, 144–145, 147–150, 160; Kutbal, 145
Kargil, 70, 72
Karim, Seikh Ahmed, 118
Karnah, 95–96, 139
Kashmir Raha da Katha, 91
Kashmir stag, 43
Kashmir University, 174

Index

Kashmir Valley, xvii–xviii, 6, 13, 45, 103, 127, 130–131; mountaineers, 41
Kashpat village, 71
Kashyap rishi, 82
Katarnag gali, 38, 41
Katha Kazinag, 94, 100–101; Nala, 97
Kats gali, 116
Kaukut: gali, 4; peak, 1, 3–4
Kazi Khan Dhar, 106
Kazim Phai bar, 40
Kazinag, 94, 96, 100
Kazi nag Dhar, range, 85, 94, 100–102, 105–107; ridge, 100
Kazinag National Park, 105
Kel nar, 27, 30
Kenawain village, 121–122
Keran, 89–93, 95, 139–140; farmer tourist camp, 90–91; Indian, 90–92; in POK, 91; sector, 89, 91; tehsil, 90
Khabhi ki gali, 122
Khaiyar, 77; Forest Rest House, 18
Khalana nala, 102–103
Khan, Ali Mardan, 120, 165
Khan, Asaf (brother of Nur Jahan), 168
Khanchi kol, 116
Khaniyar, 155
Khanpora, 141
Khashrari gali, 125
Khodmarg, 154
Khrew, 37, 39, 42–44, 146–147, 151
Khumarial, 82, 84
Khursi nala, 109
Khushal sar, 157–159; lakes, 157
Khushkidar nar, 122
Kibla: glacier, 31; nala, 31; pass, 31
Kinari Darkush peak, 68
Kinari gah cascades, 68–69

Kisar: gali, 73; nala, 73; sar, 73
Kishenganga, 51, 59, 67–75, 77–78, 80–81, 85–86, 88–91, 93–96, 101, 135–140; dam, 73–74, 94; gorge, 71; as Neelam in Pakistan, 74, 89, 91; river, 75, 90; valley, 67–68, 70, 72, 137; waters, 74
Kishir sar, 124–125
Kishtwar, 6–11, 13, 17, 21, 28, 32
Kithol nar, 60
Knight, Captain, 178
knolls, 30, 90, 124
Koh-i-Nur or Mountain of Light, 32, 40
Kokaran nar valley, 56
Kokarnag, 9
Koka sar, 40
Kokernag, 3, 12–13, 24
Kolahoi (highest peak), 2, 4, 7, 18, 21, 23–25, 28–29, 35–36, 38–42, 44, 48, 64, 66; nala, 35–36
kols, 145
Kol sar, 65
Kongdogri alp, 108
Kongdor ridge, 80
Kongwattan, 125
Kon nag, 17, 21, 29, 33, 39, 41
Kontar nag, 111
Koragbal, 79
Kounsar, 127; gali, 123
Kounsarnag, 118–127; gali, 123; Hindu pilgrimage spot, 124; lake, 123; nar, 103
Krala Nangal gali, 112–113
Kralpora, 92
Krasnak peak, 18
Krepin gali, 18, 20
Kripanwali gali, 81
Krishan bar, 58

Krishansar, 58; lake, 57, 135
Kubbi nar, 66
Kulan, 60
Kulgam, 125–126, 128–129, 132, 144–146
Kullan, 60
Kullu, 7
Kun, 2, 7
Kundabal village, 175
Kundnagar, Mohammad Rashiduddin, 159
Kunzalwan dam, 78
Kunzalwan in Gurez, 94
Kupwara, 79–95, 97, 99–101, 119, 132, 137–140; sub-division of Handwara, 99
Khusro, Amir, 171

Lachipora Wildlife Sanctuaries, 105
Ladakh, 31, 52, 54, 68, 90, 93
Lahore, 93, 118, 177
Lake Garda, 124
lakes, 11, 17, 19, 21, 36–42, 44, 46–52, 57–62, 65–69, 94, 108–109, 111–113, 118–125, 127–128, 131, 137–138, 151–152, 155–161, 163–164, 175; Chohar nag, 11; of Katar nag, 39; in Srinagar, 160
Lakhath gali, 35, 40, 51–52
Lakshmidor, 111
Laksukh sar, 122–123
Lal Gam, 115
Lalitaditya, King, 14, 20
Lalpur, 82
Lam: nadi, 46; nar, 45–48
Land Customs Stations in Kashmir, 95
Langinai, 16, 18–21, 26; nar, 16; river, 20–21; valley, 18–19, 21
Larikpur village, 42

Laripora village, 40
Larnu, 8
Lavnag, 82
Lawang gali, 65
Leepa valley, 94, 100–101
Leepa valley—Channian, 100
Leh, 50, 54, 135
Letters from India and Kashmir, Duguid, 14
Lichudalai, 47
Lidder, 13–16, 19–21, 24–25, 39, 45, 47, 52, 134; confluence of East and West, 23; East, 23, 25–27, 29, 34, 41, 48; eastern tributaries, 19; river, 15, 19, 23, 48; valley, 19, 23, 44; West, 23–25, 34–35, 38–41, 47, 49
Lidderwat, 36, 39–40, 46–47, 49, 127; alp, 39; campsite, 37; forest, 39
Lidru, 20–21
Limber, 105; nala, 106; stream, 105
limestone mining, 43
Line of Control (LOC), 6–7, 35–36, 40–41, 51, 60, 63–64, 71–72, 74–75, 79–81, 85–96, 101, 103, 105–106, 138–139, 141–142, 152–153
Lippa nala, 101
Loigul gali, 64, 66
Lokut (small) Baib nar, 69
Lokut (small) Bangus, 98
Lokut (small) Chhumahai nar, 47
Lokut (Smaller) Dal, 156
Lolab, 79, 81–86, 140; kol, 81, 85; palm, 82; river, 81; valley, 82, 84, 87, 94, 140
Lonivald pass, 11
lower Langinai valley, 20
Ludarwan, 81

Index

Machaal or Machil/Matchil, Machil, 86–88, 139–140; nala, 86, 88; river, 87; sector, 87, 93; stream, 86; as Valley of Fake Encounters, 86
Machoi West, 31
Madani, Syed Mohammad, 174
Madmati or Bod kol river, 66–67, 75, 77–78, 137; nala, 77; valley, 67
Magam, 114
Magri gali, 95
Mahadeo, 44, 153; nar, 49, 153; peak, 49
Mahagunas pass, 27, 29–30
Mahar regiment, 92
Maidanan village, 105
Makalwain nala, 69
Makdoomi, Hazrat Hamza, 139
Malinson Girls school, 155
Manasbal, 174–175; lake, 135, 175; village, 175
Manchhar nadi, 82
Mandu peak, 128
Mandwan peak, 45
Mangan dub lake, 61
Mangat nala, 129
Manigam, 61, 65
Manners, J. Lt Col, 154
Mason, Kenneth, 33, 40, 63
Manzgam, 126
Maqam, 82–83
Maraz (South Kashmir), 132
Marchoi nala, 61
Margan, 10–11; gali, 8–12; pass, 10–11, 17–18, 66, 119; slopes, 11
marg gali, 105
Mar sar lake, 37, 39–40, 44, 46, 49–50, 60
Martand, 13–14, 74; canal, 14, 20
Martand temple, 14, 20
Martshoi nala, 61
Mason, Kenneth, 21
Mastrok bar, 61; pass, 61
Mastrokhar sar lake, 61
Matehund, 18
Mawar: nar, 6; valley of, 140
meadow, 3, 5–9, 11, 23, 25–26, 37–38, 43–46, 52–54, 61, 63, 97–99, 107, 109–122, 124, 126; Astaanmarg, 29; Bangus, 99, 127; of Chitardolu, 59; Dandabari, 47; Dubjan, 117; Dudhpathri, 114; Gulmarg, 108; Harnag, 41; Hawkwas, 126; Hirpora, 117; Honabacha's stony, 41; Kallan, 35–36; Lidderwat, 36; Thajiwas, 53–54; of Waghabal, 48
medicinal plants, 58
Mianmarg gali, 73
Minuartia kashmirica, 34
Mir Behri, 157
Miyingul, 75
Mohammed, Kashmir Bakshi Ghulam, 137
Mohand Marg, 65–66, 167
Moldari, 99
Moore, Thomas, 178
Morina wallichiana, 34
Moses, 38, 41, 78
motorable roads, xvii, 2, 4, 18, 20, 38–39, 44, 48, 52, 71–74, 78–79, 83, 88–89
Mughal gardens, 2, 13, 15, 133–134, 151, 162–164, 166–167, 173, 176; in Srinagar, 164
Mughals, 110–111, 117–118, 142, 150, 152–153, 160, 163, 166, 168–170, 172, 178
Munawar lake, 47

Mungshungan nar, 59–60, 63
Muqam Shah Wali village, 139
Murdari gali, 85–86, 88
Musa (Moses) Sab-in-Qabr glacier, 41
Musa Mashid—Moses's Mosque, 116
Musa or Alayhi Salam, 38
Musa Sabin Qabr, 38
Muzaffarabad, 7, 69, 75, 92–93, 95, 104, 140
Nachian, 94
Nafron nar, 38
Nagabal nar, 44; tributary, 45
Nagaputan gali, 17
Nagasari, 85
Nagbal, 135
Nageen lake, 151, 156, 159–160
Nagmarg gali, 83
nags (lakes), 39
nahar (King's canal), 171
Nai Sarak, 158
Najibullah, Mohammed, 141
Nallah Amir Khan channel, 159
Nallah Mar, 157–158
Nambalan nar, 46, 48–49
Namche Barwa, 32
Nanak, Guru, 134
Nandakain, 47
Nandan sar, 121–122
Nand kol lake, 59–60, 63–64
Nandmarg, 5
Nanga Parbat, 32, 37, 55, 63, 66–67, 73, 86, 88, 94, 99, 107–108
Narazdan nar, 93, 97–98
Narbug nar, 12
Naruab village, 59, 69
Naseem Bagh, 164, 167, 173–174
Nasiruddin, Mullah Mir Sayyid, 155
Nasta Chun: gali, 94, 98; pass, 94
Naubug nar, 8, 10–12, 18

Naugam nar, 2–3, 178
Naugbug nar, 12
Nau Kaan, 62
Nau nar, 29–30
Nawab Bazar bridge, 149
Nawa nar, 85
Nawan gali, 85
Nehru, Jawaharlal, 53, 145
Nekbatun, 25, 41
Neve, Arthur, Maj., 31–33, 40–41, 52, 54
Neve, E.F., 31–33, 40, 52, 54
NH 1, 31, 50, 60, 135–136, 150
NH 44, 1–2, 42, 60, 128, 133, 145–147, 150
Nichang, highest peak, 24, 28, 32–33, 135
Nichnai, 57, 68; bar, 57–60, 69; nar, 53, 57; pass, 53
Nilagrar, 52, 56; village, 55
Nila nag, 40, 52
Nilkanth, passes of, 111
Nilli nar, 11
Nilnag, 143
Nilnai: gali, 67; nala, 52; nar, 55, 67
Nishat Bagh, 137, 153, 157, 164, 167–170
Northwards, 134
Nowhatta Golf Course, 160
Nun, 2
Nunkhel: gali, 128; nar, 128
Nur-afza garden, 173
Nuranag, 14, 57, 60–61, 64–65, 74
Nur-e-Chamb, 172
Nur Jahan, 13, 136, 154, 168, 170–172, 174–177
Nussu gali, 128
Nusu ghat, 78
Nyusu gali, 129

Index

Obliwas nar, 45
old Mughal Road, 118–119, 172
olives/zaitoon, 103
Omuwah nar, 2–3
orchards, 1, 4, 8, 43–45, 48, 78, 81, 130–131, 134–135, 145, 148, 175, 177
Owur: nala, 20; stream, 47

Pachakul alp, 125
Pachhagam, 128
paddy fields, 78, 82–83
Padshahi Bagh, 133–134
Pahalgam, 17, 20, 23, 26, 34, 37–38, 100, 104, 134; bridges, 19; golf course, 40; road, 14, 20, 47; town, 24
Pahalwanpora village, 137
Pahlipora village, 106
Pakistani Dudhnial, 91
Pakistan-Occupied Kashmir (POK), 7, 51, 67, 69, 72–74, 88–95, 100–101, 103, 105, 110–111, 137, 139, 141
Palat gali, 70–71
Pambach, 47; gali, 44; Khod lakes, 44, 46
Pambagai: gali, 46–47; lake, 46–47
Pampore, 131, 146, 150–151; saffron fields of, 42, 150
Pandanpathri or Pandavlary, 112
Pandrethan, 74, 151; temple, 149, 153
Pandshur: bar, 69; galis, 57
Pangwas nala, 67
Panjtarni, 27, 30
Pantha Chowk, 150–152
Panzgam, 98
paramilitary camps, Pantha Chowk, 150–151
Parasing peaks, 122–123
Parbury, Florence Tyzack, 178
Pari Mahal Mughal Garden (Fairy Palace), 151, 153, 164, 166–167
Parkyan (Farkhiyan gali), 90, 93, 98
Partition, 90–91, 95, 141
Pashat nar, 60
pashmina, 149
Patalwan gali, 73
Pathans, 141
Pathar Masjid, 153–154
Pathri Jinjar, 100
Pattan, 74
Patwalmarg Gali, 12, 17, 19
Pazmal gali, 128
peaks, 1, 19, 24–27, 32, 35–38, 50–55, 64, 67, 85–86, 99, 109–110, 130, 145, 153–154;: Banilmarg, 45; Brahma Sakli, , 123–126, 144; Buttress, 29, 41; Chhang, 114; Chinamarg, 113; craggy, 2; Deo Masjid, 50; Didam Gali, 129; Gagiari, 45; Haramukh, 62–63, 68, 111; Hiurbagwan, 51; Hodsar Bal, 47; Houen Heng, 129; K1, K2, K32, 63; Kajpathar, 33; Kanari, 3; Kaukut, 1, 3–4; Kinari Darkush, 68; Kolahoi, 7, 9, 13, 18, 21, 23, 28, 39, 40–42, 44, 48, 52, 66; Krasnak, 18; Mahadeo, 49; Mandu, 128; Mandwan, 45; Nichang 24, 28, 32–33, 135; Parasing, 122–123; Prishi, 121; Rabimarg, 41; Romesh Thong (Sunset Peak), 102, 112, 116–118, 121; Safapora, 175; Tatakuti, 102, 114–117; Viju, 76; Wawdor, 8; Zabarwan 166
peasant s, 15, 78, 155

Index

Peer gali, xviii, 110–121, 123, 144, 150, 165, 172
Phraslun, 25–26
Phuti Pansal gali, 123
pilgrim: campsites, 29; paths, 92
pilgrimage, 27–30, 74, 107, 137, 166
pines, 2, 79, 82, 84, 104, 126, 166
Pir Panjal, 1–7, 9, 17, 19, 23, 25, 27, 102, 105, 107–115, 117–124, 128–130, 143–145; craggy peak, 2; galis on, 110; railway tunnel, 1; range, 1, 7, 45, 95, 110, 117–118, 120, 128–129; ridge, 19, 27, 104–105, 124, 128; spring, 143
Pir Pantsal Marg, 44–45, 48; gali, 44
Pissu Top, 27
Pleistocene Age, 41
Pohru river of Kupwara, 78, 137
Poshbagh nar, 6–7
Poshpathar gali, 29
Pranigam, 45
Pravarsena II, 149, 170
Prishi peak, 121
Pulwama, 132, 143, 146–147
Punch, 106, 110–111, 113, 115–116, 119; summits, 116
Punjab, 90, 103, 110–111, 129, 137, 140
Pushwarnar, 88
Putakhan, 93; gali, 81, 93
Putwalmarg Gali, 5, 7, 17

Qazigund, xviii, 1–2, 128, 145–146; in Kulgama, 145

Rabimarg peak, 41
'Rad,' floating gardens, 157
Rahiwala Baihk, 98
Rainawari, 156
Raiyar forest, 114

Rajatarangini, Kalhan, 65, 136, 149
Rajouri, 118–119, 172, 177
Rajouri Mughal Road, 177
Rakisin nala, 59
Raman nala, 58–59, 68–70
Rambagh, 162
Ramban, 128–129
Rambiara river, 113, 119, 134, 144
Rampur village, 83
Ranadatiya, Raja, 14
Rangdori, 85
Rangmandu gali, 5
Rauta ki gali, 75, 92–93, 98
Rawalpindi, 93
Raza, Musa, 155
Razdan, 72
Razdhainangan Pass, 72, 74–77, 79–80, 88, 137
Razparyin nar, 8–10, 12
Reasi, 113, 120, 122–123
Ren gali, 3
Reshi, Baba Payamuddin, 108
Reshian gali, 101
Reshwari, 140
rest houses, 7, 82; above Sura Pharao village, 50; PWD, 7
Reyil, 60
ridge, 2–3, 5, 7, 9–10, 12, 17–19, 21, 26–27, 39–40, 44–45, 59–60, 62, 67–69, 75–76, 80–81, 83–86, 92, 98–100, 122–123, 165–167
Ringbala nar, 88
Rishi, Nund, 18, 145
Rishpur, 17–18
rivulets, 26, 33, 59, 71, 82, 106, 112, 126
Riyul drains Handil sar, 36
Romesh Thong (Sunset Peak), 102, 112, 116–118, 121

Index

Rozabal Khaniyar road, 155
Rukh, Lala, 178
Rupri, 119–120, 123; Gali, 122–123; nala, 120; nar, 119, 122–123; pass, 123; village, 120

Sadhana Top, 98
Safa Kadal, 151
Safa Kadal Serai, 149
Safapora peak, 175
Safawali: gali, 81; nar, 81
Safopora, 167
Saidpora, village, 105
Sainal sar, 67
Salamabad, 141
Sallar Kullar Road, 134
Salnai: gali, 61; sar, 61
Sandran, 3–5, 13, 15, 129, 146; river, 3, 3–5, 129, 134; valley, 4
sangam, 15, 27, 29–33, 39, 42, 133–134, 145
Sangar, 45; gali, 44–45; pass, 45–46
Sannan: gali, 122; sar, 122
Sarankut, 29; nala, 29; stream, 29
Sarbal: forest, 40; sar lake, 65–66; village, 52
Sarband reservoir, 49
Sarikul, 87
Saskat: gali, 30; pass, 29
Satburn, 84
Satkari, bridge, 52–53; village, 53; tunnel construction site, 57
Sat sar/seven lakes, 57, 59, 62, 120; bar, 64; nar, 59–60, 64
Scohalpathri village, 109
A Search for the Historical Jesus (2010), Hussnain, 155
security, 70, 79–80, 84, 137, 139
Sekhiwas, 36

Seki Pantsal Pass, 31
Sekiwas, 37
Seldori nar, 88
Sezwatyar nar, 25–26
Shab-i-Mehraj, 143
Shadipora, 61, 152, 156; village, 156
Shahabad Naugam, 3
Shah Hamdam mosque, 154
Shah Jahan, 2, 120, 134, 161, 164–166, 171–172, 174, 178
Shah kol, 4
Shah, Syed Qasim, Sufi St., 143, 162
Shah, Sultan Hassan, 161
Shaitan Daku (Devil Bandit) nar, 71
Shalabhato: nar, 93; village, 93
Shalabhatu, 91
Shalamar Bagh (Mughal Garden), 49, 148, 152–153, 161, 164, 167–171, 173
Shaliganga nala, 114–115
Shamsabari ridge, 81, 139
Shangri-la, 50, 111
Shankarcharya hill, 153
Sharab kol, 153, 169
Sharda Peeth, 73–74, 90, 93, 96, 101
Sheeshnag, 23, 25, 27–28, 36, 127; glacier, 27; lake, 7, 27; river, 24
Sheikh Noor-ud-Din Noorani Wali / Nund Rishi (shrine), 18, 20, 114, 143, 145
Shekhpur, 3–4
Shelverton, G., 62
shepherds, 5, 17–18, 25–27, 29, 31, 34, 37–40, 45–47, 61, 63, 66–67, 76, 92, 110–112, 116–117, 122–123, 125; camps, 7, 114; campfires, 120; Kashmiri, 36, 44, 122; passes, 104; path, 6, 83; Sekiwas, 37; tracks, 19

Shere-Kashmir Institute of Medical Sciences, 159
Sher Garhi fort, 151
Shikargah, 43, 147
Shikoh, Dara, 134, 151, 164, 167, 170
Shikoh Bagh, 15
Shilsar gali, 9
Shopian, xix, 113, 116, 118–119, 123, 126, 132, 143–144; Jamia Masjid, 143
Shrant nar, 86
Shri Guru Nanak Dev Ji Pehli Padshahi Gurudwara Bijbehara, 134
shrines, 20, 80, 118, 139–140, 153–154; of Rozabal, 154
Sidh Kanu Shah gali, 101
Sikandar, Sultan, 156
Sikhs, 80, 117, 120, 136, 139, 142, 176
Sikwas stream, 128
Silpathar nala, 105
Simnan, Syed, 145
Sind: river, 32–33, 37, 39, 42, 44, 49–52, 56, 59, 61, 135–136, 174–175; tributaries of, 60; valley, 44
Singh, Dogra Pratap, 154
Sing, Gulab, 176
Singh, Guru Hargobind visit to Baramulla, 141
Singh, Hari, 158
Sinkiang, 137
Sinpathar gali, 44
Sinthan: gali, 8–9; pass, xviii, 9–10
Sirpal, 56
Skardu, 137
skiing, 11; cross-country, 11
SMHS Hospital, Srinagar, 154
snowfields, 69, 128
snow ridges, 10, 25, 35, 38, 78, 98, 105

Sogam, 82
Sogput dhar, 57
Soi nar, 8–9
Sokh Sarai/old Mughal Sarai, 119
Sokian nar, 99
Sona (Gold) Lank, 160
Sona Lank, 161; as Lokut or smaller lake, 161
Sonamarg, 29, 32–33, 35, 37, 39–40, 50–57, 68, 135; meadows, 54; wooden forest rest house, 53
Sonamarg–Srinagar road, 61
Sonamus, meadows of, 50
Sonapindi gali, 85
Sona sar lake, 27, 36–37, 40, 49–50, 60
Sorus: nag, 19, 21; nar, 16, 21
Sosirwen lake, 35, 39, 41
springs, 5, 8, 12–13, 18–19, 35, 38, 43, 77, 80, 82, 85, 96, 105–107, 163–164, 166; of Khag, 143
Srinagar, 9, 37, 39, 42–45, 60, 63, 65–66, 72–73, 93, 106–110, 115–119, 129, 132, 135, 139–143, 147–160, 162, 164–165, 167, 174; Jamia Masjid of, 143; Lal Chowk, 155; Water bodies of, 156–161; water supply, 115
Srinagar Christian Mission Hospital, 31
Srinagar–Gulmarg highway, 114
Srinagar–Leh National Highway No. 1, 37
Srinagar–Sonamarg–Leh (NH 1) road, 60
Sri Thara Sahab, Singhpura, 142
Stein, Aurel, Sir, 65–66, 147
St Joseph's Convent, 141–142
St Joseph's Hospital, 141
streams, 47

Index

Sukh, 31
Sukhnag, 114, 159
Sukhnai: gali, 73; village, 11
Sukh nala, 31
Sultanpura kol, 109
Sumbal, 37, 42, 50, 60; lake, 42; nar, 50; pass, 37; village, 50
Sundar Kanth, 4, 6
Sundartop, 129
Sura Pharao villages, 50
surgical strike, 101
Sutaharan, 113

Takinizam village, 166
Tangdhar, 94–96, 140
Tangmarg, 107–108, 110, 112, 126
Taobat, 91; LOC at, 74; valley, 74; village, 74; village in POK, 89
Tareekh-e-Hassan, 14, 156
tarns, xviii, 6–7, 9, 26, 52, 58, 111, 113, 116–117, 120, 123–124, *see also* lakes
Tarsar sar lake, 36–37, 39–40, 44, 46–47, 49–50, 60
Tarwal, 135
Tashkent, 106
Tatakuti peaks, 102, 114–117
temple, 14, 74, 80, 107, 126, 136–137, 139, 151, 154; Badrakali, 80, 139; in Boniyar 104; in Handwara, 80; Martand, 14, 20; in Nuranag, Pandrethan, 14; 149, 153
tents, 18, 26, 29, 36, 46, 64, 66, 90, 108, 122; of Bakarwals, 122
textiles, 132
Thaiyan, 85; nar, 85–86; village, 85
Thajiwas: glacier, 35, 53–54, 135; nar, 53
Thanin, 27, 30, 41

Thorpe, Robert Lt, 155
Tibetan Muslim refugees, 149
Tilwankain gali, 63, 65
timber lobby, 79
Tirath Bal, 96
Tithwal, 89, 91–92, 94–98, 100; bulge, 94
tonga (single-horse carriage), 117
Tosha (soft) Maidan, 112–114, 124, 143
tourist bungalow, Indira Hut, 82
tourists, 37–39, 60, 70, 73–74, 79, 82–83, 90–91, 108, 110, 112–113, 116
tourists lodges, 82–83, *see also* homestays; rest houses
trade caravans, 93, 111
Tragbal, 74, 77
trails, 5–6, 18–19, 39, 43–44, 46, 48, 67, 70, 100, 104, 111, 113, 116
Tral lake, 37, 39, 42–47, 49, 134, 146–147
Tramkazan nar, 26
Trangkhul, 64–65; alp, 65
Transhipment Point (TP), 97
Treaty of Amritsar, 176
trees, 8, 11, 74, 78–80, 84, 104, 108, 119, 157, 162, 164–165, 174–175; felling, 132; walnut, 78, 82–83, 90, 101, 104, 131, 143, 173
Trehgam tehsil, 81
trekkers, abductions of seven foreigner, 24
trekking, 9, 11–12, 38–39, 44, 47, 51, 56–57, 60–61, 105–106, 113, 115, 121, 128, 140; to Apharwat, 108; companies, 21, 24, 37, 66; short, 24, 99, 107, 129; route, 45, 47; to Wangat-Nuranag, 61

tributaries, xvii–xix, 4–5, 8, 12, 16, 25–27, 36–37, 43–45, 65–66, 69–70, 80–81, 88, 111–112, 128–129, 144–145; of Jhelum, xix
Tsang, Huen, 149
Tsaraligund village, 42
Tson lake, 47
Tsur: bar, 58–59; nar, 59
Tulamulla village, 136
Tuliyan: nala, 21; sar, 17, 19, 21–22, 27
tunnel, 10, 74–75, 129, 146
Turigadalau gali, 18, 20
Tyndale Biscoe Boys school, 154–155

uniforms, 44, 79, 167
University of Kashmir, 11, 133
Upper Kishenganga, 73
Ura gali, 85–86, 88
Uri, 94, 102–103, 105, 107, 109; Hydel Project, 105; nala, 106; Trade Facilitation Centre in, 103
Uri-I (Gingal), 103
Urukshan gali, 105

Vailu, 8, 10, 12; bridge, 8; confluence at, 8
Vardhan, Durlab, 156
Veha gali, 47
Verinag, 2–4, 164, 177–178
Veshav, 125–126, 128, 145; meanders, 129; river, 128
Veth, 2
Vigne, G.T., 30, 161
Viju: and Madmati confluence, 78; nar, 75–78; peak, 76
Vimun nar (as Yemen by shepherds), 25, 41
violence, 24, 39, 86

VIP Guest House, 166
Vishensar lakes/Great Lakes, 57–59, 68–69, 123, 135
Vitalin Marg, 156

Wadoo, M.S., 143
Wadoora, 137
Wadura village, 78
Waghabal, 46, 48
Wakefield, W., 156
Wali, Syed Janbaz, 141
Waltara nar, 43–44
Wandar Dur, 10
Wangat, 60–61, 65
Wangat-Nuranag, trek to, 61, *see also* trekking
Warli gali, 73
Warwan: in Kishtwar, 28; valley, 11
Waskur sar, 175
Wasturwen, 43
waterfalls, 23, 25–26, 33, 60, 102, 106, 164, 168–169, 172, 176; semi-frozen, 27, 30
Wawdor peak, 8
Wayil: bridge, 61; village, 135
Wetharkut nar, 45–47
Wokhabal nar, 26
woods, 3, 44, 58, 80, 87, 102, 104
Woyil, 153
Wular lake, 66–67, 77–78, 94, 133, 136–138

Yadal gali, 100
Yamhar gali, 36, 60
Yamraz (Central Kashmir), 132
Yanga nar, 119, 121
Yemen: nar, 25, 38, 41; ridge, 41
Yemsar (lake of demons), 58
Younghusband, Francis, Sir, 24, 156, 178

Index

Yusmarg 'Meadow of Jesus,' 115–117, 143, 155

Zabarwan: mountain, 39, 44, 66, 150–151, 164–166; peak, 166; range, 44, 49, 151; ridge, 45–46, 48, 166–167
Zaingiri, 137
Zain-ud-din Wali, Sheikh, 20
Zain-ul-Abideen, Sultan (Bud Shah), 20, 152–153, 157, 161, 174
Zaisur, 109
Zajibal gali, 27, 62
Zajimarg gali, 17, 21, 125–126
Zaji nar, 125–126
Zajmarg nar, 36–37, 39–40, 46, 49
Zambakach gali, 17
Zamindar gali, 75, 88
Zanatrag stream, 43
Zand Dudinar, 88
Zanskar, 3, 7, 11
Zarhama, 81
Zarogabal, 174
zenana (women's suite), 164–165, 168–169, 171
Z gali, 88
ziarat, 46, 82, 106, 108, 118, 141, 145, 159, 162; at Charare-Sharief,' 115; Muqam Shah Wali, 80; of Saint Zaiti Shah Wali, 139
Zissar nag, 21
Zoji la, 11, 25, 31–33, 50–57, 65, 74, 135
Zojipal nar, 51
Zoon, 71
Zuastan, 45

About the Author

Romesh Bhattacharji has been trekking in Kashmir since his years in Delhi's St Stephen's College in the 1960s. His last trek was in 2012, forty-eight years after the first one. He continued his trysts with this fabled but tormented land even after he became a bureaucrat. His last posting as Chief Commissioner Customs, Amritsar, included Kashmir in his beat.

Bhattacharji is a high-altitude trekker concentrating on the remote mountains. He is also an avid photographer and has, over the decades, amassed a vast cache of photographs. He has previously authored books on Ladakh and India's Northeast.

HarperCollins *Publishers* India

At HarperCollins India, we believe in telling the best stories and finding the widest readership for our books in every format possible. We started publishing in 1992; a great deal has changed since then, but what has remained constant is the passion with which our authors write their books, the love with which readers receive them, and the sheer joy and excitement that we as publishers feel in being a part of the publishing process.

Over the years, we've had the pleasure of publishing some of the finest writing from the subcontinent and around the world, including several award-winning titles and some of the biggest bestsellers in India's publishing history. But nothing has meant more to us than the fact that millions of people have read the books we published, and that somewhere, a book of ours might have made a difference.

As we look to the future, we go back to that one word— a word which has been a driving force for us all these years.

Read.